GARDE
FACT FINDER

EDITED BY

GRAHAM CLARKE

ACKNOWLEDGEMENTS

The contents of *Gardener's Fact Finder* have been gathered over a period of time, and collated to form an invaluable reference work of gardening facts and figures. The staff and writers of *Amateur Gardening* magazine have toiled for many weeks to make this book possible, and the publishers would like to thank them all. Jane Courtier, Alison Francis and Michael Pilcher have made invaluable contributions.

Headmain Ltd, in association with the Hardy Plant Society, gave us permission to utilize information from their publication *The Plant Finder*. Our thanks to Chris Philip, the compiler for his co-operation and expertise.

Finally, our thanks go to Angela Pawsey, Secretary of the Rose Growers Association. She provided us with material from the Association's excellent *Find that Rose!* publication which was essential in the compilation of the Top 100 Roses section.

First published in 1987 by Amateur Gardening,
IPC Magazines Limited

Second revised and updated edition published in Great Britain 1993
by Hamlyn an imprint of Reed Consumer Books Limited
Michelin House, 81 Fulham Road, London SW3 6RB
and Auckland, Melbourne, Singapore and Toronto in conjunction
with Amateur Gardening, IPC Magazines Limited
Westover House, West Quay Road, Poole, Dorset BH15 1JG

This edition published in Australia in 1993 by
THE BOOK COMPANY
Exclusively distributed by THE BOOK COMPANY,
9/9 13 Winbourne Road, Brookvale,
Sydney NSW 2100, Australia

Produced by Mandarin Offset – printed in Hong Kong

ISBN 0 600 57697 3

A catalogue record for this book is available from the British Library

CONTENTS

INTRODUCTION

The *Gardener's Fact Finder* has been produced to provide a truly comprehensive, up-to-date and easy-to-follow handbook. It is full of facts, tables, charts and at-a-glance information. The book has been designed in a practical pocket size, making it perfect for carrying around the garden and excellent for consulting while at the garden centre.

Each chapter has been compiled by the experts and staff of *Amateur Gardening*, Britain's most widely-read gardening magazine.

What does the *Gardener's Fact Finder* contain? Well, the Planter's Guide will tell you which plant to grow where; there is essential cultural information on fruit, vegetables and house plants; advice on the control of plant pests and diseases, the chemicals we use, and how to freeze home-grown produce.

The directory section lists the 450 most popular hardy garden plants, the top 100 roses and the latter has a list of suppliers names and addresses. Finally, the Latin directory will tell you how to spell and pronounce all of those amazing botanical plant names – with explanations of what they actually mean.

After a few months of using the *Gardener's Fact Finder*, you'll wonder how you ever managed without it!

GRAHAM CLARKE
Editor, Amateur Gardening

A
PLANTER'S
GUIDE

T he object of this guide is to provide, in the most concise form possible, information which will enable readers to select plants most suitable for their requirements. The various lists have been kept as short as possible to avoid confusing users by offering too many alternatives. It is not claimed that those chosen are necessarily the best, for that must remain largely a matter of opinion, but they are all fine examples of their kind which must certainly be reckoned among the best. Heights given are those normally attained when the plants are well and fully grown. With some slow growing trees and shrubs it may be years before these dimensions are attained and with most it is possible to restrict size by judicious pruning. Since plants vary in their pruning requirements we have included an at-a-glance guide to help you with your choice. Most, though, will need little attention apart from an annual tidy up.

Further information regarding these plants will be found in the catalogues of nurserymen and seedsmen as well as in books of a more detailed and extensive character. The Planter's Guide is an informative index, guiding the reader in a clear, simple manner and revealing the plants most likely to please.

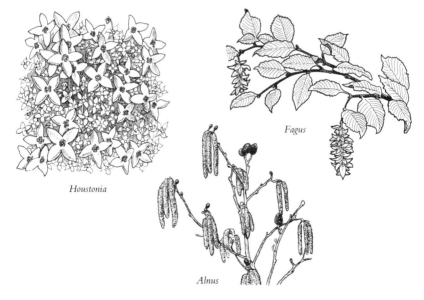

Houstonia

Fagus

Alnus

PLANTS FOR SHADY PLACES

Latin name	Popular name	Height feet	Height metres
Acanthus	Bear's breeches	4	1·2
Aconitum	Monkswood	2-5	0·6-1·5
Ajuga	Bugle	6in	15cm
Anemone hybrida	Japanese anemone	2-4	0·6-1·2
Aquilegia	Columbine	1-2	0·3-0·6
Arenaria balearica	Sandwort	1in	2·5cm
Artemisia lactiflora	White mugword	4-5	1·2-1·5
Aruncus sylvester	Goat's beard	4-6	1·2-1·8
Astrantia	Masterwort	1-2	0·3-0·6
Bergenia	Large-leafed saxifrage	1	0·3
Brunnera macrophylla		1	0·3
Campanula	Bellflower	1-5	0·6-1·5
Convallaria	Lily of the valley	9in	23cm
Cyclamen		3·2-6in	8-15cm
Dicentra	Bleeding heart	1-2	0·3-0·6
Digitalis	Foxglove	2-6	0·6-1·8
Epimedium	Barrenwort	6in-1ft	15cm-0·3m
Filipendula ulmaria 'Aurea'	Golden-leaved meadowsweet	2	0·6
Galanthus	Snowdrop	6in-1ft	15cm-0·3m
Gentiana asclepiadea	Willow gentian	2	0·6
Gillenia trifoliata	Indian physic	2	0·6
Helleborus foetidus	Bear's foot	1½	0·5
Helleborus niger	Christmas rose	1	0·3
Helleborus orientalis	Lenten rose	1½	0·5
Hemerocallis	Day lily	2-3	0·6-1
Hosta	Plantain lily	1-2	0·3-0·6
Iris foetidissima	Gladwyn	2	0·6
Lilium	Lily	1-6	0·3-1·8
Lysimachia	Loosetrife, Creeping Jenny	6in-3ft	15cm-1m
Meconopsis	Welsh poppy, blue poppy	1-5	0·3-1·5
Mertensia	Virginian cowslip	1½	0·5
Myosotis	Forget-me-not	6in	15cm
Narcissus	Daffodil	6in-2ft	15cm-0·6m
Omphalodes cappadocica	Navelwort	1	0·3
Phlox paniculata		2-3	0·6-1
Polygonatum	Solomon's seal	2-3	0·6-1
Primula acaulis	Primrose	6in	15cm
Prunella	Self-heal	6in-1ft	15cm-0·3m
Pulmonaria	Lungwort	6in-1ft	15cm-0·3m
Sanguinaria	Blood rot	6in	15cm
Saxifraga umbrosa	London pride	9in	23cm
Scilla	Squill	6in-2ft	15cm-0·6m
Thalictrum aquilegiifolium	Meadow rue	2-3	0·6-1
Tiarella	Foam flower	9in	23cm
Tradescantia virginiana	Spiderwort	1½	0·5
Trollius	Globe flower	2-3	0·6-1
Viola	Violet, pansy, viola	3·2-6in	8-15cm

HB–Hardy biennial   HP–Hardy herbaceous perennial   B–Bulb   R–Rock plant   T–Tuber

Flower colour	Season	Type	Pruning
...purple and white	mid sum – late sum	HP	after flowering
...purple, yellow	early sum – early aut	HP	after flowering
...purple	early sum	HP	
...white to rose	late sum – early aut	HP	after flowering
...various	late spr – mid sum	HP	after flowering
...white	early sum – late sum	R	
...creamy-white	mid sum – early aut	HP	mid autumn
...creamy-white	early sum – mid sum	HP	mid autumn
...white, pink	late spr – early sum	HP	mid autumn
...pink	late win – late spr	HP	deadhead
...blue	late spr – early sum	HP	deadhead
...purple, blue, white	late spr – late sum	HP, R	deadhead
...white	mid spr – late spr	HP	deadhead
...white, pink, crimson	mid spr – mid aut	T	deadhead
...rose and white	late spr – mid sum	HP	mid autumn
...various	early sum – mid sum	HP/HB	mid autumn
...white, yellow, red	mid spr – late spr	HP	early spring
...white		HP	mid autumn
...white	mid win – mid spr	B	
...purple, white	mid sum – late sum	HP	
...white and red	early sum	HP	mid autumn
...green	early sum – mid spr	HP	after flowering
...white	late aut – mid win	HP	after flowering
...white to maroon	early spr – mid spr	HP	after flowering
...yellow to crimson	mid sum – late sum	HP	after flowering
...white, lilac	mid sum – late sum	HP	deadhead
...green	early sum	HP	after fruiting
...various	early sum – early aut	B	after flowering
...yellow, white	mid sum – early aut	HP, R	late autumn
...various	late spr – mid sum	HP, HB	autumn
...blue	late spr – early sum	HP	autumn
...blue	early spr – late spr	HB, R	deadhead
...various	early spr – late spr	B	deadhead
...blue	early sum – late sum	HP	deadhead
...various	mid sum – early aut	HP	mid autumn
...white	late spr – early sum	HP	late autumn
...various	early spr – mid spr	HP	deadhead
...pink to purple	early sum – early aut	HP	deadhead
...blue, red	early spr – late spr	HP	deadhead
...white	mid spr – late spr	R	after flowering
...pink	mid spr – late spr	R	deadhead
...blue, pink, white	early spr – late spr	B	deadhead
...soft purple	late spr – early sum	HP	late autumn
...white	late spr – late sum	HP	deadhead
...blue to rose	early sum – mid aut	HP	late autumn
...yellow	late spr – early sum	HP	after flowering
...various	mid win – late sum	HP, R	deadhead

SELECTED HARDY HERBACEOUS PLANTS

Latin name	Popular name	Height feet	Height metres
Acanthus mollis★	Bear's breeches	4	1·2
Achillea 'Gold Plate'	Fernleaf yarrow	4	1·2
Aconitum 'Bressingham Spire'	Monkshood	4	1·2
Agapanthus 'Headbourne hybrids'	African lily	1-3	0·3-1
Alchemilla mollis	Lady's mantle	1	0·3
Anaphalis	Pearly everlasting	1-2	0·3-0·6
Anchusa leptophylla incana	Dwarf alkanet	1	0·3
Anemone hybrida (syn. A. japonica)	Japanese anemone	2-4	0·3-1·2
Anthemis 'Pride of Grallagh'★	Golden marguerite	2	0·6
Anthericum liliago	St Bernard's lily	1½	0·5
Aquilegia McKana hybrids	Columbine	2	0·6
Armeria 'Bee's Ruby'	Thrift	1½	0·5
Artemisia lactiflora	White mugwort	4-5	1·2-1·5
Asphodeline lutea	Jacob's rod	3-4	1-1·2
Aster novi-belgii 'Audrey'	Michaelmas daisy	1	0·3
– *A. n-b.* 'Ernest Ballard'		3	1
– *A. n-b.* 'Eventide'		4	1·2
– *A. frikartii*†		2½	0·8
– *A. n-b.* 'Margaret Rose'		1	0·3
– *A. n-b.* 'Marie Ballard'		3	1
– *A. n-b.* 'Mistress Quickly'		3-4	1-1·2
– *A. n-b.* 'Winston S. Churchill'		2½	0·8
Astible 'Fanal'		3	1
– *A.* 'Venus'		2	0·6
Astrantia	Masterwort	2	0·6
Bergenia purpurascens	Large-leaved saxifrage	9in	23cm
Bupthalmum salicifolium	Yellow ox-eye	1½-2	0·5-0·6
Campanula glomerata superba	Clustered bellflower	1½	0·5
– *C. lactiflora*	Milky bellflower	5	1·5
Catananche caerulea	Cupid's dart	2	0·6
Centaurea macrocephala	Yellow hardhead	3-4	1-1·2
– *C. montana*	Mountain cornflower	1½	0·5
Cimicifuga	Bugbane	4	1·2
Coreopsis auriculata	Tickseed	2½	0·8
– *C. verticillata*		1½	0·5
Crososmia 'Lucifer'		3	1
Delphinium 'Astolat' Group	Perennial larkspur	5	1·5
– *D.* 'Black Knight' Group		5	1·5
– *D.* 'Blue Fountains' Group		3½	1·1
– *D.* 'Blue Heaven' Group		3	1
Dianthus 'Mrs Sinkins'	Pink	9in	23cm
Dicentra	Bleeding heart	1-2	0·3-0·6
Dierama	Wand flower	3	1
Doronicum 'Harpur Crewe'	Leopard's bane	2	0·6
Echinacea purpurea	Purple coneflower	4	1·2
Echinops 'Taplow Blue'	Globe thistle	3-4	1-1.2
Erigeron	Fleabane	2½	0·8

★ Good for Foliage   † Dislikes autumn planting

Flower colour	Season	Pruning
....purple and white	mid sum – late sum	after flowering
....yellow	mid sum – late sum	late autumn....
....blue	early sum – mid sum	after flowering
...blue, white	mid sum – late sum	deadhead........
....yellow	early sum – mid sum	after flowering
....white	late sum – early aut	autumn ....
...blue	late spr – late sum	mid autumn ...
....white to rose	late sum – early aut	after flowering
....yellow	mid sum – late sum	mid autumn ...
....white	early sum	after flowering
....many colours	early sum	after flowering
....rose	late spr – early sum	deadhead........
....creamy white	late sum – early aut	mid spring......
....soft yellow	early sum – mid sum	deadhead........
....pale blue	early aut – mid aut	mid autumn ...
....rosy red	early aut – mid aut	mid autumn ...
....violet-purple	early aut – mid aut	mid autumn ...
....light blue	late sum – ear aut	mid autumn ...
....pink	early aut – mid aut	mid autumn ...
....light blue	early aut – mid aut	mid autumn ...
....deep purple	early aut – mid aut	mid autumn ...
....beetroot red	early aut – mid aut	mid autumn ...
....garnet red	early sum – mid sum	mid autumn ...
....shell pink	early sum – mid sum	mid autumn ...
....white, pink	early sum – mid sum	mid autumn ...
....rose	early spr	deadhead........
....yellow	early sum – mid sum	autumn ....
....purple	early sum – mid sum	deadhead........
....pale blue	mid sum – late sum	deadhead........
....blue	mid sum – late sum	mid autumn ...
....yellow	mid sum	mid autumn ...
....blue	late spr – mid sum	mid autumn ...
....white	late sum – early aut	late autumn....
....yellow and crimson	early sum – early aut	after flowering
....yellow	early sum – late sum	after flowering
....red	early sum – mid sum	dead leaves in early spr
....lilac	early sum – mid sum	autumn ....
....dark blue	early sum – mid sum	autumn ....
....blue	early sum – mid sum	autumn ....
....blue	early sum – mid sum	autumn ....
....white	early sum	deadhead........
....pink, white	late spr – mid sum	mid autumn ...
....pink	mid sum – late sum	mid autumn ...
....yellow	early spr – mid spr	autumn ....
....purple	late sum – early aut	mid autumn ...
....blue	mid sum – late sum	mid autumn ...
....blue, pink	early sum – late sum	autumn ....

▶

◀ ## SELECTED HARDY HERBACEOUS PLANTS

Latin name	Popular name	Height feet	Height metres
Eryngium alpinum	Alpine sea holly	3	1
– E. × tripartitum	Small-flowered sea holly	3	1
Euphorbia 'Fireglow'	Spurge	2½	0·8
– E. robbiae		2	0·6
Gaillardia 'Wirral Flame'	Blanket flower	2	0·6
Gaura lindheimeri		3–4	1–1·2
Geranium 'Johnson's Blue'	Blue cranesbill	1	0·3
Geum 'Fire Opal'	Avens	2	0·6
Gypsophila 'Bristol Fairy'	Chalk plant	3	1
Helenium 'Moerheim Beauty'	Sneezewort	4	1·2
Helianthus 'Lodden Gold'	Perennial sunflower	5	1·5
Heliopsis helianthoides gigantea		5	1·5
Helleborus corsicus	Corsican hellebore	2	0·6
– H. niger	Christmas rose	1	0·3
– H. orientalis	Lenten rose	1½	0·5
Hemerocallis	Day lily	2–3	0·6–1
Heuchera Bressingham hybrids	Alum root	2	0·6
Hosta	Plantain lily	2	0·6
Incarvillea delavayi†	Chinese trumpet flower	1½–3	0·5–1
Iris 'Cliffs of Dover'	Flag iris	3½	1·1
– I. 'Jane Phillips'		2½	0·8
– I. 'Patterdale'		3½	1·1
– I. sibirica	Siberian iris	3	1
– I. unguicularis	Algerian iris	1	0·3
Kirengeshoma	Yellow waxbells	3–4	1–1·2
Kniphofia 'Atlanta'	Red hot poker, torch lily	3½	1·1
Liatris callilepis	Kansas feather	3	1
Libertia formosa		2	0·6
Ligularia dentata	Giant ragwort	4	1·2
Limonium platyphyllum	Sea lavender	2	0·6
Linaria 'Canon Went'	Toadflax	2	0·6
Liriope muscari		1	0·3
Lupinus Russell hybrids‡	Lupin	3–4	1–1·2
Lychnis chalcedonica	Jerusalem cross	3	1
– L. coronaria	Rose campion	2	0·6
Lysimachia punctata	Yellow loosestrife	3	1
Lythrum 'Firecandle'	Purple loosestrife	3–5	1–1·5
Macleaya cordata	Plume poppy	5–8	1·5–2·4
Monarda 'Cambridge Scarlet'	Bergamot	3	1
– M. 'Croftway Pink'		3	1
Nepeta × faassenii†	Catmint	2½	0·8
Oenothera 'Fireworks'†	Golden drops	1½	0·5
Paeonia 'Duchesse de Nemours'	Peony	3	1
– P. 'Felix Crousse'		3	1
– P. 'Mme Jules Dessert'		3	1
– P. 'Sarah Bernhardt'		3	1

† Dislikes autumn planting   ‡ Dislikes lime or chalk

Flower colour	Season	Pruning
....blue	mid sum – late sum	after flowering
....blue	mid sum – late sum	after flowering
....orange-red	early sum	after flowering
....sulphur	late spr – early sum	after flowering
....red-bronze	early sum – early aut	deadhead.......
....rosy-white	mid-sum – late sum	mid autumn ...
....blue	early sum – late sum	mid autumn ...
....orange-red	early sum – late sum	after flowering
....white	early sum – late sum	mid autumn ...
....yellow-orange	late sum – early aut	late autumn ....
....yellow	mid sum – early aut	mid autumn ...
....deep yellow	mid sum – early aut	mid autumn ...
....green	mid spr – early sum	after flowering
....white	late aut – mid win	after flowering
....white to purple	early spr – mid spr	after flowering
....yellow to crimson	mid sum – early aut	after flowering
....pink to red	mid sum – early aut	mid autumn ...
....lilac, white	early sum – early aut	deadhead.......
....rose	early sum – early aut	autumn ....
....creamy white	early sum	deadhead.......
....medium blue	early sum	deadhead.......
....pale blue	early sum	deadhead.......
....white or blue	early sum	deadhead.......
....pale blue	mid win – late win	deadhead.......
....yellow	early aut – mid aut	after flowering
....yellow and red	mid sum	deadhead.......
....purple	mid sum – late sum	deadhead.......
....white	early sum – mid sum	after flowering
....yellow	mid sum – late sum	after flowering
....lavender	late sum – early aut	mid autumn ...
....pink	mid sum – early aut	autumn ....
....violet	late sum – early aut	after flowering
....crimson, pink, blue, white, yellow, red	early sum	late autumn ....
....scarlet	mid sum – late sum	autumn ....
....magenta	early sum – mid sum	autumn ....
....yellow	mid sum – late sum	late autumn ...
....magenta	mid sum – late sum	autumn ....
....pinkish-apricot	mid sum – early aut	autumn ....
....scarlet	mid sum – early aut	autumn ....
....pink	mid sum – early aut	autumn ....
....lavender	early sum – early aut	autumn ....
....yellow	early sum – early aut	mid autumn ...
....white	early sum – mid sum	mid autumn ...
....carmine	early sum – mid sum	mid autumn ...
....rose-pink	early sum – mid sum	mid autumn ...
....pink	early sum – mid sum	mid autumn ...

▶

◀ SELECTED HARDY HERBACEOUS PLANTS

Latin name	Popular name	Height feet	Height metres
Papaver 'Beauty of Livermere'	Oriental poppy	3	1
– **P.** 'Mrs Perry'		3	1
Penstemon 'Garnet'		2	0·6
Phlox 'Mary Fox'	Phlox	2½	0·8
– **P.** 'Prince of Orange'		3	1
Physostegia 'Vivid'	Obedient plant	1	0·3
Polygonum bistorta superbum	Bistort	1½	0·5
Potentilla 'Gibson's Scarlet'	Cinquefoil	1	0·1
Pulmonaria	Lungwort	6in–1ft	15cm–0·3m.
Rudbeckia 'Goldsturm'	Coneflower	2	0·6
Salvia × superba	Purple sage	3	1
Scabiosa 'Clive Greaves'†	Caucasian scabious	2	0·6
Sedum spectabile	Stonecrop	1½	0·5
Sidalcea	Prairie mallow	3–4	1–1·2
Sisyrinchium striatum	Satin flower	2½	0·8
Smilacina	False spikenard	3	1
Solidago 'Goldenmosa'	Goldenrod	2	0·6
Stachyslanata	Lamb's ear	9in	23cm
Tanacetum 'Eileen May Robinson'	Coloured marguerite	2	0·6
Thalictrum delavayi ★	Meadow blue	5	1·5
– **T.** 'Hewitt's Double'		6–7	1·8–2
Tradescantia virginiana	Spiderwort	1½	0·5
Trollius 'Goldquelle'	Globe flower	2	0·6
Veratrum album	White hellebore	3–4	1–1·2
Verbascum 'Cotswold Queen'	Mullein	4	1·2
Veronica gentianoides★	Speedwell	2	0·6

★ Good for Foliage   † Dislikes autumn planting

Aquilegia

Catananche

Flower colour	Season	Pruning
...scarlet	late spr – early sum	deadhead
...pink	late spr – early sum	deadhead
...deep red	mid sum – early aut	mid autumn
...salmon	mid sum – late sum	mid autumn
...orange	mid sum – late sum	mid autumn
...rosy-red	early aut – mid aut	mid autumn
...soft-pink	early sum – early aut	autumn
...scarlet	early sum – early aut	after flowering
...blue, red	early spr – late spr	deadhead
...yellow and black	late sum – early aut	late autumn
...purple	mid sum – early aut	late autumn
...light blue	mid sum – mid aut	late autumn
...pink	late sum – early aut	deadhead in spr
...pink, red	late sum – early aut	after flowering
...pale yellow	late spr – mid sum	autumn
...white	mid spr – late spr	late autumn
...yellow	late sum – early aut	mid autumn
...rose	early sum – mid sum	late autumn
...pink	late spr – early sum	after flowering
...mauve	mid sum – late sum	late autumn
...lilac-blue	mid sum – late sum	late autumn
...purple or rose	early sum – mid aut	late autumn
...yellow	late spr – early sum	after flowering
...white	mid sum	late autumn
...buff	mid sum – early aut	late autumn
...blue	late spr – early sum	late autumn

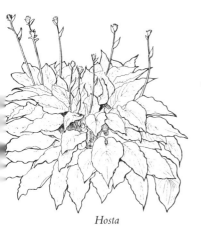

Hosta

Stachys lanata

PLANTS FOR CHALKY SOILS

Latin name	Popular name	Height feet	Height metres
Achillea	Yarrow	3·2in-5ft	8cm-1·5m
Aethionema	Stone cress	6in-1ft	15cm-0·3m
Allium	Onion	6in-3ft	15cm-1m
Alyssum saxatile	Gold dust	9in	23cm
Anemone	Windflower	3·2in-3ft	8cm-1m
Antirrhinum	Snapdragon	6in-3ft	15cm-1m
Arabis	Rock cress	6in	15cm
Armeria	Thrift	3·2in-2ft	8cm-0·6m
Aster	Michaelmas daisy	1-6	0·3-1·8
Astilbe		6in-4ft	15cm-1·2m
Aubrieta	Coloured rock cress	3·2in	8cm
Campanula	Bellflower	3·2in-5ft	8cm-1·5m
Centaurea	Cornflower	1-5	0·3-1·5
Cheiranthus	Wallflower	9in-2ft	23cm-0·6m
Chrysanthemum maximum	Shasta daisy	2-3	0·6-1
Clematis	Virgin's bower	3-4	1-1·2
Coreopsis	Tickseed	1-3	0·3-1
Crocus	Crocus	3·2in	8cm
Delphinium	Larkspur	3-7	1-2
Dianthus	Pink, carnation	6in-2ft	15cm-0·6m
Eremurus	Foxtail lily	1½-10	0·5-3
Erodium	Heron's bill	3·2in-1ft	8cm-0·3m
Erythronium	Dog's tooth violet	9in-1¼ft	23cm-0·4m
Filipendula hexapetala	Dropwort	1½	0·5
Gaillardia	Blanket flower	1-3	0·3-1
Geranium	Crane's bill	6in-2ft	15cm-0·6m
Gypsophila	Chalk plant	6in-4ft	15cm-1·2m
Helenium	Sneezewort	2-4	0·6-1.2
Helianthemum	Rock rose	1	0·3
Helianthus	Sunflower	4-6	1·2-1·8
Helleborus foetidus	Bear's foot	1½	0·5
– *H. niger*	Christmas rose	1-2	0·3-0·6
– *H. orientalis*	Lenten rose	1½	0·5
Hypericum	St. John's wort	3·2in-1ft	8cm-0·3m
Iberis	Candytuft	6in-1ft	15cm-0·3m
Iris	Flag	6in-4ft	15cm-1·2m
Lavatera	Tree mallow	3	1
Linum	Flax	1-2	0·3-0·6
Narcissus	Daffodil	6in-2ft	15cm-0·6m
Nigella	Love-in-a-mist	1½	0·5
Paeonia	Peony	2-3	0·6-1
Papaver	Poppy	1-3	0·3-1
Penstemon		2	0·6
Phlox		6in-4ft	15cm-1·2m
Polygonum	Knotweed	6in-5ft	15cm-1·5m
Potentilla	Cinquefoil	6in-2ft	15cm-0·6m
Pulsatilla	Pasque flower	4-6in	10cm-15cm

HA–Hardy annual   HHA–Half-hardy annual   HB–Hardy biennial   HP–Hardy perennial

Flower colour	Season	Type	Pruning
...white, yellow	late spr – early aut	HP, R	late autumn
...pink	late spr – mid sum	R	deadhead
...white, pink, purple	late spr – mid sum	B	deadhead
...yellow	mid-spr – early sum	R	deadhead
...white, pink, red, blue	early spr – early aut	HP, R	after flowering
...many colours	early spr – early aut	HP as HHA	
...white, pink	early spr – late spr	R	deadhead
...pink, white	mid spr – early sum	HP, R	deadhead
...many colours	late sum – mid aut	HP	mid autumn
...white, pink, red	early sum – mid sum	HP	mid autumn
...purple, pink, crimson	early spr – late spr	R	deadhead
...white, blue, purple	late spr – late sum	HP, R	deadhead
...blue, pink, yellow	early sum – early aut	HP, HA	mid autumn
...various	early spr – early sum	HP as HB	
...white	early sum – lat sum	HP	late autumn
...white, blue	early sum – early aut	HP	depends on variety
...yellow crimson	early sum – early aut	HP, HA	after flowering
...white, yellow, blue, mauve	early aut – mid spr	B	
...blue, purple, pink, white	early sum – late sum	HP, HA	autumn
...many colours	mid spr – mid sum	HP/R	deadhead
...white, yellow, pink	late spr – mid sum	HP	after flowering
...pink, carmine	early sum – early aut	R	deadhead
...white, yellow, purple	mid spr – late spr	B	after flowering
...white	early sum – mid sum	HP	mid autumn
...yellow and red	mid sum – early aut	HP, HA	deadhead
...blue to crimson	late spr – late sum	HP, R	mid autumn
...white, pink	early sum – early aut	HP, R, HA	mid autumn
...yellow to crimson	early sum – early aut	HP	late autumn
...many colours	late spr – mid sum	R	after flowering
...yellow	late sum – mid aut	HP, HA	mid autumn
...green	early spr – mid spr	HP	after flowering
...white	late aut – mid win	HP	after flowering
...white to maroon	early spr – mid spr	HP	after flowering
...yellow	early sum – late sum	R	spring
...white	late spr – late sum	R	deadhead
...many colours	mid win – mid sum	HP	after flowering
...rose, white	early sum – early aut	HA	
...blue, yellow, scarlet	early sum – late sum	HP, HA, R	mid autumn
...white, yellow, orange	early spr – late spr	B	deadhead
...many colours	mid spr – early aut	HA	
...white, pink, red, yellow	late spr – mid sum	HP	mid autumn
...various	early sum – early aut	HP, HA	deadhead
...many colours	early sum – early aut	HP, HHP	mid autumn
...many colours	late spr – early aut	HP, R	mid autumn
...white, pink, red	mid sum – early aut	HP	autumn
...many colours	early sum – early aut	HP, R	after flowering
...mauve, purple	mid spr – late spr	HP	deadhead

HHP–Half-hardy perennial   B–Bulb   R–Rock plant

►

◀ **PLANTS FOR CHALKY SOILS**

Latin name	Popular name	Height feet	Height metres
Pyrethrum	Coloured marguerite	2	0·6
Reseda	Mignonette	1	0·3
Salvia × superba	Purple sage	3	1
Sanguisorba	Burnet	2½-6	0·8-1·8
Sedum	Stonecrop	3·2in-2ft	8cm-0·6m
Sidalcea	Prairie mallow	3-4	1-1·2
Solidago	Golden rod	2-6	0·6-1·8
Stachys lanata	Lamb's ear	1	0·3
Thalictrum	Meadow rue	1-6	0·3-1·8
Thermopsis		2	0·6
Tropaeolum	Nasturtium	4in-6ft	10cm-1·8m.
Thymus	Thyme	3·2in-1ft	8cm-0·3m.
Tulipa	Tulip	6in-2½ft	15cm-0·8m.
Verbascum	Mullein	3-8	1-2·4
Veronica	Speedwell	6in-4ft	15cm-1·2m.
Viola	Pansy, violet, viola	3·2in-6in	8-15cm

HA–Hardy annual   HHA–Half-hardy annual   HB–Hardy biennial   HP–Hardy perennial

GROUND COVER PLANTS

Latin name	Popular name	Height feet	Height metres
Ajuga★	Bugle	6in-1ft	15cm-0·3m.
Alchemilla mollis	Lady's mantle	1	0·3
Anemone nemorosa	Wood anemone	4in	10cm
Bergenia★	Megasea	1	0·3
Calluna vulgaris	Ling	1-1½	0·3-0·5
Cotoneaster dammeri	Prostrate cotoneaster	6in	15cm
Epimedium	Barrenwort	9in	23cm
Genista hispanica	Spanish gorse	1-2	0·3-0·6
Geranium macrorrhizum	Crane's bill	1	0·3
Hypericum calycinum★	St. John's wort	1-1½	0·3-0·5
Lamium★	Deadnettle	6in-1ft	15cm-0·3m
Lysimachia nummularia	Creeping Jenny	6in	15cm
Pachysandra		6in-1ft	15cm-0·3m
Potentilla alba	Cinquefoil	6in	15cm
Pulmonaria	Lungwort	6in-1ft	15cm-0·5m
Saxifraga umbrosa★	London pride	1-1½	0·3-0·5
Sedum spurium	Stonecrop	4in	10cm
Thymus★	Thyme	3·2in	8cm
Vinca★	Periwinkle	1-1½	0·3-0·5
Viola labradorica	Viola	4in	10cm

HP–Hardy herbaceous perennial   S–Shrub   R–Rock plant   ★ Evergreen

Flower colour	Season	Type	Pruning
..pink, red, white	late spr – early sum	HP	after flowering
..pink and green	mid sum – late sum	HA	
..purple	mid sum – early aut	HP	late autumn....
..white, pink	mid sum – late sum	HP	late autumn....
..yellow, pink, white	early sum – early aut	HP, R	deadhead in ... spring
..pink to crimson	late sum – early aut	HP	after flowering
..yellow	late sum – early aut	HP	mid autumn ...
..pink	early sum – late sum	HP	late autumn....
..yellow, mauve	early sum – late sum	HP	late autumn....
..yellow	early sum – mid sum	HP	after flowering
..red, yellow	early sum – early aut	HA	
..pink and white	early sum – late sum	R	after flowering
..white, yellow, pink, red	early spr – late spr	B	deadhead........
..yellow, pink	early sum – late sum	HP/HB	late autumn....
..white, blue, pink	early sum – early aut	HP	late autumn....
..many colours	late spr – early aut	HP	deadhead........

HHP–Half-hardy perennial   B–Bulb   R–Rock plant

Flower colour	Season	Type	Pruning
...blue	mid spr – mid sum	HP	
..yellow	early sum – mid sum	HP	after flowering
..white, blue	early spr – late spr	HP	after flowering
..pink, red	early spr – late spr	HP	deadhead........
..pink, white	late sum – mid aut	S	after flowering
..white	late spr – early sum	S	early spring ....
..yellow, red	mid spr – late spr	HP	early spring ....
..yellow	late spr – early sum	S	early spring ....
...pink	late spr – mid sum	HP	mid autumn ...
...yellow	early sum – late sum	S	spring.............
..yellow, purple	late spr – mid sum	HP	after flowering
..yellow	mid sum – early aut	HP	late autumn....
..green	late win – mid spr	S	autumn ....
..white	mid spr – late spr	R	after flowering
..blue, red	early spr – late spr	HP	deadhead........
..pinkish white	late spr – mid sum	HP	deadhead........
..pink, red	mid sum – early aut	R	deadhead........
..pink, red, white	late spr – mid sum	R	after flowering
..blue, white	early spr – late spr	S	
..purple	early spr – late spr	HP	deadhead........

PLANTS FOR HOT DRY PLACES

Latin name	Popular name	Height feet	Height metres
Achillea	Yarrow	3·2in-5ft	8cm-1·5m
Agapanthus	African Lily	1-3	0·3-1
Alstroemeria aurantiaca	Peruvian lily	3	1
Althaea	Hollyhock	5-7	1·5-2
Alyssum saxatile	Gold dust	9in	23cm
Anagallis	Pimpernel	3·2in	8cm
Anaphalis	Pearly everlasting	1-2	0·3-0·6
Anchusa	Alkanet	1-4	0·3-1·2
Anthemis	Golden marguerite	2-3	0·6-1
Antirrhinum	Snapdragon	6in-3ft	15cm-1m
Arabis	Rock cress	6in	15cm
Armeria	Thrift	3·2in-2ft	8cm-0·6m
Aubrieta	Coloured rock cress	6in	15cm
Bupthalmum	Yellow ox-eye	1½-2	0·5-0·6
Catananche	Cupid's dart	2	0·6
Centaurea	Cornflower	1-5	0·3-1·5
Centranthus	Red valerian	2	0·6
Cerastium	Snow-in-summer	6in	15cm
Ceratostigma	Plumbago	6in-2ft	15cm-0·6m
Cheiranthus	Wallflower	3·2in-2ft	8cm-0·6m
Clarkia	Clarkia	2-3	0·6-1
Coreopsis	Tickseed	1-3	0·3-1
Dianthus	Pink	6in-1ft	15cm-0·3m
Dictamnus albus	Burning bush	2	0·6
Echinops	Globe thistle	2-5	0·6-1·5
Erigeron	Fleabane	1-2	0·3-0·6
Erodium	Heron's bill	3·2in-9in	8-23cm
Eryngium	Sea holly	2-3	0·6-1
Erysimum	Siberian wallflower	1-2	0·3-0·6
Eschscholzia	Californian poppy	6in-1ft	15cm-0·3m
Gaillardia	Blanket flower	1-3	0·3-1
Galega	Goat's rue	4-5	1·2-1·5
Gazania	Treasure flower	3·2in-6in	8-15cm
Geum	Avens	1-2	0·3-0·6
Godetia		1-3	0·3-1
Gypsophila	Chalk plant	3·2in-4ft	8cm-1·2m
Helianthemum	Rock rose	1	0·3
Iris unguicularis	Algerian iris	1½	0·5
Lavatera	Tree mallow	3-6	1-1·8
Linum	Flax	1-2	0·3-0·6
Lupinus	Lupin	2-3	0·6-1
Malope	Mallow wort	2-3	0·6-1
Mesembryanthemum	Livingstone daisy	3·2in-1ft	8cm-0·3m
Nepeta	Catmint	1-2	0·3-0·6
Nerine bowdenii	Diamond lily	1½	0·5
Oenothera	Evening primrose	6in-3ft	15cm-1m
Osteospermum	Veldt daisy	1-2	0·3-0·6
Othonna		1	0·3

HA–Hardy annual   HHA–Half-hardy annual   HB-Hardy biennial   HHP–Half-hardy perennial

Flower colour	Season	Type	Pruning
...white, yellow	late spr – early aut	HP, R	late autumn....
...blue, white	mid sum – late sum		deadhead........
...orange	mid sum – late sum		autumn..........
...various	mid sum – late sum	HP as HB/HA	after flowering
...yellow	mid spr – early sum	HP/R	after flowering
...blue, red	early sum – early aut	HA	after flowering
...white	mid sum – early sum	HP	autumn..........
...blue	late spr – mid sum	HP	mid autumn...
...yellow	mid sum – late sum	HP	mid autumn...
...various	early sum – early aut	HP as HHA	
...white	early spr – late spr	HP/R	deadhead........
...pink, white	mid spr – early sum	HP/R	deadhead........
...purple, pink, crimson	early spr – late spr	HP/R	deadhead........
...yellow	early sum – mid sum	HP	deadhead........
...blue, white	mid sum – late sum	HP	mid autumn...
...blue, pink, yellow	early spr – early aut	HP/HA	mid autumn...
...pink, red, white	early sum – mid sum	HP	mid autumn...
...white	early sum	R	autumn..........
...blue	mid sum – mid aut		deadhead........
...various	early spr – early sum	HP as HB	
...pink, red, white	early sum – late sum	HA	
...yellow, crimson	early sum – early aut	HP/HA	after flowering
...various	mid spr – late sum	HP/R	deadhead........
...white	early sum – mid sum	HP	mid autumn...
...blue	mid sum – late sum	HP	mid autumn...
...blue, pink	early sum – late sum	HP	autumn..........
...various	early sum – early aut	R	deadhead........
...blue	mid sum – late sum	HP	after flowering
...purple, yellow, orange	late spr – early sum	HP/HB	deadhead........
...various	early sum – early aut	HA	
...yellow and red	mid sum – early aut	HP/HA	deadhead........
...blue, mauve, white	early sum – late sum	HP	after flowering
...yellow, orange, black	early sum – late sum	HHP	after flowering
...yellow, orange, red	early sum – late sum	HP	after flowering
...various	early sum – late sum	HA	
...white, pink	late spr – early aut	HP/HA	mid autumn...
...various	late spr – mid sum	R	after flowering
...violet	early win – late win		after flowering
...pink, white	early sum – early aut	HP/HA	autumn..........
...blue, yellow, scarlet	early sum – late sum	HP, HA or R	mid autumn...
...various	early sum – late sum	HP/HA	late autumn....
...magenta, white	early sum – late sum	HA	
...various	early sum – late sum	HHP/HHA	deadhead........
...blue	early sum – early aut	HP	autumn..........
...pink	early aut – late aut		deadhead........
...yellow, white, pink	early sum – late sum	HP, R or HB	mid autumn...
...white, purple	early sum – early aut		mid autumn...
...yellow	late spr – early sum	R	

HP–Hardy herbaceous perennial R–Rock plant

►

PLANTS FOR HOT DRY PLACES

Latin name	Popular name	Height feet	Height metres
Oxalis	Wood sorrel	6-9in	15-23cm
Papaver	Poppy	2-3	0·6-1
Penstemon barbatus	Bearded tongue	3	1
Portulaca	Rose moss	6in	15cm
Polygonum affine		9in-1ft	23cm-0·3m
Potentilla	Cinquefoil	6in-2ft	15cm-0·6m
Pulsatilla	Pasque flower	6in	15cm
Romneya	Tree poppy	5-6	1·5-1·8
Santolina	Lavender cotton	1-2	0·3-0·6
Sedum	Stonecrop	3·2in-2ft	8cm-0·6m
Sempervivum	Houseleek	3·2in-1ft	8cm-0·3m
Sisyrinchium striatum		2	0·6
Tropaeolum	Nasturtium	6in-6ft	15cm-1·8m
Verbascum	Mullein	3-8	1-2·4
Zauschneria	Californian fuchsia	1	0·3

HA–Hardy annual   HHA–Half-hardy annual   HB–Hardy biennial

PLANTS FOR MOIST PLACES

Latin name	Popular name	Height feet	Height metres
Aruncus sylvester	Goat's beard	2-4	0·6-1·2
Astilbe		2-3	0·6-1
Caltha	King cup	1-1½	0·3-0·5
Filipendula rubra	Queen-of-the-prairie	4-5	1·2-1·5
Gunnera		4-8	1·2-2·4
Iris kaempferi	Japanese iris	2	0·6
– I. Laevigata	Water iris	2-2½	0·6-0·8
– I. sibirica	Siberian iris	3-4	1-1·2
Lysichiton	Skunk cabbage	2-4	0·6-1·2
Lythrum	Purple loosestrife	2-3	0·6-1
Lysimachia nummularia	Creeping jenny	3·2in	8cm
Mimulus guttatus	Monkey musk	1	0·3
Osmunda regalis	Regal fern	3-4	1-1·2
Persicaria campanulata	Knotweed	2	0·6
Primula beesiana		2	0·6
– P. denticulata	Drumstick primrose	1	0·3
– P. japonica		2	0·6
– P. pulverulenta		2	0·6
– P. sikkimensis	Tibetan cowslip	2	0·6
Trollius	Globe flower	2-3	0·6-1

HP–Hardy herbaceous perennial   R–Rock Plant

Flower colour	Season	Type	Pruning
....pink, yellow, white	late spr – mid sum	R	deadhead........
....various	late spr – late sum	HP/HA	deadhead........
....scarlet	mid sum – early aut		mid autumn ...
....various	mid sum – early aut	HHA	deadhead........
....pink	late sum – mid aut	HP/R	autumn ....
....various	late spr – early aut	HP/R	after flowering
....mauve, purple	mid spr – late spr		deadhead........
....white and yellow	mid sum – early aut	HP	mid autumn ...
....yellow	mid sum	HP	early spring ....
....yellow, pink, white	early sum – early aut	HP/R	deadhead........
....pink, yellow	mid sum – late sum	R	deadhead........
....yellow	early sum		autumn ....
....various	early sum – early aut	HA	
....various	early sum – late sum	HP/HB	late autumn....
....scarlet	late sum – early aut	R	early spring ....

HP–Hardy herbaceous perennial   R–Rock plant

Flower colour	Season	Type	Pruning
,....creamy-white	early sum	HP	mid autumn ...
,....pink, crimson, white	early sum – mid sum	HP	mid autumn ...
,....yellow	mid spr – late spr	HP	mid autumn ...
....pink, rose	mid sum – late sum	HP	mid autumn ...
,....very large leaves		HP	
,....various	early sum – mid sum	HP	deadhead........
,....white, blue, purple	early sum – mid sum	HP	headhead ....
,....blue, purple white	early sum – mid sum	HP	deadhead........
,....white, yellow	mid spr	HP	autumn ....
,....magenta, pink	mid sum – late sum	HP	autumn ....
,....yellow	mid sum – early aut	HP	late autumn....
,....yellow and brown	early sum – late sum	HP	late autumn....
,....fawny fronds	mid spr – mid aut		autumn ....
,....white or pink	mid sum – mid aut	HP	autumn ....
,....purple	early sum – mid sum	R	deadhead........
,....lilac, white	early spr – late spr	R	deadhead........
,....magenta	late spr – early sum	R	deadhead........
,....ruby, pink, white	late spr – early sum	R	deadhead........
,....yellow	late spr – early sum	R	deadhead........
,....yellow	late spr – early sum	HP	after flowering

SELECTED FLOWERING SHRUBS

Latin name	Popular name	Height feet	Height metres
Abelia × *grandiflora*		6–8	1·8–2·4
Azalea evergreen vars★		2–4	0·6–1·2
− *Mollis azalea*	Deciduous azalea	4–8	1·2–2·4
Berberis darwinii★	Darwin's barberry	8–10	2·4–3·1
− *B.* × *stenophylla*★		10–12	3·1–3·7
Buddleia alternifolia		12–20	3·7–6·1
− *B. davidii*	Butterfly bush	9–12	2·8–3·7
Calluna vulgaris 'Gold Haze'★	Golden heather	1½	0·5
− *C. v.* 'H.E. Beale'★	Beal's ling	2	0·6
Camellia japonica★	Japanese camellia	12–15	3·7–4·6
− *C.* × *williamsii* 'Donation'	Williams camellia	7–9	2–2·8
Caryopteris × *clandonensis*	Blue spiraea	3–5	1–1·5
Ceanothus 'Gloire de Versailles'	Californian lilac	8–10	2·4–3·1
Chaenomeles speciosa	Japanese quince	6–9	1·8–2·8
Chimonanthus praecox	Winter sweet	8–10	2·4–3·1
Choisya ternata★	Mexican orange blossom	6–9	1·8–2·8
Cistus × *cyprius*★	Rock rose	6–8	1·8–2·4
− *C.* × *purpureus*★		5–6	1·5–1·8
Clethra alnifolia	Sweet pepper	5–8	1·5–2·4
Colutea arborescens	Bladder senna	9–12	2·8–3·7
Cotoneaster franchetii★		8–12	2·4–3·7
− *C. horizontalis*	Fishbone cotoneaster	2½–4	0·8–1·2
Cytisus albus	White portugal broom	8–10	2·4–3·1
− *C.* × *praecox*	Early broom	5–7	1·5–2
− *C.* × *scoparius* vars	Common broom	6–7	1·8–2
Daphne mezereum	Mezereon	3–5	1–1·5
Erica carnea★	Winter heather	10–12in	25–31cm
− *E. cinerea*	Bell heather	12–15in	31–38cm
− *E. vagans*	Cornish heather	1–2	0·3–0·6
Escallonia 'Crimson Spire'★		8–10	2·4–3·1
Forsythia × *intermedia* 'Spectabilis'	Golden bells	8–12	2·4–3·7
Fuchsia magellanica gracilis 'Variegata'	Hardy fuchsia	4–5	1·2–1·5
Garrya elliptica★	Silk tassel bush	8–12	2·4–3·7
Genista aetnensis	Mt. Etna broom	15–20	4·6–6·1
− *G. hispanica*	Spanish gorse	2½–4	0·8–1·2
− *G. lydia*		2½–3	0·8–1
Hamamelis mollis	Witch hazel	2½–3	0·8–1
Hebe 'Autumn Glory'★	Shrubby veronica	1½–2	0·5–0·6
− *H. brachysiphon*★		4–6	1·2–1·8
− *H. pinguifolia* 'Pagei'★		9in–1ft	23cm–0·3m.
− *H. salicifolia*★	Willow-leaved veronica	4–5	1·2–1·5
Hibiscus syriacus	Syrian hibiscus	8–10	2·4–3·1
Hydrangea macrophylla	Common hydrangea	3–4	1–1·2
− *H. paniculata* 'Grandiflora'	Cone-flowered hydrangea	6–8	1·8–2·4
Hypericum calycinum★	Rose of Sharon	1–1½	0·3–0·5
− *H.* 'Hidcote'	St. John's wort	5–7	1·5–2

★ Evergreen

Spread feet	Spread metres	Flower colour	Flowering season	Pruning
6–8	1·8–2·4	fresh pink	mid sum – early aut	after flowering
3–5	1–1·5	pink, red, lilac	late spr – early sum	after flowering
4–8	1·2–2·4	yellow to red	early sum	after flowering
8–10	2·4–3·1	orange-gold	mid spr – late spr	after flowering
10–15	3·1–4·6	orange-yellow	mid spr – late spr	after flowering
15–20	4·6–6·1	purple	early sum	after flowering
9–12	2·8–3·7	purple, white	mid sum – late sum	early spring
2–3	0·6–1	white	late sum – early aut	after flowering
2–3	0·6–1	pink	late sum – early aut	after flowering
12–15	3·7–4·6	red-pink	mid spr – late spr	mid spring
7–9	2–2·8	pink	early spr – mid spr	mid spring
4–6	1·2–1·8	blue	early aut – mid aut	early spring
10–12	3·1–3·7	blue	early sum – mid aut	mid spring
6–9	1·8–2·8	red, pink, white	early spr – mid spr	train after flowering
10–12	3·1–3·7	pale yellow	early win – mid win	after flowering
8–10	2·4–3·1	white	mid spr – late spr	after flowering
7–9	2–2·8	white	early sum – mid sum	early spring
7–8	2–2·4	pink	late spr – early sum	early spring
5–8	1·5–2·4	white	late sum	early spring
9–12	2·8–3·7	yellow	early sum – early aut	early spring
8–12	2·4–3·7	pinkish	late spr	mid spring
8–10	2·4–3·1	pinkish	late spr	early spring
7–9	2–2·8	white	late spr	after flowering
6–9	1·8–2·8	yellow	mid spr – late spr	early spring
6–8	1·8–2·4	various	late spr	after flowering
3–5	1–1·5	purple, white	mid win – early spr	early spring
15–21in	38–53cm	red, white	early spr – late spr	after flowering
9–12in	23–31cm	purple, red, white	early sum – late sum	early spring
2½–3½	0·8–1·1	mixed	mid sum – early aut	early spring
8–10	2·4–3·1	red	mid sum	after flowering
8–12	2·4–3·7	yellow	early spr-mid spr	after flowering
5–7	1·5–2	carmine	early sum – mid aut	late autumn
8–12	2·4–3·7	greenish	late win – late spr	after flowering
15–18	4·6–5·5	yellow	mid sum	early spring
3–6	1–1·8	yellow	late spr – early sum	early spring
6–8	1·8–2·4	golden	late spr – early sum	early spring
6–8	1·8–2·4	yellow	early win – late win	after flowering
2½–3	0·8–1	blue	early sum – mid aut	spring
6–10	1·8–3·1	white	mid sum	spring
2–3	0·6–1	white	late spr – ear sum	spring
6–8	1·8–2·4	white	mid sum – early aut	spring
7–10	2–3·1	blue, pink, rose, white	late sum – early aut	early spring
3–4	1–1·2	blue-red, white	mid sum – early aut	early spring
6–8	1·8–2·4	white	mid sum – late sum	early spring
4–5	1·2–1·5	yellow	early sum – late sum	early spring
5–7	1·5–2	yellow	mid sum – late sum	early spring

SELECTED FLOWERING SHRUBS

Latin name	Popular name	Height feet	Height metres
Kalmia latifolia★	Calico bush	6–8	1·8–2·4
Kerria japonica 'Pleniflora'	Bachelor's buttons	6–10	1·8–3·1
Kolkwitzia amabilis	Beauty bush	6–8	1·8–2·4
Lavandula spica★	Old English lavender	1–3	0·3–1
Leycesteria formosa	Himalayan honeysuckle	6–8	1·8–2·4
Magnolia stellata	Star magnolia	5–6	1·5–1·8
Mahonia aquifolium★	Holly-leaved barberry	3–4	1–1·2
– M. japonica★	Japanese mahonia	5–7	1·5–2
Olearia haastii ★	Daisy bush	6–9	1·8–2·8
Osmanthus delavayii ★		8–12	2·4–3·7
Osmarea burkwoodii ★		9–12	2·8–3·7
Perovskia atriplicifolia	Afghan sage	5–6	1·5–1·8
Philadelphus coronarius aureus	Mock orange	9–12	2·8–3·7
– P. 'Sybille'		4–6	1·2–1·8
– P. 'Virginal'		7–9	2–2·8
Phlomis fruticosa★	Jerusalem sage	3–4	1–1·2
Pieris japonica★	Lily of the valley bush	7–10	2–3·1
Piptanthus nepalensis★	Evergreen laburnum	6–8	1·8–2·4
Potentilla fruticosa★	Shrubby cinquefoil	2–4	0·6–1·2
Pyracantha coccinea 'Mohave'★	Firethorn	10–16	3·1–4·9
– P. rogersiana flava★	Yellow firethorn	10–16	3·1–4·9
Rhododendron (hardy hybrids)★		6–12	1·8–3·7
Ribes sanguineum 'Pulborough Scarlet'	Flowering currant	9–12	2·8–3·7
Rosa 'Cantabrigiensis'	Cambridge rose	8–10	2·4–3·1
– hybrid Musks	Musk roses	4–8	1·2–2·4
– R. moyesii	Moyes' rose	9–12	2·8–3·7
– R. rugosa hybrids	Japanese rose	5–9	1·5–2·8
Rosmarinus officinalis★	Rosemary	6	1·8
Santolina chamaecyparissus★	Lavender cotton	1½–2	0·5–0·6
Senecio greyii ★	Shrubby ragwort	3–4	1–1·2
Skimmia japonica★		3–4	1–1·2
Spartium juncium	Spanish broom	9–12	2·8–3·7
Spiraea × *arguta*	Bridal wreath	6–8	1·8–2·4
– S. japonica 'Anthony Waterer'	Japanese spiraea	3–5	1–1·5
Syringa vulgaris vars.	Lilac	4–18	1·2–5·5
Tamarix ramosissima	Tamarisk	12–15	3·7–4·6
Viburnum carlesii		4–6	1·2–1·8
– V. farreri		9–12	2·4–3·7
– V. opulus 'Sterile'	Snowball tree	10–15	3·1–4·6
– V. mariesii		6–8	1·8–2·4
– V. tinus★	Laurustinus	7–10	2–3·1
Vinca minor★	Periwinkle	1–1½	0·3–0·5
Yucca filamentosa	Adam's needle	3–4	1–1·2

★ Evergreen

Spread feet	Spread metres	Flower colour	Flowering season	Pruning
8-10	2·4-3·1	pink	early sum	deadhead
6-8	1·8-2·4	golden	late spr – early sum	after flowering
6-8	1·8-2·4	pink	late spr – early sum	after flowering
1½-3	0·5-1	lavender, blue	mid sum – late sum	early spring deadhead after flowering
6-7	1·8-2	purple and white	mid sum – late sum	early spring
5-6	1·5-1·8	white	early spr – mid spr	spring
3-4	1-1·2	golden	late win – late spr	mid spring
7-12	2-3·7	lemon	late win – late spr	mid spring
8-12	2·4-3·7	white	mid sum – late sum	mid spring
10-15	3·1-4·6	white	mid spr – late spr	spring
9-12	2·8-3·7	white	mid spr	after flowering for hedges
4-5	1·2-1·5	lavender	late sum – early aut	early spring
12-15	3·7-4·6	creamy	late spr – early sum	old wood early spring
4-6	1·2-1·8	white and purple	early sum – mid sum	old wood early spring
6-8	1·8-2·4	white	early sum – mid sum	old wood early spring
3½-4½	1·1-1·4	yellow	early sum	mid autumn
8-12	2·4-3·7	white	late win – mid spr	after flowering
6-8	1·8-2·4	yellow	late spr – early sum	early spring
2-4	0·6-1·2	yellow, orange, red, white	early sum – early aut	after flowering
10-16	3·1-4·9	white	early sum	late spring – mid summer for hedges
10-16	3·1-4·9	white	early sum	late spring – mid summer for hedges
6-12	1·8-3·7	various	late spr – early sum	early spring
9-12	2·8-3·7	red	early spr – mid spr	old wood late spring
9-12	2·8-3·7	yellow	late spr – early sum	early spring
6-9	1·8-2·8	various	early sum – mid aut	early spring
10-12	3·1-3·7	crimson	early sum – mid sum	early spring
5-10	1·5-3·1	various	late spr – early aut	early spring
6-7	1·8-2	violet	mid spr – late spr	spring
2½-3½	0·8-1·1	yellow	mid sum – late sum	early spring
4-6	1·2-1·8	yellow	early sum – mid sum	deadhead
5-7	1·5-2	white	mid spr	
7-8	2-2·4	yellow	early sum – late sum	deadhead
6-8	1·8-2·4	white	mid spr – late spr	early spring
4-6	1·2-1·8	carmine	early sum – late sum	early spring
4-15	1·2-4·6	various	late spr – early sum	early spring
15-18	4·6-5·5	rosy-pink	mid sum – late sum	early spring
5-6	1·5-1·8	white	mid spr – late spr	after flowering
10-12	3·1-3·7	white	late aut – late win	mid spring
12-18	3·7-5·5	white	late spr – early sum	after flowering
9-12	2·8-3·7	white	late spr – early sum	after flowering
8-10	2·4-3·1	white	mid win – mid spr	late spring
indefinite		blue, white	early spr – late spr	
3-4	1-1·2	cream	mid sum – late sum	

SHRUBS FOR THE SHADE

Latin name	Popular name	Height feet	Height metres
Azalea kurume vars.★	Japanese azalea	2–4	0·6–1·2
– Mollis Azalea	Deciduous azalea	4–8	1·2–2·4
Aucuba japonica 'Variegata'★	Spotted laurel	6–9	1·8–2·8
Arundinaria★	Bamboo	6–15	1·8–4·6
Berberis darwinii ★	Darwin's barberry	8–10	2·4–3·1
– B. stenophylla★		10–12	3·1–3·7
Buxus sempervirens★	Box	15–18	4·6–5·5
Camellia japonica★	Japanese camellia	12–15	3·7–4·6
– C. × *williamsii* ★	William's camellia	7–9	2–2·8
Choisya ternata★	Mexican orange blossom	6–9	1·8–2·8
Cornus kousa	Flowering dogwood	12–20	3·7–6·1
Cotoneaster simonsii		10–12	3·1–3·7
Daphne mezereum	Mezereon	3–5	1–1·5
Elaeagnus ebbingei		8–10	2·4–3·1
Enkianthus campanulatus		5–7	1·5–2
Euonymus japonicus★	Japanese spindle tree	12–18	3·7–5·5
– E. fortunei ★		3–4	1–1·2
Forsythia spectabilis	Golden bells	8–12	2·4–3·7
Gaultheria shallon★	Shallon	2–6	0·6–1·8
Hydrangea macrophylla	Common hydrangea	3–4	1–1·2
– H. paniculata	Cone-flowered hydrangea	6–8	1·8–2·4
Hypericum calycinum★	Rose of sharon	1–1½	0·3–0·5
– H. patulum	St John's wort	4–6	1·2–1·8
Ilex aquifolium★	Holly	40–50	12·2–15·3
Kerria japonica	Jew's mallow	4–6	1·2–1·8
Ligustrum★	Privet	10–15	3·1–4·6
Mahonia aquifolium★	Holly-leaved barberry	3–4	1–1·2
Olearia haastii ★	Daisy bush	6–9	1·8–2·8
Pernettya mucronata★	Prickly heath	3–5	1–1·5
Pieris★	Lily of the valley bush	4–10	1·2–3·1
Prunus laurocerasus★	Cherry laurel	15–20	4·6–6·1
– P. lusitanica★	Portugal laurel	15–25	4·6–7·6
Pyracantha★	Firethorn	14–16	4·3–4·9
Rhododendron★		1–12	0·3–3·7
Ribes sanguineum	Flowering currant	9–12	2·8–3·7
Ruscus aculeatus★	Butcher's broom	1½–3	0·5–1
Skimmia japonica★		3–4	1–1·2
Symphoricarpos	Snowberry	4–8	1·2–2·4
Viburnum tinus★	Laurustinus	7–10	2–3·1
Vinca★	Periwinkle	1–1½	0·3–0·5

★ Evergreen

Spread feet	Spread metres	Flower colour	Flowering season	Pruning
...3-5	1-1·5	pink to red	late spr – early sum	after flowering
...4-8	1·2-2·4	yellow to red	late spr	after flowering
...7-9	2-2·8	white	early spr – mid spr	old stems in .... mid spring
...indefinite			year round	
...8-10	2·4-3·1	orange-gold	mid spr – late spr	after flowering
...10-15	3·1-4·6	orange-yellow	mid spr – late spr	after flowering
...15-18	4·6-5·5	greenish yellow	mid spr	topiary in late summer
...12-15	3·7-4·6	red-pink	mid spr – late spr	mid spring ......
...7-9	2-2·8	pink	early spr – mid spr	mid spring ......
...8-10	2·4-3·1	white	mid spr – late spr	after flowering
...12-15	3·7-4·6	creamy-white	late spr – mid sum	
...9-10	2·8-3·1	pinky-white	late spr	early spring.....
...3-5	1-1·5	purple-white	mid win – early spr	early spring.....
...6-10	1·8-3·1	white	early aut – late aut	mid spring ......
...4-5	1·2-1·5	yellow and red	late spr	
...12-18	3·7-5·5	white	mid sum – late sum	mid spring ......
...indefinite		white	early sum	mid spring ......
...8-12	2·4-3·7	yellow	early spr – mid spr	after flowering
...indefinite		pinky-white	late spr – early sum	mid spring ......
...3-4	1-1·2	blue-red	mid sum – early aut	early spring.....
...6-8	1·8-2·4	white	mid sum – late sum	early spring.....
...4-5	1·2-1·5	yellow	early sum – late sum	early spring.....
...4-5	1·2-1·5	yellow	mid sum – mid aut	early spring.....
...20-25	6·1-7·6	white	late spr – early sum	mid spring ......
...5-8	1·5-2·4	yellow	mid spr – late spr	after flowering
...10-15	3·1-4·6	white	mid sum	late spring and early autumn for hedges
...3-4	1-1·2	yellow	late win – late spr	mid spring ......
...8-12	2·4-3·7	white	mid sum – late sum	mid spring ......
...indefinite		white	late spr – early sum	early spring.....
...4-10	1·2-3·1	white	early spr – mid spr	after flowering
...20-30	6·1-9·2	white	mid spr	early spring.....
...20-30	6·1-9·2	white	early sum	early spring.....
...14-16	4·3-4·9	white	late spr – early sum	late spring – mid summer for hedges
...2-15	0·6-4·6	many colours	early spr – mid sum	early spring.....
...9-12	2·8-3·7	red	early spr – mid spr	old wood late spring
...indefinite		white	mid spr	early spring.....
...5-7	1·5-2	white	mid spr	
...indefinite		pinky-white	early sum – early aut	early spring.....
...8-10	2·4-3·1	pinkish	mid aut – mid spr	late spring.......
...indefinite		blue	early spr – late spr	

SCREENING TREES

Latin name	Popular name	Height feet	Height metres
Acer campestre	Field maple	25-40	7·6-12·2
– A. platanoides	Norway maple	60-70	18·3-21·4
– A. pseudoplatanus	Sycamore	70-80	21·4-24·4
Aesculus hippocastanum	Horse chestnut	70-80	21·4-24·4
Alnus glutinosa	Alder	50-70	15·3-21·4
Betula pendula	Silver birch	40-60	12·2-18·3
Castanea sativa	Spanish chestnut	60-80	18·3-24·4
Carpinus betulus	Hornbeam	50-70	15·3-21·4
Chamaecyparis lawsoniana★†	Lawson's Cypress	50-80	15·23-24·4
Crataegus monogyna	Hawthorn	20-30	6·1-9·2
Cupressocyparis leylandii	Leyland's cypress	50-75	15·3-22·9
Fagus sylvatica	Beech	80-100	24·4-30·5
Larix decidua†	Common larch	100	30·5
Picea abies★†	Norway spruce	100	30·5
Pinus sylvestris★†	Scots pine	70-100	21·4-30·5
Populus candicans 'Aurora'	Variegated poplar	40-60	12·2-18·3
– P. nigra italica	Lombardy poplar	100-120	30·5-36·6
Pseudotsuga menziesii★†	Douglas fir	100	30·5
Quercus ilex★	Holm or evergreen	50-70	15·3-21·4
– Q. robur	Common oak	60-80	18·3-24·4
Salix caprea	Goat willow	20-70	6·1-21·4
Sorbus aucuparia	Mountain ash	30-50	9·2-15·3
– S. aria	Whitebeam	20-40	6·1-12·2
– S. intermedia	Swedish whitebeam	20-40	6·1-12·2
Thuja occidentalis★†	American arborvitae	30-40	9·2-12·2
– T. plicata★†	Giant thuja	60-90	18·3-27·5
Tsuga heterophylla★†	Western hemlock	70-100	21·4-30·5

★ Evergreen   † Conifer

Acer

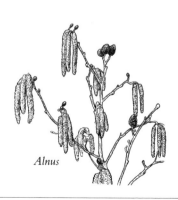

Alnus

Spread feet	Spread metres	Description	Pruning
25-35	7·6-10·7	autumn foliage	
40-50	12·2-15·3	butter-yellow foliage, autumn	
50-60	15·3-18·3	yellowish-green flowers, mid spring	
50-70	15·3-21·4	white flowers, late spring	late winter
23-35	7-10·7	reddish catkins, early spring	
25-35	7·6-10·7	silver-white bark, catkins spring	
40-50	12·2-15·3	yellowish-green flowers, mid summer	
50-60	15·3-18·3	bract-like fruits, mid spring	mid summer for hedges
15-20	4·6-6·1	quick growing	early spring
20-25	6·1-7·6	white flowers, late spring; red berries, autumn	mid summer for hedges
15-25	4·6-7·6	feathery foliage, quick growing	early autumn for hedges
70-90	21·4-27·5	good autumn colour	mid summer for hedges
30-40	9·2-12·2	light green foliage turning yellow in autumn	early spring
30	9·2	dark green foliage	early spring
20-30	6·1-9·2	green-grey foliage	early spring
20-25	6·1-7·6	leaves splashed with white	
20-25	6·1-7·6	quick growing, plant 40ft/12·2m from buildings	
50-70	15·3-21·4	grass-green foliage	early spring
45-60	13·7-18·3	grey-green leathery foliage	mid spring and early autumn for hedges
50-80	15·3-24·4	green foliage, brown in autumn	early spring
15-60	4·6-18·3	attractive catkins	early spring
25-40	7·6-12·2	white flowers, late spring – early summer, red fruits, autumn	
15-30	4·6-9·2	grey leaves, red berries	
15-30	4·6-9·2	white flowers, late spring; red fruit	
20-30	6·1-9·2	bronzy-green foliage	
20-40	6·1-12·2	dark green foliage	
40-50	12·2-15·3	grey-green feathery foliage	early summer for hedges

Salix

Sorbus

SHRUBS FOR CHALK

Latin name	Popular name	Height feet	Height metres
Arbutus unedo★	Strawberry tree	10-15	3·1-4·6
Berberis	Barberry	6-12	1·8-3·7
Buddleia davadii	Butterfly bush	9-12	2·8-3·7
Cistus	Rock rose	6-8	1·8-2·4
Chaenomeles	Japanese quince	2-10	0·6-3·1
Cotoneaster		1½-25	0·5-7·6
Cytisus	Broom	6in-8ft	15cm-2·4m
Daphne mezereum	Mezereon	3-5	1-1·5
Elaeagnus		8-10	2·4-3·1
Escallonia	Chilean gum box	5-12	1·5-3·7
Euonymus	Spindle tree	12-18	3·7-5·5
Forsythia	Golden bells	5-12	1·5-3·7
Fuchsia		1-8	0·3-2·4
Genista	Broom	6in-20ft	15cm-6·1m
Griselinia		10-15	3·1-4·6
Hebe★	Shrubbery veronica	1½-6	0·5-1·8
Helianthemum	Rock rose	9in-1ft	23cm-0·3m
Hippophae	Sea buckthorn	15-25	4·6-7·6
Hypericum	St. John's wort	1-5	0·3-1·5
Ilex★	Holly	8-20	2·4-6·1
Kerria	Batchelor's buttons	6-10	1·8-3·1
Lavandula	Lavender	1-3	0·3-1
Lonicera†	Honeysuckle	indefinite	
Philadelphus	Mock orange	3-15	1-4·6
Phlomis fruticosa	Jerusalem sage	2-3½	0·6-1·1
Potentilla fruticosa	Shrubby cinquefoil	2-4	0·6-1·2
Prunus laurocerasus★	Cherry laurel	15-20	4·6-6·1
Pyracantha	Firethorn	10-16	3·1-4·9
Ribes	Flowering currant	9-12	2·8-3·7
Rosmarinus★	Rosemary	6-7	1·8-2
Romneya	Californian tree poppy	6-7	1·8-2
Sambucus	Elder	12-18	3·7-5·5
Santolina	Lavender cotton	1½-2	0·5-0·6
Senecio greyii ★	Shrubby ragwort	3-4	1-1·2
Spartium junceum	Spanish broom	9-12	2·8-3·7
Spiraea	Bridal wreath	3-8	1-2·4
Syringa vulgaris vars.	Lilac	4-18	1·2-5·5
Tamarix	Tamarisk	12-15	3·7-4·6
Ulex★	Gorse	4-6	1·2-1·8
Viburnum		2-15	1·6-4·6
Vinca★	Periwinkle	1-1½	0·3-0·5
Weigela		6-8	1·8-2·4
Yucca	Adam's needle	3-6	1-1·8

★ Evergreen † Climbing

Spread feet	Spread metres	Flower colour	Flowering season	Pruning
.8-10	2·4-3·1	white	mid aut – late aut	mid spring
.7-15	2-4·6	orange-yellow	mid spr – late spr	after flowering
.9-12	2·8-3·7	purple, white	mid sum – mid aut	early spring
.7-9	2-2·8	white	early sum – mid sum	spring
.3-12	1-3·7	red, pink	early spr – late spr	train after flowering
.2-25	0·6-7·6	white	mid spr – mid sum	early spring
.1-8	0·3-2·4	various	mid spr – early sum	after flowering
.3-5	1-1·5	purple, white	mid win – early spr	early spring
.6-10	1·8-3·1	white	early aut – late aut	mid spring
.6-12	1·8-3·7	pink, red, crimson	early sum – mid sum	after flowering
.12-18	3·7-5·5	white	mid sum – late sum	mid spring
.7-12	2-3·7	yellow	early spr – mid spr	after flowering
.2-8	0·6-2·4	pink, red, purple, white	early sum – mid aut	late autumn
.3-15	1-4·6	yellow	late spr – mid sum	early spring
.8-10	2·4-3·1	greenish-yellow foliage		mid spring
.2½-6	0·8-1·8	various	mid spr – mid aut	spring
.1-2	0·3-0·6	various	late spr – early sum	after flowering
.15-20	4·6-6·1			late summer for hedges
.1½-7	0·5-2	yellow	early sum – early aut	early spring
.6-12	1·8-3·7	white	late spr – early sum	mid spring
.6-8	1·8-2·4	yellow	mid spr – early sum	after flowering
.1½-6	0·5-1·8	lavender	mid sum – late sum	early spring/deadhead after flowering
.indefinite		yellow, pink	early sum – mid aut	after flowering
.4-12	1·2-3·7	white	late spr – mid sum	old wood in early spring
.3½-4½	1·1-1·4	yellow	early sum	mid autumn
.2-4	0·6-1·2	yellow	early sum – early aut	after flowering
.20-30	6·1-9·2	white	mid spr	
.10-16	3·1-4·9	white	early sum	late spring to mid summer for hedges
.9-12	2·8-3·7	pink, red	early spr – mid spr	late spring
.6-7	1·8-2	violet	mid spr – late spr	spring
.8-12	2·4-3·7	white and yellow	late sum – early aut	mid autumn
.12-15	3·7-4·6	white	mid win – early aut	mid autumn for foliage
.2½-3½	0·8-1·1	yellow	mid sum – late sum	early spring
.4-6	1·2-1·8	yellow	early sum – mid sum	
.7-8	2-2·4	yellow	early sum – late sum	deadhead
.4-8	1·2-2·4	white, pink, red	mid spr – early sum	early spring
.4-15	1·2-4·6	various	late spr – early sum	early spring
.15-18	4·6-5·5	rosy-pink	mid sum – late sum	early spring
.4-8	1·2-2·4	yellow	late win – early aut	early spring
.5-18	1·5-5·5	white	mid win – mid aut	after flowering
.indefinite		blue	early spr – late spr	
.6-8	1·8-2·4	various	late spr – early sum	after flowering
.3-5	1-1·5	white, cream	mid sum – late sum	

CLIMBING SHRUBS

Latin name	Popular name	Flower colour
Actinidia deliciosa	Chinese gooseberry	buff
– A. kolomikta		variegated leaves
Campsis grandiflora	Trumpet vine of China	orange-scarlet
Ceanothus	Californian lilac	blue
Celastrus orbiculatus		
Chaenomeles speciosa	Japanese quince	red
Clematis	Virgin's bower	various
Cotoneaster horizontalis	Fishbone cotoneaster	pinkish
Eccremocarpus	Chilean glory flower	yellow, orange, red
Euonymus fortunei 'Coloratus'†		variegated leaves
Forsythia suspensa	Golden bells	yellow
Hedera vars.★	Ivy	many with variegated leaves
Hydrangea petiolaris†	Climbing hydrangea	white
Jasminum nudiflorum	Winter flowering jasmine	yellow
Jasminum officinale	Summer flowering jasmine	white
Lonicera	Honeysuckle	various
Magnolia grandiflora★	Laurel magnolia	creamy-white
Parthenocissus	Virginia creeper, Boston ivy	leaves colour in autumn
Passiflora caerulea	Passion flower	green-blue, white
Phygelius capensis	Cape figwort	red
Polygonum baldschuanicum	Russian vine	white
Pyracantha	Firethorn	white
Rosa climbing vars.	Rose	various
Schizophragma hydrangeoides†		creamy
Solanum crispum		pale heliotrope
– S. jasminoides 'Album'		white
Vitis coignetiae	Ornamental vine	
Wisteria floribunda	Japanese wisteria	blue, pink, white
– W. sinensis	Chinese wisteria	mauve, purple, white

★ Evergreen   † Self-clinging

Lonicera

Chaenomeies

Fruit	Season	Pruning
...reddish	mid sum – late sum	late winter
		late winter
	late sum	spring
	late spr – early sum	mid spring
...yellow and scarlet	late aut – mid win	late winter
...yellow	early spr, mid aut	train after flowering
...silvery silken	late spr – mid aut	depends on variety
...red	late spr, mid aut	early spring
	mid sum – early aut	mid spring
		mid spring
	early spr – mid spr	after flowering
		early spring
	early sum	
	late aut – late win	after flowering
	early sum – late sum	after flowering
	early sum – mid aut	thin shoots after flowering
	mid sum – mid aut	spring
		spring
...orange	mid sum – early aut	early spring
	mid sum – early aut	mid spring
	mid sum – mid aut	autumn
...red, orange, yellow	late spr – early sum	late spring – mid summer for hedges
...red	late spr – early aut	early spring
	mid sum	deadhead
	early sum – late sum	early spring
	mid sum – late sum	early spring
		early autumn
	late spr – early sum	late winter
	late spr – early sum	late winter

Pyracantha

Wisteria

HEDGE MAKING SHRUBS

Latin name	Popular name	Height feet	Height metres
Berberis darwinii ★	Darwin's barberry	6–8	1·8–2·4
Buxus sempervirens ★	Box	4–9	1·2–2·8
Carpinus betulus	Hornbeam	8–20	2·4–6·1
Chamaecyparis lawsoniana ★	Lawson's cypress	15–18	4·6–5·5
Cupressocyparis leylandii ★	Leyland cypress	8–20	2·4–6·1
Cotoneaster simonsii		3–5	1–1·5
Cupressus macrocarpa ★	Monterey cypress	8–12	2·4–3·7
Escallonia ★	Crimson spire	6–8	1·8–2·4
Euonymus japonicus ★	Japanese spindle tree	4–8	1·2–2·4
Fagus sylvatica	Beech	8–15	2·4–4·6
Fuchsia 'Riccartonii'		4–5	1·2–1·5
Griselinia littoralis ★		5–7	1·5–2
Ilex aquifolium ★	Holly	5–20	1·5–6·1
Lavandula ★	Lavender	1½–4	0·5–1·2
Ligustrum ovalifolium	Privet	2½–10	0·8–3·1
Lonicera nitida	Shrubby honeysuckle	4–5	1·2–1·5
Olearia haastii ★	Daisy bush	3–4	1–1·2
Osmarea burkwoodii		5–10	1·5–3·1
Prunus cerasifera	Purple plum	6–9	1·8–2·8
Pyracantha ★	Firethorn	4–8	1·2–2·4
Quercus ilex ★	Holm oak	15–20	4·6–6·1
Rhododendron ponticum ★		8–15	2·4–4·6
Rosa floribunda	Floribunda rose	2½–4	0·8–1·2
Rosmarinus ★	Rosemary	6–7	1·8–2
Santolina chamaecyparissus ★	Lavender cotton	1½–2	0·5–0·6
Tamarix ramosissima	Tamarisk	10–15	3·1–4·6
Taxus baccata	Yew	5–12	1·5–3·7
Thuja plicata ★	Arborvitae	5–12	1·5–3·7

★ Evergreen

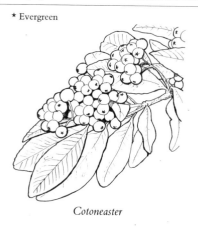

Cotoneaster

Ilex

Spread feet	Spread metres	Description	Pruning
1½–2	0·5–0·6	orange flowers	after flowering
1½–2	0·5–0·6	aromatic scent	topiary in late summer
1–1¼	0·3–0·4	retains foliage	mid summer
1½–2	0·5–0·6	green, gold and grey forms	early spring
2½–3	0·8–1	green and golden leaved varieties	early autumn
1–1½	0·3–0·5	red berries	early spring
2½–3	0·8–1	yellow leaves	early spring
1–1½	0·3–0·5	pink and red flowers, summer	after flowering
1½–2	0·5–0·6		mid spring
1–1½	0·3–0·5	retains foliage	mid summer
1½–2	0·5–0·6	purple flowers, summer	late autumn
1½–2	0·5–0·6		mid spring
1½–2½	0·5–0·8	red berries	mid spring
1–2	0·3–0·6	blue flowers	early spring/deadhead after flowering
1–1½	0·3–0·5		late spring and early autumn
1	0·3		after flowering
2–3	0·6–1	white flowers	mid spring
1½–2	0·5–0·6	white flowers	after flowering
1½–2	0·5–0·6	crimson leaves	after flowering
1½–2	0·5–0·6	orange and red berries	late spring – mid summer
1½–2	0·5–0·6		mid spring and early autumn
2–2½	0·6–0·8		
1–1½	0·3–0·5	flowers various	early spring
1–1½	0·3–0·5	scented foliage	spring
1½–2	0·5–0·6	grey leaves	early spring
1½	0·5	pink flowers	early spring
1½–2	0·5–0·6		
1–2	0·3–0·6		

Taxus

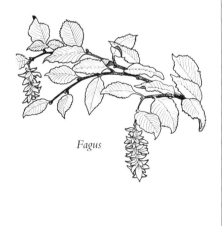

Fagus

SELECTED ROCK PLANTS

Latin name	Popular name	Height in/cm	Colour	Season
Achillea clavennae	Rock yarrow	6/15	white	late spr – early sum
– A. 'King Edward'		6/15	sulphur yellow	early sum – late sum
– A. tomentosa		6/15	yellow	early sum – late sum
Aethionema grandiflorum	Stone cress	9/23	light pink	late spr – early sum
– A. × 'Warley Rose'		6/15	pink	late spr – early sum
Ajuga reptans 'Burgundy Glow'	Bugle	6/15	blue	mid spr – late spr
Alchemilla alpina	Lady's mantle	4-6/10-15	greenish-yellow	early sum – late sum
Alyssum saxatile	Gold dust	9/23	yellow	late spr – early sum
Androsace lanuginosa	Rock jasmine	4/10	white and pink	early sum – mid sum
– A. sarmentosa		4/10	pink	late spr – early sum
Antennaria dioica	Cat's ear	3/8	white or pink	early sum – mid sum
Aquilegia bertolonii	Columbine	5/13	blue	early sum – mid sum
– A. glandulosa		9/23	blue and white	early sum – mid sum
Arabis caucasica	Rock cress	9/23	white, pink	mid spr – late spr
Arenaria balearica	Balearic sandwort	½/1	white	early sum – mid sum
– A. montana	Mountain sandwort	4/10	white	early sum – late sum
Armeria juniperifolia	Stemless thrift	2/5	pink	mid spr – late spr
– A. maritima	Thrift	6/15	pink, rose, white	late spr – early sum
Asperula lilaciflora	Stemless woodruff	2/5	pink	late spr – late sum
– A. suberosa		3/8	pink	early sum – mid sum
Aster alpinus	Alpine aster	6/15	blue	late spr – early sum
Astilbe simplicifolia★	Spiraea	9/23	pink	early sum – mid sum
Aubrieta vars.	Coloured rock cress	3/8	various	mid spr – late spr
Campanula carpatica	Bellflower	6/15	blue, white	mid sum – late sum
– C. cochleariifolia		4/10	blue, white	early sum – mid sum
– C. garganica		4/10	blue	mid sum – late sum
– C. portenschlagiana		4/10	blue	early sum – late sum
– C. poscharskyana		6/15	blue	early sum – late sum
Ceratostigma plumbaginoides		6-9/15-23	blue	late sum – early aut
Cheiranthus 'Harpur Crewe'	Wallflower	12/30	yellow	mid spr – early sum
Chrysanthemopsis hosmariense		10/25	white	late spr – mid aut
Convolvulus cneorum	Shrubby convolvulus	18/46	white	late spr – late sum
– C. sabatius		trailing	lilac blue	early sum – late sum
Cyclamen coum	Hardy cyclamen	3/8	crimson	late win – early spr
– C. hederifolium		4/10	pink, white	early aut – mid aut
Dianthus gratianopolitanus	Cheddar pink	6/15	pink	late spr – early sum
– D. deltoides	Maiden pink	6/15	pink, crimson	early sum – late sum
– D. pavonius		4/10	rose and buff	early sum – late sum
Diascia cordata		9/23	pink	early sum – early aut

Selected Rock Plants

Latin name	Popular name	Height in/cm	Colour	Season
Dryas octopetala	Mountain avens	3/8	white	late spr – early sum
Erigeron 'Elstead Pink'	Fleabane	9/23	soft pink	early sum – late sum
Erinus alpinus		3/8	pink, red, white	late spr – early sum
Erodium reichardii 'Roseum'	Heron's bill	1/3	pink	late spr – mid aut
Festuca glauca	Blue fescue	6/15	glaucous foliage	early sum – mid sum
Gentiana acaulis	Gentianella	4/10	purple	mid spr – early sum
– *G. asclepiadea*	Willow gentian	2-4/5-10	purple	early sum – late sum
– *G. farreri*		5/13	electric blue	late sum – mid aut
– *G. septemfida*		6/15	blue	mid sum – late sum
– *G. sino-ornata*	Autumn gentian	6/15	blue	early sum – late aut
– *G. verna*	Spring gentian	3/8	blue	mid spr – late spr
Geranium × 'Ballerina'	Crane's bill	4/10	pink	late spr – mid sum
– *G. cantabrigiense*		4/10	shell pink, white	late spr – early sum
– *G. sanguineum striatum*	Lancastrian crane's bill	3/8	pink	early sum – mid sum
Gypsophila repens	Creeping gypsophila	4/10	pink	early sum – late sum
Helianthemum	Rock rose	2-3/5-8	various	late spr – early sum
Hepatica nobilis		6/15	blue, pink, white	early spr – mid spr
Hypericum coris	St John's wort	6/15	yellow	early sum
– *H. olympicum*		12/30	yellow	mid sum – late sum
– *H. o. minus*		2/5	deep yellow	early sum – late sum
Iberis saxatilis	Perennial candytuft	2/5	white	late spr – early sum
– *I. sempervirens*		6-12/15-30	white	late spr – early sum
Linum arboreum	Shrubby flax	9/23	yellow	late spr – late sum
– *L. narbonense*	Perennial flax	18/46	blue	early sum – early aut
Lithodora 'Grace Ward'	Gromwell	6/15	blue	late spr – early sum
– *L. oleifolia*		6/15	sky blue	late spr – early sum
Myosotis alpestris 'Ruth Fischer'	Forget-me-not	2/5	blue	mid spr
Nierembergia repens★		2/5	white	mid sum – early aut
Omphalodes cappadocica		6/15	bright blue	mid spr – late spr
– *O. verna*★		6/15	blue	mid spr – early sum
Onosma alboroseum		9/23	pink tinged	early sum – mid sum
– *O. tauricum*	Golden drop	9/23	yellow	early sum – late sum
Othonna cheirifolia		9-12/23-30	yellow	early sum – mid sum
Oxalis enneaphylla	Wood sorrel	3/8	white or blush	late spr – early sum
– *O. rosea*		6/15	rose	mid spr – early aut
Parahebe lyallii	Veronica	6/15	white	early sum – early aut
– *P.* 'Miss Willmott'		6/15	pinkish lilac	early sum – late sum
Penstemon alpinus		8/20	light blue	late spr – early sum
– *P. heterophyllus*		10/25	blue	early sum – late sum

★Cool, partially shaded place

SELECTED ROCK PLANTS

Latin name	Popular name	Height in/cm	Colour	Season
Phlox douglasii	Moss pink	3/8	various	late spr – early sum
– P. divaricata laphami		9/23	lavender blue	late spr – early sum
– P. subulata		3-6/8-15	various	late spr – early sum
Polygonum affine	Himalayan knotweed	10/25	red	mid sum – mid aut
– P. vaccinifolium	Alpine knotweed	6/15	pink	late sum – mid aut
Potentilla aurea 'Plena'	Cinquefoil	3/8	yellow	late spr – mid sum
– P. × tonguei		3/8	orange	early sum – late sum
Primula auricula	Auricula	6/15	various	mid spr – late spr
– P. denticulata★	Drumstick primrose	12/30	lilac, white	early spr – mid spr
– P. frondosa★		3/8	rosy-lilac	mid spr – late spr
– P. juliae★		2/5	crimson	early spr – mid spr
– P. juliana★		3-6/8-15	pink to crimson	early spr – mid spr
– P. marginata		6/15	lavender	early spr
Pulsatilla vulgaris	Pasque flower	8/20	mauve, purple	mid spr – late spr
Ramonda myconi★	Rosette mullein	6/15	lilac	late spr – early sum
Saponaria ocymoides	Soapwort	6/15	pink, carmine	mid sum – late sum
– S. × olivana		2/5	light pink	late spr – mid sum
Saxifraga aizoon	Silver saxifrage	2-9/5-23	white, pink, yellow	early sum – mid sum
– S. × apiculata	Cushion saxifrage	3/8	yellow	early spr – mid spr
– S. burseriana		2/5	white	early spr – mid spr
– S.cochlearis		3-6/8-15	white	early sum – mid sum
– S. cotyledon	Silver saxifrage	24/61	white and red	early sum – mid sum
– S. × 'Cranbourne'		1/3	pink	early spr – mid spr
– S. oppositifolia		1/3	white to crimson	early spr – mid spr
– S. 'Sanguinea Superba'★		6/15	crimson	mid spr – early sum
– S. umbrosa★	London pride	6-12/15-30	pink	late spr – early sum
Sedum cauticola	Stonecrop	4/10	carmine	mid sum – early aut
– S. kamtschaticum 'Variegatum'		6/15	deep yellow	early sum – early aut
– S. lydium		1/3	white	early sum
– S. pulchellum		3/8	pink	early sum – late sum
– S. rupestre		6/15	yellow	mid sum
– S. spathulifolium		2/5	yellow	early sum
– S. spurium		3/8	rose to crimson	mid sum – late sum
Sempervivum tectorum	Houseleek	6/15	rose	early sum – mid sum
– S. arachnoideum	Cobweb houseleek	3/8	rose	early sum – mid sum
Silene schafta	Catchfly	6/15	rosy-red	late sum – early aut
Sisyrinchium angustifolium	Blue-eyed grass	9/23	blue	mid spr – late sum
Soldanella montana		4/10	blue	mid spr – late spr

SELECTED ROCK PLANTS

Latin name	Popular name	Height in/cm	Colour	Season
Solidago cutleri	Alpine golden rod	9/23	yellow	early aut – mid aut
– S. virgaurea		6/15	deep yellow	early sum – mid sum
Synthyris reniformis		6/15	blue	mid spr – early sum
Thymus serpyllum	Wild thyme	prostrate	pink, crimson, white	early sum – late sum
Veronica gentianoides 'Nana'		8/20	pale blue	late spr – early sum
– V. teucrium prostrata		3/8	blue	early sum – late sum
– V. saturejoides		3/8	deep blue	late spr – early sum
Viola cornuta★	Horned violet	9/23	white to violet	late spr – mid sum
Zauschneria californica	Californian fuchsia	12/30	scarlet	late sum – mid aut

★ Cool, partially shaded place

Raised beds ideal for growing alpines

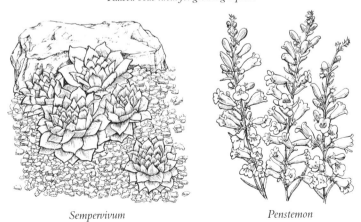

Sempervivum   *Penstemon*

PLANTS FOR PAVING

Latin name	Popular name
Acaena buchananii	New Zealand burr
– A microphylla	
Achillea 'King Edward'	Rock yarrow
– A. clavennae	
Arenaria balearica	Balearic sandwort
– A. caespitosa	Stemless sandwort
– A. purpurascens	Purple sandwort
Armeria maritima	Thrift
Campanula cochleariifolia	Bellflower
– C. garganica	
– C. poscharskyana	
Erodium reichardii	Heron's bill
Geranium pylzowianum	Crane's bill
– G. sanguineum striatum	
Gypsophila cerastiodes	
– G. repens	
Hedyotis michauxii	Bluetts
Mazus reptens	
Oxalis acetosella	Wood sorrell
Phlox douglasii	Moss pink
Potentilla nitida	Cinquefoil
Raoulia australis	
– R. glabra	
Saxifraga moschata	Mossy saxifrage
Sedum dasyphyllum	Stonecrop
– S. lydium	
– S. spathulifolium	
– S. spurium	
Silene acaulis	Stemless catchfly
Thymus serphyllum	Thyme
Veronica prostrata	

Geranium

Erodium

Description	Pruning
...tiny, fern-like, grey-green leaves	
...small bronzy leaves, red burr-like flowers	
...grey-green leaves, sulphur-yellow flowers in summer	
...grey-green leaves, white flowers in summer	
...close carpets of green, minute white flowers	
...moss-like leaves. There is a yellow-leaved variety	
...moss-like leaves, lilac flowers in spring	
...cushions of narrow leaves, heads of pink or crimson in	deadhead
...late spring – early summer	
...nodding white or blue bells on threat-like stems in early summer	deadhead
...starry blue flowers in summer	deadhead
...widely creeping plant with starry blue summer flowers	deadhead
...small pink flowers all summer	deadhead
...pretty divided leaves, pink flowers late spring – early summer	after flowering
...close mats of leaves covered with small pink flowers in summer	after flowering
...small white, pink-veined flowers all summer	deadhead
...narrow leaves and small pink or white flowers	deadhead
...blue and white flowers late spring – early summer. Likes a shady place	deadhead
...small mauve flowers, late spring – early summer on green carpet	deadhead
...pink flowers in spring, shamrock leaves	
...white, pink or mauve flowers in early summer	
...silvery carpets with rose-pink flowers late spring – early summer	
...a close carpet of silver	
...similar to the above but green	
...mossy foliage, white or pink flowers mid spring – early summer	
...grey, succulent leaves; pale pink flowers, early summer	deadhead
...bronze-red leaves, white flowers, early summer	deadhead
...fleshy grey or purple leaves	deadhead
...pink to crimson flowers in late summer	deadhead
...compact cushions, pink flowers in spring	
...aromatic carpets with white, pink or crimson flowers	autumn
...bright blue flowers in summer	deadhead

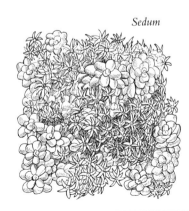

Sedum

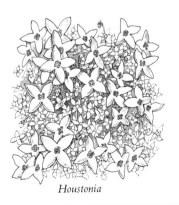

Houstonia

SEASIDE PLANTS

Latin name	Popular name	Height feet	Height metres
Agapanthus	African lily	2-3	0·6-1
Alyssum	Gold dust	3·2-9in	8-23cm
Amaryllis belladonna	Belladonna lily	2	0·6
Anagallis	Pimpernel	1	0·3
Anchusa	Alkanet	1-5	0·3-1·5
Armeria	Thrift	3·2in-2ft	8cm-0·6m
Aubrieta	Coloured rock cress	3·2in	8cm
Calendula	Pot marigold	1½	0·5
Centranthus	Red valerian	2	0·6
Cheiranthus	Wallflower	1-2	0·3-0·6
Clarkia	Clarkia	2	0·6
Convolvulus	Convolvulus	6in-1½ft	15cm-0·5m
Crambe	Plumed seakale	5	1·5
Crinum		3	1
Dianthus	Pink, carnation	6in-2ft	15cm-0·6m
Echinops	Globe thistle	2-4	0·6-1·2
Eryngium	Sea holly	2-3	0·6-1
Erysimum	Wallflower	1-2	0·3-0·6
Eschscholzia	Californian poppy	1	0·3
Gazania	Treasure flower	6in	15cm
Godetia	Godetia	9in-2ft	23cm-0·6m
Helianthemum	Rock rose	1	0·3
Iris unguicularis	Algerian iris	12	3·7
Kniphofia	Torch lily, red hot poker	2-7	0·6-2
Lavatera	Tree mallow	2-5	0·6-1·5
Limonium	Statice	6in-2ft	15cm-0·6m
Linum	Flax	1-2	0·3-0·6
Lupinus	Lupin	2-3	0·6-1
Lychnis	Campion	1-3	0·3-1
– L. chalcedonica	Jerusalem cross	3	1
Malope	Mallow	3	1
Mesembryanthemum	Livingstone daisy	6in-1ft	15cm-0·3m
Matthiola	Stock	1-3	0·3-1
Montbretia		2	0·6
Nemesia		9in	23cm
Nerine bowdenii	Diamond lily	1½	0·5
Oenothera	Evening primrose	6in-3ft	15cm-1m
Osteospermum	Veldt daisy	1-2	0·3-0·6
Oxalis	Wood sorrel	3·2-9in	8-23cm
Papaver	Poppy	2-3	0·6-1
Petunia		1-1½	0·3-0·5
Primula auricula	Auricula	3·2-6in	8-15cm
Saponaria	Soapwort	3·2in-2ft	8cm-0·6m
Sedum	Stonecrop	3·2in-1½ft	8cm-0·5m
Silene	Catchfly	3·2in-2ft	8cm-0·6m
Tagetes	Marigold	6in-3ft	15cm-1m
Tulipa	Tulip	9in-2ft	23cm-0·6m
Zinnia		1-2½	0·3-0·8

HA–Hardy annual   HHA–Half-hardy annual   HB–Hardy biennial   HP–Hardy perennial

Flower colour	Season	Type	Pruning
..blue, white	mid sum – early aut	HP/HHP	deadhead
..white, yellow	late spr – early aut	R, HA	after flowering
..pink	late sum – mid aut	B	after flowering
..blue, red	early sum – late sum	HA	
..blue	late spr – mid sum	HP	
..pink, crimson, white	mid spr – mid sum	R	deadhead
..various	mid spr – early sum	R	deadhead
..yellow, orange	early sum – early aut	HA	
..pink, red, white	early sum – mid sum	HP	deadhead
..various	mid spr – early sum	HP/HB	mid autumn
..pink, crimson, white	mid sum – late sum	HA	
..various	late spr – early aut	R, HA	
..white	mid sum – late sum	HP	
..pink, white	late sum	B	
..various	late spr – late sum	HP/R	deadhead
..blue	mid sum – late sum	HP	deadhead
..blue, white	mid sum – late sum	HP	mid autumn
..yellow, orange	late spr – early sum	HP/HB	autumn
..various	early sum – early aut	HA	
..yellow, orange	early sum – late sum	HHP	deadhead
..pink to crimson	early sum – early aut	HA	
..various	late spr – early aut	HP	
..sky-blue	late aut – early spr	HP	after flowering
..yellow, red	early sum – early aut	HP	deadhead
..pink, white	mid sum – late sum	HP/HA	autumn
..various	mid sum – late sum	HP, HHA	after flowering
..various	late spr	HA	
..various	late spr – late sum	HP/HA	late autumn
..white to crimson	early sum – late sum	HP	deadhead
..scarlet	mid sum – late sum	HP	deadhead
..rose, crimson	mid sum – early aut	HA	
..various	late spr – late sum	HHP	deadhead
..various	late spr – late sum	HHA	
..yellow, orange, crimson	late sum – early aut	HP	early spring
..various	early sum – late sum	HHA	
..pink	early aut – late aut	HP	deadhead
..yellow	early sum – early aut	HP/HB	mid autumn
..white, purple	early sum – early aut	HP	mid autumn
..pink, yellow	late spr – early aut	HP/R	deadhead
..various	late spr – early aut	HP/HA	deadhead
..various	early sum – early aut	HHA	
..various	late spr – mid sum	HP/R	deadhead
..white to rose	late spr – early aut	HP, R, HA	late autumn
..various	early sum – early aut	HP/R	deadhead
..white to rose	late spr – early aut	HP, R, HA	
..yellow, orange and crimson	early sum – early aut	HHA	
..various	late win – early spr	B	deadhead
..various	mid sum – early aut	HHA	

HHP–Half-hardy perennial   B–Bulb   R–Rock plant

SELECTED ORNAMENTAL TREES

Latin name	Popular name	Height feet	Height metres
Acer grosseri hersii	Snake-bark maple	30	9·2
– *A. negundo* 'Variegatum'	Box elder	30	9·2
– *A. palmatum*	Japanese maple	15	4·6
Amelanchier lamarckii	Snowy mespilus	25	7·6
Betula pendula 'Dalecarlica'	Swedish birch	60	18·3
– *B.* 'Youngii'	Weeping birch	25	7·6
Catalpa bignonioides	Indian bean tree	40	12·2
– *C.* 'Aurea'	Golden Indian bean tree	30	9·2
Cercis siliquastrum	Judas tree	20	6·1
Cornus florida rubra	Flowering dogwood	15	4·6
– *C.* × *kousa*	Flowering dogwood	20	6·1
Cotoneaster frigidus		20	6·1
Crataegus × *lavallei*	Thorn	20	6·1
Davidia involucrata	Handkerchief tree, dove tree	50	15·3
Fagus sylvatica 'Dawyck'	Dawyck beech	50	15·3
Fraxinus ornus	Manna ash	50	15·3
Ginkgo biloba	Maidenhair tree	70	21·4
Gleditsia 'Sunburst'	Golden honey locust	20-30	6·1-9·2
Halesia tetraptera	Snowdrop tree	20	6·1
Koelreuteria paniculata	Golden rain tree	15-30	4·6-9·2
Laburnum vossii	Golden rain	30	9·2
Liriodendron tulipfera	Tulip tree	60	18·3
Liquidambar styraciflua	Sweet gum	50	15·3
Magnolia denudata	Lily tree, yulan	25	7·6
– *M. sieboldii*		15	4·6
– *M.* × *soulangiana*		25	7·6
Malus 'Eleyi'	Red crab	25	7·6
– *M. floribunda*	Japanese crab	20	6·1
– *M.* 'John Downie'	Crab apple	35	10·7
– *M.* × *robusta*	Siberian crab	35	10·7
– *M.* 'Golden Hornet'	Crab apple	35	10·7
Mespilus germanica	Medlar	20	6·1
Metasequoia†	Dawn redwood	50-100	15·3-30·5
Morus nigra	Black mulberry	35	10·7
Nothofagus obliqua	Rebel beech	30-60	9·2-18·3
Prunus 'Amanogawa'	Fastigiate cherry	25	7·6
– *P. avium*	Gean	30	9·2
– *P.* × *blireana*	Double myrobalan	15	4·6
– *P. cerasifera* 'Pissardii'	Purple plum	20	6·1
– *P.* 'Kanzan'	Japanese cherry	35	10·7
– *P. persica* 'Klara Mayer'	Double flowering peach	15	4·6
– *P. sargentii*	Sargent's cherry	30	9·2
– *P. serrula*	Birch-bark cherry	30	9·2
– *P.* 'Shidare-zakura'	Cheal's weeping cherry	15	4·6
– *P. subhirtella* 'Autumnalis'	Winter-flowering cherry	20	6·1
– *P.* 'Tai haku'	Japanese cherry	30	9·2
– *P.* × *yedoensis*	Fastigiate cherry	25	7·6
Pyrus salicifolia 'Pendula'	Weeping pear tree	20	6·1

† Conifer

Spread feet	Spread metres	Description	Pruning
..20	6·1	striped bark	
..25	7·6	variegated leaves	
..15	4·6	coloured and divided leaves	
..25	7·6	white flowers in mid spring	
..30	9·2	fern-like leaves	
..20	6·1	weeping habit	
..45	13·7	large leaves, spotted white, flowers mid summer	
..50	15·3	golden foliage	
..20	6·1	rosy-purple flowers, late spring – early summer	
..15	4·6	pink 'flowers' in late spring	mid spring
..15	4·6	white 'flowers' in early summer	mid spring
..25	7·6	red berries in autumn	early spring
..20	6·1	scarlet fruits in autumn	
..40	12·2	white 'flowers' in late spring	
..12	3·7	narrow column	
..50	15·3	creamy-white flowers, attractive fruits	
..50	15·3	yellow foliage in autumn	
..15	4·6	feathery yellow leaves	
..20	6·1	white flowers in late spring	
..15	4·6	feathery leaves, plumes of yellow flowers	
..25	7·6	yellow flowers in late spring – early summer	
..35	10·7	greenish-yellow flowers	
..40	12·2	rich autumn tints	late autumn
..25	7·6	white flowers in mid spring	
..20	6·1	white flowers in early summer	
..25	7·6	white to purple flowers in mid – late spring	
..30	9·2	crimson flowers, mid – late spring	early spring
..25	7·6	pink flowers, mid – late spring	early spring
..30	9·2	yellow and red fruits	early spring
..35	10·7	white flowers, red fruits	early spring
..25	7·6	yellow fruits	early spring
..25	7·6	white flowers, edible fruit	early spring
..20	6·1	light green foliage colouring in autumn	spring
..30	9·2	crimson, blackberry-like fruits	
..25	7·6	fast growing, small elm-like leaves	
..8	2·4	double pink flowers, spring	
..25	7·6	double white flowers, late spring	
..15	4·6	double pink flowers, early spring	
..20	6·1	pink flowers, purple leaves	
..35	10·7	double pink flowers, spring	
..15	4·6	double pink flowers, mid spring	
..25	7·6	pink flowers, mid spring	
..15	4·6	peeling mahogany bark	
..15	4·6	double pink flowers, weeping habit	
..25	7·6	pink flowers, late autumn – early spring	
..30	9·2	white flowers, late spring	
..25	7·6	white flowers, mid spring	
..15	4·6	grey foliage, white flowers	

◄ # SELECTED ORNAMENTAL TREES

Latin name	Popular name	Height feet	Height metres
Quercus robur fastigiata	Cypress oak	40	12·2
Robinia pseudoacacia 'Frisia'	Golden false acacia	30	9·2
Salix chrysocoma	Golden weeping willow	50	15·3
Sorbus aucuparia	Mountain ash	40	12·2
– S. aria 'Majestica'	Whitebeam	30–40	9·2–12·2
– S. intermedia	Swedish whitebeam	35	10·7
– S. sargentiana	Sargent's mountain ash	25	7·6
Taxodium distichum†	Swamp cypress	100	30·5

† Conifer

SEASIDE SHRUBS

Latin name	Popular name	Height feet	Height metres
Arbutus unedo★	Strawberry tree	15–25	4·6–7·6
Berberis darwinii★	Darwin's barberry	8–10	2·4–3·1
Buddleia davidii	Butterfly bush	9–12	2·8–3·7
Camellia		7–15	2–4·6
Ceanothus★		15–20	4·6–6·1
Cistus★	Rock rose	2½–3	0·8–1
Cotoneaster frigidus		15–25	4·6–7·6
Cupressus macrocarpa★	Monterey cypress	50–75	15·3–23
Cytisus scoparius	Broom	5–8	1·5–2·4
Elaeagnus★		8–12	2·4–3·7
Escallonia★		6–12	1·8–3·7
Euonymus japonicus★	Japanese spindle tree	12–18	3·7–5·5
Garrya elliptica★	Silk tassel bush	8–12	2·4–3·7
Griselinia★		10–15	3·1–4·6
Hippophae rhamnoides	Sea buckthorn	15–25	4·6–7·6
Hydrangea		6–8	1·8–2·4
Lupinus arboreus	Tree lupin	4–6	1·2–1·8
Mahonia aquifolium★	Oregon grape	3–5	1–1·5
Olearia haastii★	Daisy bush	6–9	1·8–2·8
Osmanthus delavayi★		7–12	2–3·7
Phlomis fruticosa★	Jerusalem sage	2½–3½	0·8–1·1
Pittosporum tenuifolium		8–12	2·4–3·7
Quercus ilex★	Holm oak	50–70	15·3–21·4
Spartium junceum	Spanish broom	9–12	2·8–3·7
Ulex★	Gorse	5–6	1·5–1·8
Viburnum tinus★	Laurustinus	7–10	2–3·1

★ Evergreen

Spread feet	Spread metres	Description	Pruning
.12	3·7	narrow column	
.25	7·6	ferny yellow leaves	
.50	15·3	golden bark, weeping habit	early spring
.30	9·2	white flowers, red fruits	
.25	7·6	leaves white beneath	
.35	10·7	red fruits in autumn	
.20	6·1	orange-red fruit, rich autumn foliage	
.40	12·2	feathery green foliage, colours in autumn	

Spread feet	Spread metres	Flower colour	Season	Pruning
18-25	5·5-7·6	pinkish	mid aut – early win	mid spring
8-10	2·4-3·1	orange	mid spr – late spr	after flowering
9-12	2·8-3·7	mauve	late aut – mid spr	after flowering
7-15	2·4·6	red, pink, white	late aut – mid spr	mid spring
12-18	3·7-5·5	blue, pink	late spr – early sum	mid spring
5-6	1·5-1·8	white	early sum	early spring
20-40	6·1-12·2	white	early sum – mid sum	early spring
15-24	4·6-7·3			early spring
6-9	1·8-2·8	yellow	late spr – early sum	after flowering
10-15	3·1-4·6			mid spring
6-12	1·8-3·7	pink or red	early sum – mid sum	after flowering
12-18	3·7-5·5	white		mid spring
8-12	2·4-3·7	yellow	late winter	after flowering
8-10	2·4-3·1			mid spring
15-20	4·6-6·1			mid summer
7-9	2-2·8	blue-red	mid sum – early aut	early spring
6-8	1·8-2·4	yellow	early sum	
3-5	1-1·5	yellow	late win – late spr	mid spring
8-12	2·4-3·7	white	mid sum – late sum	mid spring
9-12	2·8-3·7	white	mid spr	spring
4-5	1·2-1·5	yellow	early sum	mid autumn
5-8	1·5-2·4	purple	late spr	mid spring
45-60	13·7-18·3			mid spring and early autumn for hedges
7-8	2-2·4	yellow	early sum – late sum	deadhead
6-8	1·8-2·4	yellow	late win – early aut	early spring
8-10	2·4-3·1	pinkish	mid aut – mid spr	after flowering

TREES AND SHRUBS FOR WET PLACES

Latin name	Popular name	Height feet	Height metres
Alnus glutinosa	Alder	50-70	15·3-21·4
Betula nana	Dwarf birch	2-4	0·6-1·2
Cornus alba	Dogwood	7-9	2-2·8
Hippophae rhamnoides	Sea buckthorn	15-25	4·6-7·6
Populus (all species)	Poplar	40-50	12·2-15·3
Pterocarya	Wing nut	50-80	15·3-24·4
Salix (all species)	Willow	5-50	1·5-15·3
Sambucus	Elder	6-15	1·8-4·6
Taxodium distichum	Swamp cypress	80-100	24·4-30·5
Viburnum opulus 'Sterile'	Snowball tree	10-15	3·1-4·6

SELECTED BULBS

Latin name	Popular name	Height feet	Height metres
Allium	Ornamental onion	1-4	0·3-1·2
Amaryllis belladonna	Belladonna lily	2	0·6
Anemone coronaria	Poppy anemone	1	0·3
Brodiaea	Spring star flower	6-9in	15-23cm
Chionodoxa	Glory of the snow	6in	15cm
Colchicum	Autumn crocus	6in	15cm
Crinum	Crinum	3	1
Crocus	Crocus	6-9in	8-23cm
Erythronium	Dog's-tooth violet	6in-1ft	15cm-0·3m
Fritillaria imperialis	Crown imperial	3	1
– *F. meleagris*	Fritillary	1	0·3
Galanthus	Snowdrop	6-9in	15-23cm
Galtonia	Summer hyacinth	3	1
Gladiolus	Gladiolus	1-5	0·3-1·5
Hyacinthus	Hyacinth	9in-1ft	23cm-0·3m
Iris	Iris	6in-1ft	15cm-0·3m
Ixia	African corn lily	1½	0·5
Leucojum	Snowflake	6in-1½ft	15cm-0·5m
Lilium	Lily	1-8	0·3-2·4
Montbretia	Montbretia	1½-2	0·5-0·6
Muscari	Grape hyacinth	6in	15cm
Narcissus	Daffodil, lent lily	6in-2ft	15cm-0·6m
Ornithogalum	Star-of-Bethlehem	1-2	0·3-0·6
Ranunculus asiaticus	Turban ranunculus	9in	23cm
Sparaxis	Harlequin flower	6in-1ft	15cm-0·3m
Sternbergia	Lily-of-the-field	6in	15cm
Tigridia	Tiger flower	1½-2	0·5-0·6
Tulipa	Tulip	1-2	0·3-0·6
Zephyranthes	Flower of the west wind	6in	15cm

Spread feet	Spread metres	Description	Pruning
.25–35	7·6–10·7	reddish catkins, early spring	
		useful for stream margins	
.9–11	2·8–3·4	red shoots autumn and winter	mid spring
.15–20	4·6–6·1	orange berries early autumn onwards	mid summer
.35–40	10·7–12·2	green or silvery foliage, catkins	
.30–40	9·2–12·2	long green catkins in summer followed by winged seed	
.8–40	2·4–12·2	green or silvery foliage, catkins	early spring
.6–10	1·8–3·1	flat clusters of white flowers in early – mid summer followed by black or red cherries	early spring
		soft green foliage, rich brown in autumn	
.12–18	3·7–5·5	white flowers, late spring – early summer	after flowering

Flower colour	Season	Type
.various	late spr – mid sum	autumn
.pink	early aut – mid aut	mid summer
.various	mid spr – early sum	autumn/spring
.blue, violet, lilac	mid spr – late spr	autumn
.blue	mid spr	autumn
.white, lilac	early aut – mid aut	mid summer
.white, pink	mid sum – late sum	autumn
.various	mid win – early spr	mid summer
.various	early spr – late spr	autumn
.yellow, orange, red	late spr	autumn
.purple, white	mid spr – late spr	autumn
.white, green	mid win – early spr	autumn/spring
.creamy white	mid sum – late sum	autumn
.various	early sum – early aut	spring
.various	mid spr – late spr	autumn
.various	mid win – mid sum	autumn
.various	early sum	spring
.white, pink	early spr – mid sum	autumn
.various	early sum – early aut	autumn/spring
.yellow, orange, red	late sum – early aut	spring
.blue	early spr – mid spr	autumn
.yellow, white, red	early spr – late spr	autumn
.white	early sum	autumn
.various	late spr – early sum	autumn/spring
.various	late spr – early sum	spring
.yellow	mid aut – late aut	mid summer
.various	mid sum – late sum	spring
.various	late win – late spr	autumn
.white	early aut	spring

RECOMMENDED TULIP BULB VARIETIES

Name	Class	Colour	Height in/cm
'Apeldoorn'	DH	scarlet	24/61
'Ancilla'	K	soft pink	6/15
'Aristocrat'	D	lilac-rose	28/71
'Artist'	V	tangerine and green	12/30
'Big Chief'	DH	old rose	26/66
'Blue Parrot'	P	violet-blue	24/61
'Burgundy'	L	deep purplish-violet	18/46
'Cantata'	F	orange-scarlet	9/23
'China Pink'	L	pink	22/56
'Corona'	K	yellow with red and yellow heart	6/15
'Diana'	E	white	12/30
'Fantasy'	P	rose and green	18/46
'Golden Springtime'	DH	golden yellow	26/66
'Groenland'	V	pink and green	20/51
'Gudoschnick'	DH	yellow and cerise	24/61
'Holland Glorie'	DH	orange red	20/51
'Ibis'	E	rose pink	12/30
'Keizerskroon'	E	red and yellow	18/46
'Mariette'	L	pink	26/66
'Mount Tacoma'	DT	white	22/56
'Mrs John T. Scheepers'	D	yellow	24/61
'Orange Emperor'	F	pure orange	15/38
'Orange Favourite'	P	orange and green	18/46
'Peach Blossom'	DT	deep rose	12/30
'Princeps'	F	vermilion	12/30
'Queen of Bartigons'	D	salmon pink	28/71
'Queen of Sheba'	L	scarlet brown	20/51
'Red Emperor'	F	vermilion	18/46
'Red Parrot'	P	deep scarlet	28/71
'Renown'	D	carmine red	30/76
'Rockery Beauty'	F	blood red	8/20
'Shakespeare'	F	salmon	5/13
'Stresa'	K	yellow and red	7/18
'Sunkist'	D	yellow	22/56
'Sweetheart'	F	lemon yellow	17/43
'Sweet Harmony'	D	soft yellow	26/66
'Texas Gold'	P	yellow	22/56
'The First'	K	white and red	8/20
'Triumphator'	DT	deep rose	10/25
'West Point'	L	yellow	20/51
'White Triumphator'	L	white	28/71
'Yellow Dover'	DH	buttercup yellow	26/66

D–Darwin   DH–Darwin hybrid   L–Lily-flowered   F–Fosteriana   P–Parrot
E–Early flowering   K–Kaufmanniana   DT–Double tulips   V–Viridiflora

Recommended daffodil bulb varieties

Name	Class	Colour	Height in/cm
'Actaea'	P	white and red	18/46
'April Tears'	TR	yellow	7/18
'Barrett Browning'	SC	white and orange-red	17/43
'Beersheba'	T	white	14/36
'Binkie'	LC	sulphur yellow	16/41
'Birma'	SC	yellow and orange-red	18/46
'Bridal Crown'		white and lemon	16/41
'Carbineer'	LC	golden yellow	18/46
'Carlton'	LC	yellow	18/46
'Cheerfulness'	PZ	creamy white	19/48
'Dove Wings'	C	white and primrose	12/30
'Easter Bonnet'	LC	white and pink	17/43
'February Gold'	C	golden yellow	15/38
'Flower Drift'	D	white and orange	15/38
'Fortune'	LC	yellow and orange	24/61
'Geranium'	PZ	pure white and orange scarlet	16/41
'Golden Ducat'	D	yellow	18/46
'Golden Harvest'	T	yellow	20/51
'Ice Follies'	LC	white and primrose	16/41
'Irene Copeland'	D	white and yellow	14/36
'Jenny'	C	white	12/30
'Kilworth'	LC	white and orange-red	19/48
'King Alfred'	T	golden yellow	24/61
'Kingscourt'	T	yellow	16/41
'Liberty Bells'	TR	lemon yellow	12/30
'Magnificence'	T	golden yellow	14/36
'Mount Hood'	T	white	18/46
'Peeping Tom'	C	yellow	14/36
'Petit Four'	D	white and red	15/38
'Queen of Bicolours'	T	yellow	17/43
'Scarlet Gem'	TZ	yellow and orange	15/38
'Sempre Avanti'	LC	cream and orange	16/41
'Silver Chimes'	TR	white and pale primrose	10/25
'Spellbinder'	T	sulphur yellow	17/43
'Tete-a-Tete'	C	yellow and orange	8/20
'Texas'	D	yellow and orange	17/43
'Thalia'	TR	white	16/41
'Trevithian'	J	yellow	14/36
'Trousseau'	T	white to pale cream	18/46
'Unsurpassable'	T	buttercup yellow	20/51
'Verger'	SC	white and red	16/41
'White Lion'	D	white	18/46

LC–Large-cupped   SC–Small-cupped   T–Trumpet   TR–Triandus   P–Poeticus
PZ–Poetaz   D–Double   TZ–Tazetta   J–Jonquil   C–Cyclamineus

SELECTED ANNUALS AND BIENNIALS

Latin name	Popular name	Height in	Height cm
Adonis aestivalis	Summer adonis	12	30
Ageratum	Ageratum	4-12	10-30
Agrostemma milas	Corn cockle	36	91
Alyssum maritimum	Sweet alyssum	3-4	8-10
Amaranthus caudatus	Love-lies-bleeding	24	61
– A. tricolor		24	61
Anagallis	Pimpernel	6	16
Anchusa 'Blue Angel'	Annual alkanet	9	23
Antirrhinum	Snapdragon	8-36	20-91
Asperula orientalis	Woodruff	12	30
Bartonia aurea		18-24	46-61
Begonia semperflorens	Begonia	6-9	16-23
Brachycome	Swan river daisy	15	38
Calandrinia umbellata	Rock purslane	6	16
Calendula	Pot marigold	18	46
Callistephus	Annual aster	12-36	30-91
Campanula medium	Canterbury bell	30-36	76-91
Celosia	Cockscomb, Prince of Wales' feather	12-18	30-46
Centaurea cyanus	Cornflower	12-36	30-91
– C. moschata	Sweet sultan	18	46
Chrysanthemum carinatum	Annual chrysanthemum	18	46
– C. coronarium		36	91
Clarkia	Clarkia	24	61
Cleome	Spider flower	36	91
Cobaea	Cups and saucers	Climber	
Convolvulus	Convolvulus	6-12	16-30
Coreopsis	Calliopsis	12-36	31-91
Cosmos	Cosmea	24-36	61-91
Delphinium ajacis	Larkspur	3-4ft	1-1·2m
Dianthus barbatus	Sweet william	18	46
Dianthus caryophyllus	Carnation	12-18	30-46
–D. chinensis	Indian pink	12	30
Digitalis	Foxglove	5-6ft	1·5-1·8m
Dimorphotheca	Star of the Veldt	12-18	30-46
Echium plantagineum	Viper's bugle	12	30
Eschscholzia	Californian poppy	12	30
Euphorbia marginata	Snow on the mountain	18-24	46-61
Gaillardia pulchella	Annual gaillardia	24	61
Godetia	Godetia	9-30	23-76
Gypsophila elegans	Annual gypsophila	18	46
Helianthus annuus	Annual sunflower	2-8ft	0·6-2·4m
Helichrysum	Everlasting	18-24	31-61
Helipterum (acroclinium)	Everlasting	12	30
Iberis coronaria	Candytuft	9-12	23-30
Impatiens balsamina	Balsam	12-18	30-46
– I. sultani	Busy lizzie	9-15	23-38
Ipomaea	Morning glory	climber	

HA–Hardy annual　　HHA–Half-hardy annual　　HB–Hardy biennial　　HP–Hardy perennial

Flower colour	Season	Type
..scarlet	mid sum – late sum	HA
..blue	early sum – early aut	HA
..lilac-pink	early sum – mid sum	HA
..white, purple	early sum – early aut	HA
..purple	mid sum – late sum	HHA
..coloured leaves		HHA
..scarlet, blue	early sum – late sum	HA
..blue	early sum – mid sum	HA
..various	early sum – early aut	HP as HHA
..blue	early sum – mid sum	HA
..yellow	early sum – late sum	HA
..white, pink, red	mid sum – early aut	HHA
..white, pink, blue	mid sum – early aut	HHA
..crimson	early sum – late sum	HHA
..yellow, orange	late spr – mid aut	HA
..various	mid sum – early aut	HHA
..blue, pink, white	late spr – early sum	HB
..yellow, scarlet, crimson	mid sum – early aut	HHA
..blue, pink, white	early sum – early aut	HA
..various	early sum – early aut	HA
..various	mid sum – early aut	HA
..white, yellow	mid sum – early aut	HA
..white to crimson	early sum – early aut	HA
..pink, purple	mid sum – late sum	HA
.green and purple	late sum – early aut	treat as HHP
.various	mid sum – late sum	HA
.yellow, crimson, orange	early sum – early aut	HA
.white, pink, crimson	late sum – early aut	HHA
.various	early sum – late sum	HA
.white to crimson	early sum	HP as HB
.various	mid sum – early aut	HHA
.various	early sum – late sum	HA
.various	early sum – mid sum	HP as HB
.various	mid sum – early aut	HA
.blue, pink, white	early sum – late sum	HA
.various	early sum – mid aut	HA
.green and white leaves		HA
.yellow, pink, red	early sum – late sum	HHA
.white to crimson	early sum – early aut	HA
.white, pink	early sum – early aut	HA
.yellow	mid sum – early aut	HA
.various	mid sum – late sum	HHA
.various	mid sum – late sum	HHA
.white to purple	early sum – early aut	HA
.various	mid sum – late sum	HHA
.various	early sum – early aut	HHA
.blue, rose, red	early sum – late sum	HHA

HHP–Half-hardy perennial

SELECTED ANNUALS AND BIENNIALS

Latin name	Popular name	Height in	Height cm
Jacobaea		12	30
Kochia	Summer cypress	12	30
Lathyrus odoratus	Sweet pea	climber	
Lavatera trimestris	Mallow	30	76
Layia elegans	Tidy tips	18	46
Leptosyne		12	30
Limonium bonduellii	Annual statice	15	38
– L. sinuatum		15	38
Limnanthes	Meadow foam	6	16
Linaria maroccanna	Annual toadflax	8-12	20-30
Linum grandiflorum	Annual flax	12	30
Lobelia erinus	Annual lobelia	3-6	8-16
Malcomia	Virginian stock	6-8	16-20
Malope	Mallow	36	91
Matthiola	Brompton and east lothian stock	15-18	38-46
– M. bicornis	Night-scented stock	12	30
– M. incana	Ten week stock	12-36	30-91
Mesembryanthemum oriniflorum	Livingstone daisy	3	8
Mimulus tigrinus	Annual musk	12	30
Mirabilis Jalapa	Marvel of Peru	24	61
Myosotis	Forget-me-not	6-9	16-23
Nemesia	Nemesia	8-18	20-46
Nemophila	Baby blue-eyes	6	16
Nicotiana	Jasmine tobacco	18	46
Nigella	Love-in-a-mist	18	46
Papaver rhoeas	Shirley poppy	24	61
– P. somniferum	Opium poppy	24	61
Petunia	Petunia	12-18	30-46
Phacellia		9	23
Phlox drummondii	Annual phlox	6	16
Portulaca	Rose moss	6	16
Reseda ordorata	Mignonette	12-18	30-46
Rhodanthe	Everlasting	12	30
Rudbeckia hirta	Annual coneflower	24-36	61-91
Salpiglossis	Salpiglossis	24	61
Salvia splendens	Scarlet sage	12	30
–S. horminum	Clary	18	46
Saponaria vaccaria	Annual soapwort	24	61
Scabiosa atropurpurea	Sweet scabious	35	89
Silene pendula	Annual catchfly	6	16
Tagetes africana	African marigold	6-36	16-91
– S. erecta	French marigold	6-15	16-38
– S. signata	Dwarf marigold	9	23
Tropaeolum majus	Nasturtium	6 & climber	16
Ursinia		12	30
Verbena	Vervain	9-15	23-38
Viscaria	Annual catchfly	12	30
Zinnia	Zinnia	12-30	30-76

HA–Hardy annual   HHA–Half-hardy annual   HB–Hardy biennial

Flower colour	Season	Type
..various	mid sum – early aut	HHA
..foliage	late sum – early aut	HHA
..various	early sum – late sum	HA
..pink, white	mid sum – early aut	HA
..yellow and white	early sum – mid sum	HHA
..yellow	early sum – early aut	HA
..yellow	mid sum – late sum	HHA
..blue, white	mid sum – late sum	HHA
..yellow, white	late spr – early sum	HA
..various	early sum – early aut	HA
..scarlet	early sum – late sum	HA
..blue, white	early sum – early aut	HHA
..various	early sum – early aut	HA
..rose, crimson	mid sum – early aut	HA
..various	late spr – early sum	HB
..purplish	early sum – late sum	HA
..various	mid sum – late sum	HHA
..various	mid sum – late sum	HHA
..various	mid sum – late sum	HHA
..blue	early spr – late spr	HB
..various	early sum – late sum	HHA
..blue	mid sum – late sum	HA
..white and lime-green to crimson	mid sum – early aut	HHA
..blue, purple, white	early sum – late sum	HA
..various	early sum – late sum	HA
..various	early sum – late sum	HA
..various	early sum – early aut	HHA
..blue	mid sum – late sum	HA
..various	late sum – early aut	HHA
..various	mid sum – late sum	HHA
..yellow and white, red	mid sum – late sum	HA
..pink, white	mid sum – late sum	HB
..yellow to crimson	mid sum – early aut	HHA
..various	mid sum – early aut	HHA
...scarlet, pink, purple	mid sum – early aut	HHA
..lilac to purple	mid sum – early aut	HA
...white, pink	early sum – early aut	HA
..various	early sum – early aut	HA
...white to crimson	early sum – early aut	HA
...yellow, orange	mid sum – early aut	HHA
...yellow, orange and crimson	mid sum – early aut	HHA
...yellow, orange	mid sum – early aut	HHA
..various	mid sum – early aut	HA
...orange	mid sum – early aut	HHA
...various	mid sum – early aut	HHA
...various	early sum – early aut	HA
...various	mid sum – early aut	HHA

SPRING BEDDING PLANTS

Latin name	Popular name	Height in/cm	Colour	Type
Alyssum saxatile	Gold dust	9/23	yellow	HP/R
Anemone	Windflower	6-12/16-30	various	HP
Arabis	Rock cress	9/23	white	HP/R
Aubrieta	Coloured rock cress	3/8	various	HP/R
Bellis perennis	English daisy	6/16	pink and white	HP
Bellis perennis florepleno	Double daisy	6/16	white to crimson	HP
Campanula medium	Canterbury bell	12-24/30-61	violet	
Cheiranthus	Wallflower	1-1½ft/ 0·3-0·5m	various colours	HP/HB.
Crocus	Crocus	3-6/8-16	various	B
Erysimum	Alpine wallflower	6/16	yellow	HB
Hyacinthus	Hyacinth	9-12/23-30	various colours	B
Iberis sempervirens	Candytuft	6-12/16-30	white	HP
Myosotis	Forget-me-not	6-9/16-23	blue	HB
Muscari	Grape hyacinth	3/8	blue and white	B
Narcissus	Daffodil	12-24/30-61	white, yellow and red	B
Primula auricula	Auricula	6/16	various	HP
– P. polyantha	Polyanthus	6/16	various colours	HP
– P. vulgaris	Primrose	6/16	various	HP
Tulipa	Tulip	12-24/30-61	various colours	B
Viola cornuta hybrida	Viola	3-6/8-16	various	HP
– V. tricolor hybrida	Winter-flowering pansy	3-6/8-16	various	HP

HB–Hardy biennial   HP–Hardy perennial   B–Bulb   R–Rock plant

Bellis perennis florepleno

Primula auricula

SUMMER BEDDING PLANTS

Latin name	Popular name	Height ft/m	Flower colour	Type
Abutilon thompsonii	Abutilon	3-4/1-1·2	mottled foliage	HHP
Alyssum maritimum	Sweet alyssum	3·2in/8cm	white or purple	HHA
Amaranthus caudatus	Love-lies-bleeding	2/0·6	purple trails	HHA
– A. tricolor		2/0·6	coloured leaves	HHA
Antirrhinum	Snapdragon	9in-3ft/23cm-1m	various colours	HHA
Ageratum	Ageratum	3·2in-1ft/8cm-0·3m	blue	HHA
Begonia (fibrous)	Begonia	6-9in/15-23cm	white, pink, red	HHA
– B. (tuberous)		1/0·3	various colours	HHP
Calceolaria integrifolia	Calceolaria	1/0·3	yellow	HHP
Callistephus	Annual aster	1-3/0·3-1	various colours	HHA
Campanula medium	Canterbury bell	1-3/0·3-1	blue, pink, white	HB
Canna	Indian shot	3/1	various colours	HHP
Celosia plumosa	Prince of Wales' feather	1½/0·5	yellow or scarlet	HHA
Centaurea ragusina	Dusty miller	1-1½/0·3-0·5	grey foliage	HHP
Chrysanthemum coreanum	Korean chrysanthemum	2-3/0·6-1	various colours	HHP
– C. frutescens	Marguerite	2/0·6	white, yellow	HHP
– C. parthenium aureum	Golden feverfew	1-2/0·3-0·6	golden foliage	HP
Cleome	Spider flower	3/1	pink or purple	HHA
Coleus	Coleus	1/0·3	variously coloured foliage	HHP
Cuphea miniata	Firefly	1/0·3	red	HHA
Dahlia	Dahlia	1-6/0·3-1·8	various colours	HHP
Datura arborea	Angel's trumpet	4-6/1·2-1·8	white	HHP
Dianthus barbatus	Sweet william	1½/0·5	white to crimson	HB
– D. heddewigii	Japanese pink	6in-1ft/15cm-0·3m	various colours	HHA
Echeveria		6in/15cm	grey rosette of leaves	HHP
Echium	Viper's bugloss	1/0·3	blue	HA
Fuchsia	Fuchsia	1-4/0·3-1·2	various colours	HHS
Heliotropium	Heliotrope	1-3/0·3-1	purple	HHA
Iberis	Candytuft	6in-1ft/15cm-0·3m	various colours	HA
Kochia	Summer cypress	1/0·3	green foliage turning crimson	HHA
Lobelia erinus	Annual lobelia	3·2-6in/8-15cm	blue, white	HHA
– L. tenuior		1/0·3	blue	HHA
– L. t. 'Compacta'		9in/23cm	blue	HHA
Matthiola incana annua	Ten-week stock	1-3/0·3-1	various colours	HHA
Nemesia	Nemesia	9in-1½ft/23cm-0·5m	various colours	HHA
Nemophila maculata		6in/15cm	blue and white	HA
– N. menzeisii	Baby blue eyes	9in/23cm	blue and white	HA
Nicotiana	Jasmine tobacco	1½/0·5	various colours	HHA

HHA–Half-hardy annual   HB–Hardy biennial   HP–Hardy perennial
HHP–Half-hardy perennial   HHS–Half-hardy shrub

▶

Summer bedding plants

Latin name	Popular name	Height ft/m	Flower colour	Type
Pelargonium zonale	Zonal-leaved geranium	1-2/0·3-0·6	various colours, some with variegated leaves	HHP
– P. inequale	Ivy-leaved geranium	6in-4ft/15cm-1·2m	various colours	HHP
Penstemon	Penstemon	1-2/0·3-0·6	various colours	HP/ HHP
Perilla atropurpurea		2/0·6	bronze-purple leaves	HHA
Petunia Multiflora	Petunia	6in-1ft/15cm-0·3m	various colours	HHA
– P. Grandiflora		6in-1ft/15cm-0·3m	various colours	HHA
Phlox drummondii	Annual phlox	6in/15cm	various colours	HHA
Portulaca		6in/15cm	various colours	HHA
Ricinus communis	Castor-oil plant	4-5/1·2-1·5	ornamental foliage	HHA
Salvia splendens	Scarlet sage	1/0·3	scarlet, pink, purple	HHA/ HHP
Senecio cineraria		1-4/3-1·2	grey foliage	HHP
Schizanthus wisetonensis	Butterfly flower	1½/0·5	various colours	HHA
Tagetes erecta	African marigold	1-3/0·3-1	yellow/orange	HHA
– T. patula	French marigold	9in-1ft/23cm-0·3m	orange/brown	HHA
Verbena hybrida	Vervain	9in-1¼ft/ 23cm-0·4m	various colours	HHA
Viola tricolor hybrida	Pansy	3·2-6in/8-15cm	various colours	HP
– V. comuta hybrida	Viola	3·2-6in/8-15cm	various colours	HP
Zea mays 'Variegata'	Variegated maize	4-5/1·2-1·5	cream-striped foliage	HHA
Zinnia	Zinnia	1-2½/0·3-0·8	various colours	HHA

HHA–Half-hardy annual   HP–Hardy perennial   HHP–Half-hardy perennial

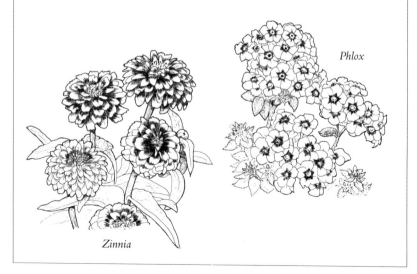

Phlox

Zinnia

FRUIT

AND

VEGETABLES

All vegetables need to be sown at the correct spacing and the right time for optimum results. The following tables give the right sowing times and the correct final spacing after thinning or planting. However, there is no need to follow the recommendations slavishly as you will still get acceptable crops from slight variations – use the tables as a guide.

New varieties of vegetables appear every year, and some need different cultivation methods to the old established varieties – follow recommendations on the seed packet. Catalogues produced by major seed companies contain a great deal of information and are essential reading.

Few people have the space to plant fruit trees in orchards these days, but the fruit charts will give you an idea of the relative space each form of tree will occupy. The new, very dwarfing rootstocks have made a great impact, giving controllable trees ideal for today's smaller gardens.

Many gardeners are disappointed by poor fruit crops because they don't have the right trees to pollinate each other. Plant two varieties that are good pollination partners and both will give you bumper crops – the apple pollination chart will tell you which to choose.

When planning your fruit and vegetable gardens, don't forget the most important aspect of all – grow only what you and your family like. It's amazing how often keen gardeners will include a crop because it fits into the space, rotation or timing perfectly.

Next point to consider is the amount to grow. Crops like lettuce and radishes, which need to be eaten as soon as they are ready, should be sown in small amounts at intervals to give successional harvests: crops such as leeks can be grown in larger quantities because they will 'stand' for a considerable time without deteriorating. If you have a freezer, you can grow plenty of peas, raspberries and other crops that freeze well.

The best planned vegetable plots have crops available throughout the year, but if your plot is not large enough for such perfection, just grow the crops you like best and that are at their most delicious picked straight from the garden.

To keep celery stems white and succulent, blanch them by tying cardboard around them to exclude the light.

VEGETABLES TO BE SOWN IN A SEEDBED AND TRANSPLANTED

Vegetable	Sow	Plant	In/cm between rows	In/cm between plants
Broccoli	early spr– late spr	late spr – mid sum	29/75	29/75
Brussels sprouts	early spr – mid spr	late spr – early sum	29/75	29/75
Cabbage, spring	mid sum – late sum	early aut – mid aut	17·5/45	12/30
Cabbage, autumn and winter	mid spr	early sum – mid sum	24/61	24/61
Calabrese	early spr	late spr	29/75	29/75
Cauliflower	late win – early spr	late spr – early sum	24/61	24/61
Celery	late win – early spr	early sum – mid sum	4ft/1·2m	10/25
Kale	mid spr – late spr	mid sum – late sum	29/75	29/75
Leek	mid win (g/house)	early sum	18/46	12/30
	early spr	early sum	18/46	12/30
Onion	mid win (g/house)	late spr – early sum	16/41	3/8
Marrow	early spr (g/house)	late spr	24/61	30/76

LIFE OF VEGETABLE SEEDS

Store your vegetable seeds in a cool, dry and dark place. On average they will last:

Seeds	Years	Seeds	Years
Beans	3	Melon	5
Beetroot	4	Onion	1-2
Broccoli	5	Parsley	2-3
Brussels sprouts	5	Parsnip	1-2
Cabbage	4-5	Pea	3
Carrot	3-4	Pepper	4
Cauliflower	4-5	Pumpkin	4
Celery	5-6	Radish	5
Chinese cabbage	5	Salsify	2
Cucumber	5-6	Scorzonera	2
Kale	5	Seakale	1-2
Kohl rabi	5	Spinach	5
Leek	3	Sweetcorn	1-2
Lettuce	4-5	Tomato	4
Marrow	5-6	Turnip	5

VEGETABLES TO BE SOWN IN THE ROW AND THINNED

Vegetable	Sow	In/cm between rows	In/cm between plants
Beans, broad	early spr – mid spr	9/23	9/23
Beans, French	mid spr – late spr	18/46	4/10
Beans, runner	late spr	24/61	6/16
Beetroot	mid spr – late spr	12/30	4/10
Cabbage, summer	early spr – mid spr	18/46	18/46
Carrots	early spr – early sum	6/16	½-2/1-5
Endive	mid spr – late sum	12/30	12/30
Kohl rabi	mid spr – late sum	15/38	6/16
Lettuce	early spr – late sum	12/30	6-12/16-30
Onion, spring	early spr	4/10	1/3
Parsley	early spr – late sum	12/30	6/16
Parsnip	early spr – mid spr	12/30	6/16
Peas	early spr – early sum	18/46	5/13
Radish, summer	early spr – late sum	6/16	½/1
Radish, winter	mid sum – late sum	9/23	6/16
Salsify and scorzonera	early spr – mid spr	15/38	8/20
Seakale beet	early spr – mid spr	15/38	10/25
Spinach, summer	early spr – mid sum	12/30	8/20
Spinach, winter	mid sum – late sum	12/30	8/20
Swede	late spr – early sum	15/38	8/20
Turnip, summer	early spr – mid sum	12/30	6/16
Turnip, winter	mid sum – late sum	15/38	6/16

GERMINATION RATE

Bean, broad	75%	Carrot	50%
Bean, dwarf	75%	Onion	60%
Bean, runner	60%	Parsnip	45%
Beet	50%	Pea	70%
Cabbage	70%	Swede	75%
Cauliflower	60%	Turnip	75%

The germination rate of raw, unpelleted seed is affected by soil and weather conditions at sowing time, as well as the quality and age of the seed. There are also differences between varieties. Sow seeds with the poorest germination rates rather more thickly.

FRUIT DISTANCES/HEIGHTS

Fruit	Feet between trees	Metres between trees	Feet between rows	Metres between rows
Apples				
Standard	33	10	20	6·1
Half standard	20	6·1	20	6·1
Bush	12	3·7	12	3·7
Dwarf bush	6	1·8	13	4
Dwarf pyramid	4	1·2	7	2
Espalier	16	4·9	(on walls)	
Cordon	3	1	6	1·8
Pears				
Standard	26	8	26	8
Half standard	22	6·7	22	6·7
Bush	14	4·3	14	4·3
Dwarf pyramid	8	2·4	4	1·2
Soft Fruit				
Strawberries	3	1	1½	0·5
Raspberries	6	1·8	1½	0·5
Red currants	8	2·4	4	1·2
Black currants	8	2·4	4	1·2
Gooseberries	8	2·4	4	1·2
Blackberries	8	2·4	12	3·7
Loganberries	8	2·4	8	2·4

	Comments	Height ft	Height m
Apple rootstocks			
M27	Very dwarfing	5	1·5
M9	Dwarfing	6	1·8
M26	Semi-dwarfing	10	3·1
MM106	Semi-vigorous	10–12	3·1–3·7
Pear rootstocks			
Quince A	Semi-vigorous	10–15	3·1–4·6
Quince C	Semi-vigorous	12–18	3·7–5·5
Plum rootstocks			
St Julien A	Semi–dwarfing	10–12	3·1–3·7
Pixy	Dwarfing	8–10	2·4–3·1

APPLE POLLINATION CHART

Early flowering	Mid season flowering	Late flowering
Egremont Russet	Blenheim Orange, Bountiful,	Ashmead's Kernel
Idared	Bramleys Seedling, Charles Ross,	Golden Delicious
Lord Lambourne	Cox's Orange Pippin, Crispin,	Howgate Wonder
Ribston Pippin	Discovery, Laxton's Fortune,	Orleans Reinette
	Greensleeves, Grenadier, James	Red Ellison
	Grieve, Jupiter, Merton Knave,	Laxton's Superb
	Spartan, Sunset, Worcester	Suntan
	Pearmain	

Choose apples from the same or adjacent groups for good pollination: i.e. an early flowering variety is unlikely to pollinate a late flowering variety, but both may be pollinated by a mid season flowering variety.

FREEZING HOME PRODUCE

Until you owned a freezer it always seemed that everything in the garden was ready to eat at the same time in too great a quantity. Now, 'grow now eat later' is really true.

Aim at freezing a variety of crops rather than 100lb/45kg of one in particular; so that the variety of frozen produce is much greater.

This section is all about freezing your own home-grown fruit and vegetables, but in your enthusiasm to get produce into the freezer, don't neglect the pleasure of eating fresh from the garden. This can never be bettered, even though freezing is by far the best method of preservation that is available to us today.

BASIC RULES FOR FREEZING FRUIT AND VEGETABLES

- Pick crops at their optimum point of maturity and freshness.
- Aim to get them straight from garden to the freezer in shortest possible time.
- Gather vegetables if possible in the cool of the morning.
- Do not freeze blemished fruit.
- Keep produce cool to prevent wilting if delayed.
- Wash vegetables, grade into uniform sizes (rejecting all but perfect ones) and trim as necessary.
- Wash fruit carefully and quickly only if necessary.
- Blanch vegetables for the correct time.
- Cool vegetables in iced water.
- Drain, pack in correct containers, seal and freeze.
- Freeze in manageable quantities so that you can observe the above rules without carelessness of timing.
- Freeze in portions suitable for family consumption or open freeze.

- Do not use galvanized iron, copper or chipped enamel utensils, which may taint and discolour fruit.
- Protect from the air in order to avoid discolouration.
- The secret of good freezing is quick freezing, so make sure to: Use the fast freeze switch to give you the low temperatures you need for freezing anything more than just single packs.
- Always keep food stored at the correct storage temperature of 0°F/18°C.
- Never overload the freezer by freezing more than 10% of its total capacity in any 24 hours.

Additional tips:

- Exceeding recommended storage items will lead to loss of flavour, colour, texture and aroma.
- Always store food in order of freezing so that packages which have been frozen longest are used first; this ensures that the frozen food is used in rotation.
- Use packaging materials which are guaranteed to be moisture-vapour-proof.
- All frozen fruit should be thawed in its unopened packaging.
- In emergencies both fruit and vegetables can be thawed quickly by placing the food, still wrapped, in lukewarm water or under a running tap.

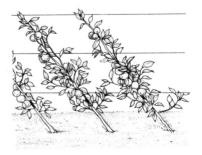

Cordon-shaped fruit trees.

HOW TO FREEZE VEGETABLES

Vegetable	Storage time	Select	Prepare
Asparagus	12 months	Young tender stalks; discard limp or woody ones lengths	Grade to thickness of stalk; trim off tough end and any scales. Wash, cut to even lengths LARGE STALKS
Aubergine	6-9 months	Firm, ripe aubergines with rich gloss on skin; reject those which appear wrinkled or dull	Do not peel, cut into ½in/1cm slices and, if doing large quantities, slice into salted water before blanching to prevent discolouration
Beans (French and runner)	12 months	Young, tender, preferably stringless beans	Top, tail and leave whole if small, otherwise cut and slice, not too thinly
Beetroot	6 months	Small ones about 1½in/4cm in diameter	Cook completely or will have poor texture after freezer storage. Peel after cooking
Broad beans	12 months	Small young pods	Shell and grade for size
Broccoli	12 months	Well-coloured green, purple or white compact heads with tender stalks. Pick before buds fully open. Discard limp or woody parts	Grade for size. If necessary soak for 30 min in salted water to remove insects. Wash thoroughly and cut into even-sized pieces suitable for serving
Brussels Sprouts	12 months	Small, firm, sprouts of good colour	Remove loose outer leaves and stem. Wash thoroughly, soaking in salt water if necessary. Grade for size

Blanching time Boiling water	Steam	Freeze and pack	Thawing and cooking
SMALL STALKS 2 min	3 min	Cool quickly, drain well and pack in suitable quantities or open freeze. Pack in plastic boxes to avoid damage boiling water	Thaw just enough to separate for more even cooking – for 5-10 min in
MED STALKS 3 min	4.5 min		
4 min	6 min		
Do not blanch in bundles or water will not penetrate to the centre			
Ideally, do this immediately after preparation. 4 min		Cool quickly, dab dry with kitchen paper and open freeze	Cook from frozen by frying in butter for about 5 min
WHOLE BEANS 2-3 min	3-4 min	Cool quickly, drain, pack suitable quantities in polythene bags or plastic bags or plastic boxes, or open freeze	Cook from frozen in boiling water, whole 7-8 min; sliced 5-6 min
CUT BEANS 2 min	3 min		
SLICED BEANS 1 min	2 min		
		Cool quickly and rub off skins. Slice large ones in ½in/1cm slices	Cold – thaw unopened in refrigerator. Hot – reheat and serve with white sauce
SMALL 2 min	3 min	Cool quickly, drain and open freeze or pack in suitable quantities in polythene bags or plastic boxes	Cook from frozen in boiling water 8-10 min
LARGE 3 min	4 min		
THIN STALKS 3 min	4 min	Cook quickly, drain well and pack in suitable quantities or open freeze. Pack in plastic boxes to avoid damage – place stalks and buds alternatively to give more compact parcel	Thaw just enough to separate for more even cooking – for 5-8 min in boiling water
MED STALKS 4 min	5 min		
THICK STALKS 5 min	6 min		
Steam probably better to avoid damage to heads			
SMALL 3 min		Cool quickly, drain well and pack in suitable quantities or open freeze. Pack in polythene bags or plastic boxes	Cook from frozen in boiling water 5-8 min
MED 4 min			

►

HOW TO FREEZE VEGETABLES

Vegetable	Storage time	Select	Prepare
Cabbage	6 months	Choose young crisp cabbage	Shred
Capsicum (red and green peppers)	9-12 months	Firm crisp peppers with glossy skins	Remove stalks and seeds
Carrots	12 months. Even unblanched carrots keep 9-12 months	Young carrots	Remove tops and tails, wash well. Should not be necessary to scrape young carrots. Scrape the medium sized ones and slice into rounds for stews. May be skinned after blanching
Cauliflower	6 months	White, clean and solidly formed head	Break cauliflower into even sized florets 1-2in/3-4cm in size or very small ones 4-5in 10-13cm may be left whole. Wash and if necessary soak in salted water for 30 min to remove insects
Celeriac	6 months		Wash well and peel. Cut into slices ½-1in/ 1-3cm. Cook completely if desired for purée
Celery	9 months. Stew pack 3 months	Young celery for hearts. Discard stringy stalks	Wash thoroughly. Trim hearts to compact shape. Cut stalks to 1-2in/3-5cm pieces
Corn on cob	12 months	Uniformly matured; when kernels are well rounded and milk is thin and sweet, not starchy	Remove husk and silk, wash and grade for size

| Blanching time | | Freeze and pack | Thawing and |
Boiling water	Steam		cooking
1½ min A little vinegar (1-2 tbs) helps to improve colour		Cool quickly, drain and pack in suitable quantities in polythene bags or plastic boxes	Cook from frozen
For short term storage (up to 2 months) may be frozen unblanched, preferably left whole for easy stuffing. Otherwise halve, slice or dice as desired. Blanching time 2-3 min depending on size		Cool rapidly, dab dry and pack into polythene bags or plastic boxes	Cook from frozen
WHOLE 4 min Not necessary to blanch for use in stews, etc		Cool quickly, drain and pack in suitable quantities in polythene bags. Stew pack carrots in large bag	Cook from frozen in boiling water 5-8 min
3 min SMALL WHOLE 5 min A little lemon juice added to blanching water keeps florets firm and good colour	4½ min	Cool quickly, drain and pack in suitable quantities or open freeze in polythene bags or plastic boxes	Cook from frozen in boiling water 8-10 min
3-4 min Add lemon juice for good colour		Cool quickly, dab dry and pack in polythene bags or boxes. Pack purée in boxes leaving headspace	Cook from frozen in boiling water 10 min. Serve with white or cheese sauce
HEARTS 5 min PIECES 3 min Not necessary for stew packs		Cool quickly, drain and pack in suitable quantities in polythene bags or plastic boxes. Stew pack in large bag	Cook from frozen. Hearts 10-12 min. Pieces 5 min in boiling water
SMALL COBS 5 min MED COBS 6½ min LARGE COBS 8 min		Cool quickly, drain and pack singly or in pairs in polythene bags	Must be completely thawed before cooking, approximately 3-4 hours at room temperature. Then cook in boiling water 8-10 min

▶

HOW TO FREEZE VEGETABLES

Vegetable	Storage time	Select	Prepare
Courgettes	12 months	Small courgettes about 3–4in/8–10cm long and ½–1in/1–3cm in diameter. Fresh and crisp when cut	Wash, do not peel, top and tail, and cut in half lengthways or slice in ½in/1cm slices
Globe artichokes	12 months	Medium size head. Cut only when ready to freeze	Remove outer leaves and stalk; wash thoroughly. Remove 'hairy' choke from centre
Kale	9 months	Young, tender, tightly-curled leaves; discard dry, discoloured coarse ones	Remove leaf from stalk and wash leaves thoroughly
Kohlrabi	12 months	Young, tender stems	Trim stalks and leaves; wash and peel thinly, slice in ½in/1cm slices
Leeks	6 months	Young, clean leeks	Cut off excess green and root; easier to be sure of removal of grit if sliced
Mushrooms		Very fresh, clean and white ones	Trim stalk. Leave button whole. Slice large ones, wipe with clean damp cloth. Fry in butter 1-2 min
Onions	Unblanched stew pack and fried up to 3 months, others 6 months	Crisp, firm, fresh onions, large for slicing and chopping, and small button	Peel, slice, chop or leave button onions whole

| Blanching time | | Freeze and pack | Thawing and |
Boiling water	Steam		cooking
VERY SMALL WHOLE 1 min 1½ min or fry in butter 1 min or completely cook with garlic and tomato		Cool quickly (butter fried and completely cooked ones are best cooled in refrigerator) and pack in polythene bags, plastic boxes or foil dishes depending on final cooking. Leave ½-1in/ 1-3cm headspace	Cook from frozen by frying for 5-10 min or reheating in lidded pan
WHOLE ARTICHOKES 7 min HEART ONLY 5 min A tablespoon of lemon juice in blanching water helps retain colour		Cool quickly, dab well and pack in rigid containers as spiky leaves may pierce polythene bags	Cook from frozen in boiling water about 10-15 min
1-2 min		Cool quickly, drain and dry. Pack in polythene bags. May be chopped after blanching	Cook from frozen in boiling water for 8 min
3 min		Cool quickly, and pack in suitable quantities in polythene bags or plastic boxes	Cook from frozen in boiling water 5-6 min
1 min		Cool quickly, and pack in suitable quantities in good quality containers to prevent odour transfer	Cook from frozen in boiling water 5-10 min
		Cool quickly in refrigerator, pack in suitable quantities in plastic boxes or open freeze	Cook from frozen, frying for about 5 min
Chopped onions, pack unblanched; sliced onion rings, floured and blanched in oil for 3 min. Whole onions 2 min 4 min		Cool quickly, pack in suitable quantities in good quality containers to prevent odour transfer	Cook from frozen. Whole onions 5-10 min in boiling water; floured rings deep fat fry 2-3 min

▶

HOW TO FREEZE VEGETABLES

Vegetable	Storage time	Select	Prepare
Parsnips, Swedes, Turnips	9-12 months blanched; 8-10 months for purée; up to 3 months for stew pack	Small, young and fresh parsnips. Only freeze if plenty of storage space in freezer	Remove tops, wash, peel and slice thinly
Peas	12 months	Young, fresh, sweet, tender peas with crisp, green shells	Pod, not necessary to wash
Potatoes	12 months	Clean, unblemished specimens	New – scrape
	2 months		Old – roast or Duchesse
Red cabbage	12 months blanched 6 months completely cooked	Firm crisp heads	Shred
Spinach	12 months	Young, fresh, crisp and tender leaves of good green colour, without heavy midribs	Wash thoroughly, cut off stems, may be cooked and sieved before freezing
Tomatoes	Up to 12 months	Choose firm ripe tomatoes	Just bag and freeze or make purée or sauce

| Blanching time | | Freeze and pack | Thawing and |
Boiling water	Steam		cooking
Not necessary for stew pack for short storage period; completely cook and purée		Cool quickly and pack in suitable quantities in polythene bags or plastic boxes. Leave headspace for purées	Cook from frozen in boiling water 8-12 min. Thaw purée unopened until soft 2-3 hours at room temperature then gently reheat
SMALL PEAS 1 min MED PEAS 1½ min	1½ min 2 min	Cool quickly, drain and pack in suitable quantities in polythene bags or open freeze and pack	Cook from frozen in boiling water 5-8 min
2 min		Cool quickly, open freeze all potatoes. Pack new and roast in polythene bags Pack Duchesse carefully in polythene container	Cook from frozen in boiling, salted water 5-10 min. Reheat roast from frozen in hot oven, or thaw and deep fry. Glaze Duchesse while still frozen, thaw slightly, then reheat in hot oven
1½ min		Cool quickly, drain and pack in suitable quantities in polythene bags or plastic boxes. Or may be completely cooked with onions and and apples, and frozen	Cook from frozen
Blanch in small quantities to ensure heat penetration 2 min		Cool quickly, drain and pack in suitable quantities in polythene bags or plastic boxes. Leave ½in/1cm headspace for sieved	Just enough to separate leaf for more even cooking in very little boiling water, or butter 6-8 min
		Polythene bags for whole tomatoes. Cool purée quickly and pack in plastic containers leaving headspace	Cook from frozen by grilling or frying. Heat purée slowly in lidded pan

HOW TO FREEZE FRUIT

Fruit	Select	Prepare	Freeze and pack
Apples	Good quality for slices. Others for purées	Wash, peel, core and slice. Use ascorbic acid to prevent discolouration. Use windfalls, bruised and fluffy apples for purée. Cut away blemished part and completely cook	Dry pack but blanch for 2 min then cool in iced water. Sugar pack. Syrup pack – medium Purée
Apricots	Firm, ripe evenly coloured fruit	Wipe, do not peel, halve and stone. Prepare quickly using ascorbic acid to prevent discolouration. Under-ripe fruit – completely cook in syrup. Over-ripe fruit – completely cook and purée	Sugar pack syrup pack – medium
Bilberries & Blueberries	Firm, ripe berries	Wash, drain and dab dry	Dry pack. Syrup pack – medium
Blackberries	Firm, plump, fully ripe berries. Discard for freezing over or under-ripe fruit	Wash only if necessary. Drain and dab dry	Dry pack – for subsequent jam making. Sugar pack. Syrup pack – medium
Currants (black, red and white)	Clean, dry, fully ripe fruit. Discard green or wrinkled ones	Top and tail. Wash, drain and dab dry	Dry pack – for subsequent jam making Sugar pack. Syrup pack – medium
Cherries	Red freeze better than black or white. Choose firm but fully ripe fruit	Remove stalks, wash, drain and remove the stones, which tend to flavour fruit during storage	Sugar pack. Syrup pack – medium
Damsons	Ripe but firm fruit	Halve and stone skin if possible as skin toughens on freezing	Syrup pack – heavy. Use ascorbic acid to prevent discolouration

HOW TO FREEZE FRUIT

Fruit	Select	Prepare	Freeze and pack
Gooseberries	Slightly under-ripe gooseberries	Top, tail, wash and drain, or cook completely	Sugar pack. Syrup pack – heavy
Grapes	Firm but fully ripe fruit. Smaller the grape the better	Remove from bunch, wash and dab dry	Sugar pack – medium
Greengages	Ripe but firm fruit	Halve and stone, skin if possible as skin toughens on freezing	Syrup pack – heavy. Use ascorbic acid to prevent discolouration
Loganberries	Firm, plump, fully ripe berries	Wash only if necessary. Discard for freezing over or under-ripe fruit	Dry pack for subsequent jam making. Sugar pack. Syrup pack – medium
Mulberries	Do not pick until fully ripe and really black	Sort over and only wash if necessary	Sugar pack, coating each fruit well with sugar
Peaches	Firm, fully ripe peaches	Skin if possible without plunging into water; otherwise into boiling water for 30 seconds and then into cold; halve, remove the stone and slice if desired; use ascorbic acid to prevent discolouration	Sugar pack. Syrup pack – heavy
Pears	Choose strong flavoured, ripe pears	Peel and slice, and cook in boiling medium sugar syrup syrup for 1-1½ minutes	Syrup pack – medium. Use ascorbic acid added to prevent discolouration
Plums	Ripe but firm fruit	Halve and stone, skin if possible as skin toughens on freezing	Syrup pack – heavy. Use ascorbic acid to prevent discolouration

▶

HOW TO FREEZE FRUIT

Fruit	Select	Prepare	Freeze and pack
Raspberries	Top quality just ripe fruit	Wash only if necessary and grade for size if possible	Dry pack. Sugar pack. Purée
Rhubarb	Only young tender stalks	Wash and cut into 1-2½ in/3-6 cm lengths	Blanch in boiling water 1 minute. Drain, dry and cool. Dry pack. Syrup pack – medium
Strawberries	Just ripe unblemished fruit	Remove hulls, wash only if necessary. May be sliced, mashed, puréed or left whole	Dry pack for specially selected prime fruit mainly for decoration and for subsequent jam making. Sugar pack. Syrup pack – heavy

RECOMMENDED VARIETIES

VEGETABLES

Beetroot: Detroit Little Ball, Boltardy.
Broad Beans: Jubilee Hysor, Imperial Green Longpod, Hylon.
Broccoli: Purple Sprouting, Calabrese Corvet.
Brussels Sprouts: Achilles, Citadel, Peer Gynt.
Carrots: Amsterdam Forcing, Bangor, Nantes Tip Top.
Cauliflower: Snow's Winter White, All The Year Round, Dok.
Courgettes: Zucchini, Gold Rush.
French Beans: Masterpiece, Sprite.
Kale: Frosty.
Kohlrabi: Rowel.
Peas: Little Marvel, Tristar, Onward.
Runner Beans: Mergoles, Achievement Polestar.

Spinach: Novak, seakale beet, perpetual spinach.
Sweetcorn: Sunrise, Sweet Nugget, Sundance.
Tomatoes: Gardener's Delight, Big Boy.

FRUIT

Apples: Bramley's Seedling, Grenadier.
Blackberries: Ashton Cross, Bedford Giant.
Blackcurrants: Ben Sarek, Ben Lomond.
Gooseberries: Invicta, Leveller.
Pears: Williams.
Plums: Czar, Victoria, Warwickshire Drooper.
Raspberries: Glen Clova, Delight, Leo.
Rhubarb: Cawood Delight.
Strawberries: Tonto, Tyee, Totem.

PLANTS
IN THE
HOME

With more and more people using flowering plants and foliage plants to decorate their homes it's as well to know a little bit about them to guarantee success.

The following pages contain a wealth of useful information with tables on the best plants for light, shady, warm and cool rooms, a guide to the top 30 flowering plants and top 30 foliage plants and details of cultural disorders, pests and diseases that you may encounter.

PLANTS FOR LIGHT ROOMS

Light rooms are those that get some sun. For most of the year the plants selected for lighter rooms can be grown right in the window.

The 12 plants listed overleaf grow best in bright light, and lose much leaf colour and produce fewer flowers if they don't get enough.

Bright light encourages strong growth, so it is down to us to provide the other essential elements – a regular supply of water (with some drying out between applications), a balanced supply of plant foods, adequate-sized pots and a suitable potting mixture.

During winter months we suffer much lower light intensity, when daylength is also drastically reduced. It is important to turn plants regularly so that they do not become lopsided. During winter we cannot give our house plants too much light. Move them around the house, if necessary, to see that they get the maximum amount available.

Other plants that would thrive here include bougainvillea, many succulents including the low-growing and taller echeverias, hoyas, the variegated-leaved tradescantias and poinsettia.

PLANTS FOR SHADY ROOMS

No plant will survive without some light, and plants grown in inadequate light become drawn and pale, flowerless and give no real pleasure. This is why it is important to choose the right plant for shady corners or hallways that are darker than the average room.

A position out of direct summer sun but in good indirect light is preferred by most popular house plants.

The plants chosen for this sort of situation are those from the partially shaded places in the wild that grow successfully, albeit perhaps more slowly.

Plants grown in shade or semi-shade should not be moved suddenly to a brightly lit position or they will get 'scorched'. Make sure you acclimatize any plants to brighter light gradually.

Practically all ferns will thrive in this kind of light; many palms will tolerate it

PLANTS FOR LIGHT ROOMS

Latin name	Popular name	Height in/cm	General comments
Ananas comosus 'Variegatus'	Variegated pineapple	18-24/46-61	Takes on best colour in full sun
Asparagus densiflorus sprengeri	Asparagus fern	12-18/30-46	Shade from hottest summer sun
Beloperone guttata	Shrimp plant	12-14/30-36	Cut back annually to prevent leggy growth
Crassula argentea (now officially *C. ovata*)	Money or Jade plant	12-14/30-36	Easy. Look out for variety called Hummel's Sunset (pink and orange markings)
Euphorbia milii	Crown of thorns	12-14/30-36	Red or yellow flowered forms and a dwarf kind are available
Gynura sarmentosa	Purple velvet plant	12/30	Renew frequently as young plants are best
Hippeastrum hybrids	Amaryllis	to 18/46	Give full sun after flowers fade, feed regularly and 'bake' in the garden until leaves yellow in autumn
Passiflora caerulea	Passion flower	climber – train around hoop	Prune drastically in spring
Pelargonium domesticum hybrids	Regal geranium	12-24/30-61	Keep in full sun and allow the mixture to dry out a little between waterings
– P. hortorum hybrids	Zonal geranium	12-24/30-61	
– P. peltatum hybrids	Ivy-leaved geranium	12-24/30-61	
Plectranthus oertendahlii	Swedish ivy	trailer to 18/46	Pinch out growing tips regularly to encourage side-shoots and renew each spring
Setcreasea purpurea	Purple heart	sprawler to 16/41	Keep in full sun and a little on the dry side
Thunbergia alata	Black-eyed Susan	climber – train around canes	Treat as an annual and discard when flowering stops

Plants for shady rooms

Latin name	Popular name	Height ft/m	General comments
Agloeonema commutatum	Painted drop-tongue	18in/46cm	An easy plant that grows slowly. Provide extra humidity by standing on moist pebbles. Can last for years
Aspidistra elatior	Cast-iron plant	2/0·6	Never over-water. The variegated-leaved form needs a little more light. Otherwise very easy
Begonia rex	Painted-leaf begonia	12in/30cm	Available in very wide colour range. Small-leaved forms are often more tolerant. Don't over-water, especially in winter.
Calathea makoyana	Peacock plant	up to 2/0·6	Keep air humid by standing on moist pebble-filled trays. Hand spray in warm weather
Cyperus afternifolius	Umbrella plant	up to 2/0·6	Keep pot standing in shallow dish of water throughout the year. Feed fortnightly. Cut off at base any faded 'reeds'
Cyrtomium falcatum	Holly fern	18-24in/46-61cm	Very easy plant. Keep glossy leaves free of dust. Give slightly better light during short winter days
Davallia fejeensis	Rabbit's foot fern	up to 2/0·6	Excellent in large hanging basket when the furry rhizomes trail over the edge. Keep moist but don't over water
Fatshedera lizei	Tree ivy	best kept to below 2/0·6	Provide some thin cane support, repot annually and renew when old plant loses lower leaves. Pinch out growing tips to encourage side shoots. The variegated-leaved variety needs a little more light. These plants are also suitable for cool rooms
Fittonia verschaffeltii	Snakeskin plant	around 6in/16cm	Never allow to dry out completely or leaves will shrivel. Keep barely moist at all times. Provide high humidity. Pinch out regularly to induce bushy

▶

PLANTS FOR SHADY ROOMS

Latin name	Popular name	Height ft/m	General comments
Howea belmoreana	Kentia palm	to 6/1·8	Very tolerant of a wide range of growing conditions. Slow growing, expensive and worth caring for. Keep fronds clean by frequent sponging. Do not damage growing tip, or plant will die.
Pellaea rotundifolia	Button fern	6in/16cm	Very low growing, spreading over potting mixture. Keep thoroughly moist at all times and humidity high
Platycerium bifurcatum	Stag's horn fern	12/30cm	Best grown on slab of bark or wood. Keep humidity high and constantly moist at the roots. Dunk in a bowl of water periodically. Avoid using pesticides as they do more harm than good. Scale insects might appear

for quite long periods and marantas and their relatives will enjoy it provided warmth comes with it.

PLANTS FOR WARM ROOMS

For the purposes of this guide, 'warm' is considered to be at least 60°F/15°C. It is the temperature in which we, and plants from tropical and sub-tropical areas feel comfortable. There is little we can do to bring down the temperature in summer if it begins to soar, although frequent watering and a correspondingly high level of humidity will ensure that the plants don't suffer.

Plants in warm rooms need to be kept moist at the roots at all times and the extra humidity should be provided by standing pots on generous-sized trays or saucers filled with moist pebbles, or by packing damp peat between the pot and an outer container.

Many plants will continue to grow through the winter in such temperatures and may even continue to flower, but this is only likely if there is enough light available.

Avoid standing plants close to radiators and other heating appliances during winter as the air there becomes too dry, and brown, crispy leaf tips and patches will develop. Unfortunately many radiators are fitted immediately below the windows – the lightest position in the room and the best possible sites for our plants during short winter days. Hot, dry air rising from the radiator can be baffled by widening windowsills or by the use of large plant trays fitted on to the sills.

PLANTS FOR COOL ROOMS

Even completely unheated rooms – possibly bathrooms and some kitchens – offer

PLANTS FOR WARM ROOMS

Latin name	Popular name	Height ft/m	General comments
Anthurium andreanum	Flamingo flower	up to 20in/51cm	Extra humidity must be provided. Support flower stalks with thin canes. Give medium bright light throughout the year. Use a very open peat-based mixture
Brassaia actinophylla (syn. *Schefflera actinophylla*)	Queensland umbrella plant	to 6/1·8	Air should be humid. Clean leaves regularly with a damp sponge. Water thoroughly but allow some drying out between applications
Caladium hortulanum hybrids	Angel wings	14in/36cm	The paper-thin leaves will shrivel if the mixture dries out, keep moist while in active growth. Stop watering when leaves yellow in autumn. Rest almost completely dry. Give bright light but avoid direct summer sun
Cordyline terminalis	Good luck plant	to 6/1·8	Often called *Dracaena terminalis*. In warmth a relatively easy plant if kept moist
Chrysalidocarpus lutescens	Golden feather palm	to 7/2	A thinner, clumpier palm than kentia palm (*Howea belmoreana*), with very attractive yellow reed-like stems. Give bright light without hot sun; right in the window for winter
Dizygotheca elegantissima	False aralia	to 6/1·8, usually much shorter	Reluctant to form side shoots; grow several plants together in one pot for best bushy effect. See that air is humid by standing on gravel-filled trays
Epipremnum aureum (syn. *Scindapsus aureus*)	Devil's ivy	trailer or climber to 6/1·8	A philodendron relative that revels in warmth. Allow to trail or train. Keep moist
Episcia cupreata hybrids	Flame violet	creeping – rarely more than 6in/16cm	Demand high humidity and good filtered light. Keep mixture moist at all times and do not overpot, they can be grown in half pots or shallow pans

▶

◀

PLANTS FOR WARM ROOMS

Latin name	Popular name	Height ft/m	General comments
Peperomia caperata	Emerald ripple	rarely more than 8in/20cm	Beautiful textured deep green leaves, strange cream-coloured flowerspikes. Can easily be over-watered – allow considerable drying out between applications
Philodendron erubescens	Redleaf or blushing philodendron	6/1·8	Several red-leaved hybrids are now freely available (Red King, Red Emerald and Burgundy). The species is still one of the best. Keep air humid, in good light without direct sun and handle gently, the leaves tear easily
Pilea cadierei	Aluminium plant	12in/30cm	Easy and very tolerant. Don't over-pot as they make nice bushy plants in pots apparently too small for them
Saintpaulia hybrids	African violet	8in/20cm	There is a vast range of colours, flower shape and habit. The trailing forms are catching on. Give them all the good things in life, warmth, good bright light (no burning sun), relatively small pots, peat-based mixture and allow a little drying out between water applications

house plants a temperature of around 55°F/13°C (including the warmth dissipated from the heated part of the home, and that caused by direct sunshine).

Such temperatures suit many plants (including ivies and fatsias – which both suffer from browning of the leaves and die-back at higher temperatures).

The advantages of cooler rooms are that any flowers that are produced, last so much longer. Spring-flowering bulbs last twice as long in a cool room as can be expected in much warmer places. Some ferns find these conditions most accept-able, and akin to their natural habitats.

There is a warning, however. Don't let plants get too cold, see that they are not left behind drawn curtains, and so cut off from whatever warmth there is within the room, and don't let leaves touch the glass of the window. On a frosty night these leaves will freeze on to the window and die when they thaw out.

The cooler the room, the higher the relative level of humidity. Plants that would need very regular watering if grown in a warm room, will last that much longer under cooler conditions.

PLANTS FOR COOL ROOMS

Latin name	Popular name	Height ft/m	General comments
Aloe variegata	Partridge-breasted aloe	under 12in/30cm	Are better as house plants than in the greenhouse. Give bright indirect light
Bilbergia nutans	Queen's-tears	14in/36cm	Very easy, virtually hardy. A rosette of leaves. Flowers only once, but many offsets are made
Cycas revoluta	Sago palm	2/0·6	Very slow growing. Tough needle-like leaves and a woody base. 'Antique' plants that are becoming very popular
Dracaena marginata	Madagascar dragon tree	rarely more than 4/1·2	The most tolerant dracaena indoors. Bare-stemmed, tufted-topped plants are now regularly available. Also splendid variegated-leaved forms (called 'Rainbow Plants'). These need slightly brighter light and a bit more warmth
Grevillea robusta	Silk oak	up to 5/1·5	Much used in municipal summer bedding, but also a good house plant, giving a soft feathery but tall fern-like look to the indoor garden. Being Australian they love the sun, but will grow well in a little shade
Hedera helix	Ivy	climber or trailer up to 4/1·2	Much prefers it cool. Pinch out growing tips regularly to induce side shoots. Watch out for aphids on young shoots particularly in early spring. Keep moist at all times. Renew regularly
Jasminum polyanthum	Jasmine	climber (rather rampant) to 6/1·8	Beautifully scented but needs curbing if to be kept within bounds
Phoenix canariensis	Canary Island palm	6/1·8	Almost our toughest palm. Rather prickly fronds and when older a chunky base
Plumbago auriculata (syn. *P. capensis*)	Cape leadwort	climbing to 6/1·8	Although South African very near to being hardy. Grows apace and will withstand cutting hard back

▶

PLANTS FOR COOL ROOMS

Latin name	Popular name	Height ft/m	General comments
Primula malacoides	Fairy primrose	15in/38cm	There is now a wide range of flower colour from which to choose. Keep moist at all times. Give good light to encourage the development of late winter and early spring flowers
Saxifraga stolonifera	Mother-of-thousands	6in/16cm	Totally hardy, surviving quite severe frosts. There is a very attractive pink-leaved variety ('Tricolor') which won't take the cold
Sparmannia africana	Indoor lime	4/1·2	Very attractive and long-flowering shrub for a large window area. White flowers appear in early summer

HOUSE PLANT CARE

Containers There are basically two main types of pot: clay and plastic. Clay (or terracotta) pots are the traditional type that have, after many years of decline, begun to gain once more in popularity. Still, plastic pots are preferred by many gardeners because they are lightweight, robust and easy to clean.

Apart from the standard pot, which is available in a multitude of sizes, you can get half-pots, seed pans, seedtrays and many, many more in a wide range of colours, styles and materials. Choose the pot to suit the plant and situation.

Composts The seemingly endless range of composts can be split into two main groups: loam-based and peat-based. The former varies a lot in quality and is difficult to handle. Peat-based composts are light and clean to work with and can be tailored for any plant requirements.

There are three mainstream peat-based composts: sowing, potting and general purpose. The difference between them mainly lies in their levels of nutrients – sowing compost having the least and potting the most, with general purpose slotted between.

There are other composts available which suit specific groups of plants like bulbs, orchids, cacti and an ericaceous compost for lime-hating azaleas.

All house plants should be checked regularly by assessing growth rate and the amount of water they need. Roots persistently growing through the drainage hole in the base of the pot is a tell-tale sign of a pot-bound house plant. To make certain, tip the plant out of its pot and check the root system – if it is filling the container it's time to repot.

Only use a pot one or, at the most, two sizes larger and choose a compost similar to the one the plant is already in.

Watering Death by waterlogging is probably the most common cause of fatalities in house plants. Beginners often make the mistake of giving plants little and often when it comes to watering then compound the error by applying the same amount of water all year round. This invariably causes a steady decline in the plants well-being.

It is impossible to give a general rule for watering house plants, although you will find that plants in clay pots will require more water than those in plastic containers.

The amount of water required, though, depends mainly on what type of plant you are growing, how big it is, the environment in which it is kept and the time of year. If it's hot and the plant is in active growth water requirement will be at its highest. Watering must be done by observation and not just as a routine.

You can water your plants either using a watering can or by the immersion method. Choose a can with a long thin spout, then fill the pot up to the rim. Then return to each plant and remove any water remaining in the drip saucer.

The immersion method is particularly good for plants that don't like their crowns to get wet. Simply plunge the pot into water and leave it for 20-30 minutes, then remove it and let it drain.

Fertilizers All plants require a regular supply of balanced nutrients. These are taken up by the roots from the compost. Although a potting compost contains a good supply of nutrients, this will only last for about six weeks after potting. Therefore, a food supplement is needed.

Feeding house plants is best done using a soluble proprietary fertilizer as this is quickly absorbed by the plants. However, food sticks, tablets and mats all perform perfectly well.

Feed most house plants every couple of weeks between early spring and mid autumn. Some winter-flowering plants will need feeding until the flowers fade.

Reduce feeding slowly before abstaining altogether during the dormant period. Do not feed plants more than they require. A build up of salts caused by an overdose of fertilizers can cause problems.

HOUSE PLANT TROUBLES

A healthy plant needs the correct light, moisture, temperature, soil and nutrients. An imbalance in any one of these factors can lead to disaster. If a plant is looking poorly for no apparent reason look for some problems with the cultural conditions.

Flower failure Plants that produce lush foliage instead of flowers are probably being over-fed. High potash fertilizers encourage flowering. Some plants need pruning or training while others have to reach a certain age first. The plant may be kept too warm or cool. Some plants require drier soil to encourage flowering. Dry air causes flowers to fade quickly. Even though there are many benefits to central heating, it does cause the atmosphere to become extremely dry.

CHECK feeding, necessary pruning, watering, temperature and humidity.

Poor growth Normal during the winter months but caused by over-watering or a nutrient deficiency during the growth period. Other causes include insufficient light, or the plant may be pot bound.

CHECK watering, feeding, light levels, condition of root system.

Wilting Most commonly due to lack of water, especially during the summer months. Also caused by high temperatures or too much light. Alternatively root rot may be the cause.

CHECK position and watering regime. Correct if necessary. Severe root rot is fatal but mild attacks can be controlled. Check also for signs of soil pests and root damage.

TOP FLOWERING PLANTS

Latin name	Popular name	Height in	Height cm
Aechmea fasciata	Urn plant	2ft	0·6m
Aeschynanthus speciousus	Basket plant	Trailing to 2ft	0·6m
Begonia semperflorens	Wax begonia	6–12	16–30
Campanula isophylla	Star-of-Bethlehem	Trailing to 14	36
Catharanthus roseus	Madagascar periwinkle	Around 12	30
Chrysanthemum morifolium hybrids	Chrysanthemum	Around 12	30
Clivia miniata	Kaffir lily	2ft	0·6m
Columnea banksii	Goldfish plant	Trailing to 24	61
Cyclamen persicum hybrids	Cyclamen	to 12	30
Epiphyllum hybrids	Orchid cactus	2ft	0·6m
Euphorbia pulcherrima	Poinsettia	Ideally not more than 2ft/0·6m	
Exacum affine	Persian violet	12	30
Guzmania lingulata	Scarlet star	Flower stalks to 14in/36cm	
Hibiscus rosa-sinensis hybrids	Rose of China	24in/61cm but need drastic spring pruning	
Hippeastrum hybrids	Amaryllis	Flower stalk to 24in/61cm	
Hyacinthus hybrids	Hyacinths	14	36
Impatiens wallerana hybrids	Busy Lizzie	Ideally under 12in/30cm but New Guinea hybrids to 24in/61cm	
Kalanchoe blossfeldiana hybrids	Flaming Katy	Under 12	30
Pelargonium domesticum hybrids	Regal geranium	12–18	30–46
Primula obconica hybrids	Poison primrose	12–14	30–36
Rhipsalidopsis gaertneri	Easter cactus	8–10	20–25
Rhododendron simsii hybrids	Azalea	9–12	23–30
Saintpaulia hybrids	African violet	8	20
Schlumbergera bridgesii and modern hybrids	Christmas cactus	8–10	20–25
Sinningia speciosa hybrids	Gloxinia	12	30
Streptocarpus hybrids	Cape primrose	12	30

General comments

.Long-lasting pale pink flowerhead. Each rosette of leaves flowers only once

.Orange flowers with yellow markings. Must have high humidity to do well, stand in warmth on moist pebble-filled trays

.New hybrids are low growing and floriferous. Must have good light for close growth. Young seedlings can be bought cheaply in the spring and these flower quickly and into late autumn

.Starts to flower in late summer, continues late into the autumn. Flowers may be white or pale blue. Leafstalks are very brittle – handle with care. Renew every spring

.Pink, mauve or white flowers. Best discarded when flowers become fewer. Water plentifully

.Today's pot chrysanthemums have usually been treated with a dwarfing compound to keep them low and compact

.Splendid and striking early spring-flowering. Like to be left undisturbed for three or four years and to have a cool, virtually dry winter rest. Use John Innes No. 3 potting compost

.Scarlet flowers with yellow lines at throat. In warm, moist, well-lit position can flower most of the year

.Some dwarf forms are sweetly scented. Standard kinds come in a wide range of colours, all can be retained for future years if placed in the garden for the summer

.Very wide range of colours now available in medium and large flowered hybrids. Like warmth and high humidity, feed with tomato-type fertilizer once flowerbuds start to form

.Although forms can now be had that do not insist upon being 'blacked out' they are short-day plants and will only produce flowers and bracts when days are short

.Value for money as their flowering season is very long. Best thrown away as flowers cease

.Many dwarf forms (minor is one) are available. Bracts stay colourful for some weeks

.Must be hard pruned to keep within reasonable bounds. Feed weekly with a tomato-type fertilizer once flowerbuds start to appear

.Keep fed and in bright sun after flowerhead fades until leaves yellow in late summer/early autumn. Give totally dry winter rest

.See that newly-planted bulbs have 10 weeks in cool and dark. Gradually accustom them to light, keep as cool as possible until flowerbuds are well clear of the neck of the bulbs

.Small plants are available (for use in bedding) in early spring and these quickly come into bloom and flower throughout the summer and autumn. New Guinea hybrids normally have variegated leaves and very large flowers although growth is much stronger

.Modern hybrids are in a wide range of sparkling colours. Although traditionally a short-day plant they can now be bought throughout the year

.Older plants can be most striking when they carry several large heads of bloom. In mid/late summer (if plants have finished flowering) they should be cut hard back, placed in the garden for a few weeks and rested for say 3-4 weeks

.Beware, the fine hairs can cause skin irritation (or worse). Long-flowering

.Can flower right up to early summer. Young plants are best and stem cuttings (of 2 or 3 'links') root easily in late summer

.Best kept cool, flowers will last longer that way. Plunge in pot in the garden but don't forget to water and feed in summer

.Wide range of colours available. Avoid getting the foliage wet

.Flowers from Christmas onwards (a hybrid called 'Evita' can still be in bloom in early summer). Treat as Easter cactus

.The best forms for indoors are those with a relatively close habit – it is the trumpet-shaped flowers we are after, not huge leaves. Must have high humidity and once leaves and flowers have developed must not dry out at the root

.The named varieties that originated with the John Innes Institute (JI hybrids) are without doubt the best forms

TOP FOLIAGE PLANTS

Latin name	Popular name	Height ft	Height m
Adiantum raddianum	Delta maidenhair	2	0·6
Aglaeonema commutatum	Painted drop-tongue	18in	46cm
Asparagus setaceus (syn. *A. plumosus*)	Asparagus fern	Some climb to 4ft/12m	
Begonia 'Tiger Paws'	Tiger Paws	8in	20cm
Calathea makoyana	Peacock plant	Up to 2	0·6
Chamaedorea elegans 'Bella'	Parlour palm	3	1
Chlorophytum comosum	Spider plant	Cascading plant-bearing stolens to 3ft/1m	
Cissus antarctica	Kangaroo vine	Climber to 6ft/1·8m	
Cissus rhombifolia (syn. *Rhoicissus rhomboidea*)	Grape ivy	Climber to 6ft/1·8m	
Codiaeum variegatum pictum	Croton	3	1
Coleus blumei	Flame nettle	Up to 2	0·6
Dieffenbachia maculata	Dumb cane	to 5	1·5
Dracaena deremensis 'Warneckii'	Dragon tree	to 4	1·2
Fatshedera lizei	Tree ivy	Best kept to below 2ft/0·6	
Fatsia japonica	Japanese fatsia	4	1·2
Ficus benjamina	Weeping fig	5	1·5
Ficus elastica 'Decora'	Rubber plant	6	1·8
Hedera helix hybrids	Ivy	Climbing or trailing	
Heptapleurum arboricola	Parasol plant	6	1·8
Hypoestes sanguinolenta (syn. *H. phyllostachya*)	Polka-dot plant	Keep to 8in/20cm by pinching out tips	
Maranta leuconeura	Prayer plant	Usually under 12in/30cm	
Monstera deliciosa	Swiss cheese plant	6ft/1·8m or more	
Nephrolepis exaltata	Boston fern	18in	46cm
Philodendron scandens	Sweetheart plant	4	1·2
Phoenix roebelenii	Miniature date palm	3	1
Radamachera sinica (syn. *Stereospermum chelonoides*)		2	0·6
Sansevieria trifasciata laurentii	Mother-in-law's tongue	Up to 4	1·2
Tradescantia fluminensis	Wandering Jew	Trailing to 20in/51cm	
Yucca elephantipes	Yucca	5	1·5

General comments

..Keep constantly moist but never sodden. Cut down old fronds each spring

..'Silver Queen' is the most popular. An easy plant to grow

..Not a fern, makes thick fleshy roots that push up potting mixture – allow room for this trait when potting and repotting

..Becoming very popular. Renew frequently as young plants are by far the best

..Keep air humid in warm weather by standing plant on moist pebbles

..One of the easiest of palms. Never grows tall and produces clusters of yellow bead-like flowers when mature

..Easy, best leaf colour contrast when grown in bright light but keep moist. Another plant that makes thick fleshy roots

..Tolerant of a wide range of growing conditions. Train on trellis or allow to trail

..Leaves of a darker green than *C. antarctica*, divided into three leaflets. The form 'Ellen Danica', with crinkled leaf edges, is the most attractive

..Leaves of many hues. Loves warmth, good light and a relatively high level of humidity

..Simple but beautifully marked leaves that can have strong or muted colour contrast. Nip out the flowers once seen

..Large-leaved, normally heavily spotted with cream. Some lower leaf loss is inevitable, leaving bare but not unattractive stems. Beware toxic sap

..A variety with white leaf striping, some have more some less stripes. Easy in warmth

..Needs a cane for support. Pinch out tips to encourage sideshoots

..Needs plenty of space. The form 'Moseri' is a little shorter and a variegated-leaved kind – 'Variegata', with just narrow white leaf edging – likes a little more warmth and light

..Very elegant. Some good variegated-leaved kinds – 'Hawaii', 'Golden Princess' and 'Starlight'

..Still very popular despite the fact that so many are seen. 'Black Prince' is almost black, and three or four variegated-leaved forms are readily available

..Prefers cool conditions. Pinch out regularly and keep moist at all times

..The golden-tipped form 'Golden Capello' is much the best form and easy to grow. Watch out for scale insects

..Some really brilliant sorts are now on sale which have much more pink than green in their leaves. Give really good light to retain best leaf colour

..Several forms are available, including the red-veined *M. leuconeura erythroneura*. Avoid bright sun and keep moist at the roots all the time

..Best leaf divisions and slits develop on mature plants in good-sized pots. Air layer when it hits the ceiling

..Good in hanging baskets or stood on a pedestal. Keep moist at the roots at all times and repot frequently

..Easy and trouble-free. If gaps between leaves get extended during winter due to insufficient light, cut back in spring

..The most graceful date palm but one needing a warm room. Reduce watering during winter

..Now becoming very popular. Watch out for scale insects which often attack this plant. Plants of all sizes are around

..Easy, provided that it is not overwatered during the winter. A wet potting mixture and cold will cause leaf bases to rot. The dwarf form 'Hahnii' provides a different, squat shape

..Best renewed frequently as older plants lose their lower leaves. Pinch out growing tips regularly to encourage bushy growth. Best leaf colour contrast is obtained by growing in really bright light and keeping a little dry at the roots

..Bare-stemmed specimens (called stick yuccas) and virtually stemless specimens (called tip yuccas) can be bought. Both are the same plant, one is just much older than the other. Can go in a sheltered position in the garden for the summer

PESTS
AND
DISEASES

Anyone who has ever grown plants will know that there's a whole army of pests and diseases lurking in the garden just waiting to attack – or so it seems! When a problem does occur, it's often difficult to know exactly what's causing it and what you can do about it. Accurate identification and swift action are often the keys to keeping your plants alive and healthy, so you need to be on your toes at all times.

The first essential is to be observant, so that you notice as soon as something is amiss. This means taking a little time simply to look at your plants every few days. Examine the growing points of one or two for insects, and turn over a few leaves to check the undersides, where pests often congregate. Within a short time you will be able to quickly pick out plants that are not thriving.

The next step is finding out exactly what the problem is and what you should do about it, and this is where our quick reference charts have an important part to play. Armed with them you should be able to identify and treat all the major pests and diseases you are likely to come across – and can look forward to a garden that's blooming with health!

Don't forget that chemical treatment is not always necessary. Prompt action can often prevent a disease or pest ever reaching damaging proportions: picking off and destroying a leaf in the very early stages of infection, for example, can pre-

vent the problem spreading to the rest of the plant. Knowing when and where pests and diseases are likely to attack can also be helpful: removing the growing tips of broad beans once the first clusters of pods are swelling will often completely avoid infestations of black aphids, and taking care to avoid splashing water on greenhouse plants in cool conditions will help prevent fungus diseases occurring.

When chemicals are necessary, remember to use them in strict accordance with the directions at all times. Ensure they are suitable for both plant and problem in question; spray or dust when plants are not in flower and observe the stated interval between treatment and harvest of edible crops. Choose products of short persistance whenever possible – that is, where crops can be eaten within a day or two of spraying. The product label will give you full details.

Leaves affected by the fungal disease, rust.

QUICK GUIDE TO FLOWER PESTS

Pest	Symptoms	Plants affected	Control
Aphids	Masses of small, long-legged, usually black, green or greyish insects clustered on soft, fleshy shoots and leaves	Many types but especially common on roses, hollyhocks, viburnums, sweet peas, nasturtiums, and cinerarias	Spray with contact insecticides such as pirimicarb
Birds	Seedlings uprooted and flowers torn by pecking	Many different bedding and shrubby ornamentals	Install scaring devices. Chemical repellents may work but need regular renewal
Bulb flies	Bulbs give rise to pale and distorted leaves and poor or no flowers. Bulbs softened and contain greyish maggots	Hyacinths, narcissi and other bulbous plants	Destroy affected bulbs, buy new stock from a reputable source and examine carefully before planting
Caterpillars	Leaves eaten systematically from margins inwards either by single caterpillars or small colonies clustered together	Ornamental shrubs are probably worst affected; perennial herbaceous plants sometimes	Pick off by hand, taking care with irritating insect hairs, or spray with resmethrin, bioresmethrin or permethrin
Cutworms	Similar to leather jackets; dingy caterpillars in soil	Many types, but especially chrysanthemums, dahlias and primulas	Cultivate ground thoroughly. Protect young plants by applying chlorophos at planting time
Earwigs	Shiny brown insects with pincers at the rear occur on and among flower petals, eating out irregular holes	Many, but large-flowered types such as dahlias and chrysanthemums are particularly susceptible	Spray with permethrin, or dust with pirimiphos-methyl in late evening and maintain good hygiene

▶

QUICK GUIDE TO FLOWER PESTS

Pest	Symptoms	Plants affected	Control
Eelworms	Very varied; generally poor growth. Bulbs are soft and have rings of discoloured tissue within. Chrysanthemum leaves wilt (lowest first)	Very many plants; common on narcissi and similar bulbous plants. The leaf symptoms occur only on chrysanthemums	Always buy planting stock from reputable sources. Once land is contaminated, do not grow the same crop on the plot for at least three years
Leaf miners	Blotches or irregular, maze-like, meandering patterns on leaves	Most plants; commonly azaleas, lilacs, chrysanthemums and primulas	Pick off affected leaves and burn them. Spray with malathion as an added precaution
Leather jackets	Leaves turn yellow and wilt. Brownish caterpillar-like larvae	Many types of seedlings and mature plants	Cultivate new ground regularly and thoroughly
Red spider mites	Plants decline and are festooned with cobwebs containing masses of minute, reddish mites	Chrysanthemums, carnations, pelargoniums, fuchsias and roses outdoors	Apply water mist spray to prevent mites establishing. Attacks may be checked by regular application of pyrethrum
Slugs and snails	Irregular holes, often very extensive, in leaves and shoots. Slime trails present on and around affected plants	All fleshy plants, but especially hoyas, some types of campanula, irises, primulas and lilies	Pick off slugs and snails in late evening. Place commercial slug baits regularly around susceptible plants

QUICK GUIDE TO FLOWER PESTS

Pest	Symptoms	Plants affected	Control
Thrips	Masses of tiny, irregular fleck–like markings on flowers and leaves. Minute black 'thunder-flies' on flowers	Roses and gladioli most importantly, but privet, lilac and carnations, among others, can also be affected	Spray with rotenone as soon as symptoms are seen
Whiteflies	Tiny, moth-like insects infest plants and cover them with sticky honeydew	Honeysuckles, rhododendrons, azaleas, viburnums and others	Spray with a synthetic pyrethroid insecticide as soon as insects are seen, and repeat at regular intervals
Wireworms	Plants decline; golden–yellow maggot-like larvae tunnel into fleshy shoots and stems	Many types, but gladioli, primulas, dahlias and anemones worst affected	Avoid using compost made from old turf. Maintain good cultivation and weed control
Woodlice	Holes gnawed in roots and in leaves and stems, usually close to ground level	Seedlings of all kinds; also mature lupins, petunias, pansies and chrysanthemums	Clear away garden debris. Seek out woodlouse colonies in spring and kill them with boiling water

Slugs and snails

Whitefly

QUICK GUIDE TO FLOWER DISEASES

Disease	Symptoms	Plants affected	Control
Bulb rot	Bulbs, corms or tubers softened and discoloured, often with mould growth	Most types of plant producing bulbs, corms or tubers although narcissi are often affected severely	Destroy any affected bulbs. Obtain new stock, plant them on a fresh site, and routinely dip them in systemic fungicide before planting
Canker	Large, blister-like swellings or depressions on stems of woody plants	Many types of garden tree; ash is probably affected most commonly	Cut out affected branches. Do not plant new stock close to old, cankered trees
Damping off	Seedlings die in patches in boxes; sometimes mould develops after pricking out	Especially common on bedding plants such as alyssum, antirrhinums, petunias, tagetes	Destroy all seedlings from an affected box. Always use clean seed boxes and water, and sterile compost
Grey mould	Soft, brownish decay of stems, stem bases, leaves, buds and flowers, usually accompanied by a fluffy grey mould growth	Most types of flowering plant can be affected under cool, moist conditions	Always maintain strict hygiene – remove dead heads and other moribund plant parts promptly
Honey fungus	Trees and shrubs die in ones and twos; toadstools may be present at the stem base. Roots are decayed	Almost all types of tree and shrub	Affected trees must be felled, uprooted and as much as possible of the root system and the surrounding soil dug out. Do not replant the same site with new stock for two years

QUICK GUIDE TO FLOWER DISEASES

Disease	Symptoms	Plants affected	Control
Leaf spots	Small, discoloured patches on the leaves; very variable in size and shape	Almost every type of ornamental plant; black spot on roses is probably the best known of all	First, be sure that the spotting is really causing any damage. If so, spray with fungicide
Powdery mildew	Powdery white coating to leaves, stems, buds and flowers. Affected parts may be twisted and distorted	Most garden flowers; probably commonest on Michaelmas daisies, lupins, roses, aquilegias and doronicums	Spray at 2-3 week intervals with a systemic fungicide based on benomyl
Root rot	Leaves become yellowed and begin to wilt. The entire plant gradually dies back and roots are blackened and decayed	Many types of flower and ornamental shrub	Rarely practical to cure affected plants – correct some underlying cause of stress such as waterlogging
Rust	Tiny, powdery pustules, mostly on the leaves. Individual pustules may be black, brown, yellow or orange	Hollyhocks, mahonias, roses, antirrhinums and others	Spray with Bordeaux mixture or mancozeb
Sooty mould	Sticky black covering to foliage; plants may decline in vigour	Many types of trees, shrubs and perennials but less common on bedding plants	Control the insects that secrete honeydew on which moulds grow
Wilt	Above-ground effects similar to root rot (above), except that the lower leaves are always affected first. Stems bear dark streaks within when cut	Many types of plant, but particularly serious on carnations	Difficult, as there are no reliable chemical treatments. Prevent by rigorous attention to hygiene; replace affected plants with new stock on a fresh site

QUICK GUIDE TO VEGETABLE PESTS

Pest	Symptoms	Plants affected	Control
Aphids	Dense clusters of long-legged, variously coloured insects, sometimes covered with a waxy powder and exuding sticky honeydew	Beans are often affected with black aphids; brassicas with masses of powdery grey ones	Pinch out broad bean shoots in spring. Clear away old brassica crops. Use pirimicarb insecticide
Eelworms	Many different symptoms, difficult to diagnose. Tiny spherical or yellowish 'cysts', clustered on affected roots; overall growth poor	Potatoes and tomatoes	Do not grow potatoes or tomatoes on the affected land for seven years
Flea beetles	Masses of tiny holes in leaves, especially those close to soil level. Small, jumping beetles may also be present	Brassicas are worst affected; especially swedes, turnips and radishes	Clear away garden debris. Protect with Gamma-HCH dust around young plants
Flies	Foliage becomes reddened and later wilts. Ultimately the entire plant is stunted and feeble. The roots are mined by whitish maggots	Brassicas of all kinds, carrots, onions, parsnips and celery	Mix chlorophos into soil around young plants. Sow carrots sparsely to avoid the need for thinning
Leaf caterpillars	More or less rounded holes: leaves reduced to a skeleton of veins in severe attacks. Various greenish caterpillars most common	Many types of plant but brassicas are almost always worst affected	Pick off by hand or spray thoroughly with a synthetic pyrethroid insecticide

QUICK GUIDE TO VEGETABLE PESTS

Pest	Symptoms	Plants affected	Control
Leather-jackets	Roots and base of stem eaten away. Plants wilt and shrivel. Dingy brown, caterpillar-like larvae may be found in soil	Many different plants but lettuces and brassicas are often the most severely affected	Cultivate new ground regularly and thoroughly. After persistent attacks, protect with chlorophos at planting
Pod caterpillars	Almost no visible external symptoms but seeds within pods are holed by tiny, black-headed, maggot-like grubs	Peas	Sow pea crops early or late to avoid late summer flowering. Spray with permethrin one week after flowers appear; repeat two weeks later
Root aphids	Plants wilt, shrivel and die. When pulled up, masses of tiny off-white insects can be seen among the roots	Lettuces	Destroy affected plants. Leave ground free of lettuces for 12 months or grow resistant varieties
Slugs and snails	Tubers extensively mined; large seeds eaten before they germinate; leaves and leaf-stalks holed; seedling stems eaten through at ground level	Potatoes, lettuces, brassicas and celery, among many others	Pick off slugs and snails in late evening. Place commercial slug baits regularly around susceptible plants
Soil caterpillars (cutworms)	Plants wilt, often suddenly, as stem is eaten through at ground level. Brownish caterpillars found in soil nearby. Worst in dry seasons	Many different plants: brassicas, lettuces, carrots, celery and potatoes are among those most commonly affected	Cultivate ground thoroughly. Protect young. plants by applying chlorophos at planting

QUICK GUIDE TO VEGETABLE DISEASES

Diseases	Symptoms	Plants affected	Control
Blight	Leaves develop soft brownish patches with white mould beneath. Tomato fruits develop hard brown rot; potato tubers become affected with a soft, reddish rot	Potatoes and outdoor tomatoes	Do not dump old potato and tomato debris in the garden. Spray potatoes fortnightly with mancozeb from mid summer in damp seasons
Clubroot	Plants wilt and become stunted. Roots swollen and hugely distorted	All brassicas and related plants	Prevent by raising plants in sterilized compost. Treat by dipping transplants in thiophanate-methyl dip
Damping off	Young seedlings die in patches, usually while still in the seed box. Slightly larger seedlings may develop wiry stems	All types of vegetable but probably commonest on brassicas and lettuces	Destroy all seedlings from an affected box. Always use clean seed boxes and water, and sterile compost
Downy mildew	Small, angular, dead brown patches of leaf tissue with white or off-white mouldy growth beneath	Lettuces are most important; brassicas less so	Spray with mancozeb, from when half of the plants have emerged until within two weeks of cutting
Ghost spot	Small, circular white spots on ripe fruit	Tomatoes – this problem is commonest in greenhouses but can occur outdoors also	Maintain thorough hygiene by regular removal of dead leaves. Spray with benomyl to check attacks
Grey mould	A soft, brownish rot accompanying fluffy, grey mould growth on growing and stored vegetable produce	Most types of vegetable are liable to be affected in cool, damp conditions, either growing in the garden or in store	Dispose of affected material promptly. If symptoms are seen sufficiently early, spray with systemic fungicides

QUICK GUIDE TO VEGETABLE DISEASES

Disease	Symptoms	Plants affected	Control
Leaf spot	Variously sized spots on the leaves; sometimes a general decline in vigour and shrivelling of the leaves	Many types of vegetable, but most serious on celery	Spray with systemic fungicides such as thiophanate-methyl when symptoms are seen; repeat two weeks later
Neck rot	Stored bulbs soften around the neck region and develop greyish mould growth	Onions	Routinely wash onion seed with benomyl before sowing. Do not dump old onions in the garden
Parsnip canker	Softening around the crown with black, purple or orange-brown discolouration of the affected tissues	Parsnips	Where severe attacks have been experienced, grow the resistant variety, 'Tender and True'
Powdery mildew	Powdery white coating to leaves and other plant parts	Most common on brassicas	Spray at 2-3 week intervals with carbendazim
Virus	Various leaf discolourations and distortions, sometimes with reduced yield and generally poor growth	Many vegetables but only really serious on potatoes	Maintain good, routine aphid control and renew potatoes with fresh certified seed stock each season
White rot	Base of stem softened and covered with cottony white mould	Onions and related plants	Do not grow onions on contaminated land. Treatment as for 'neck rot'

QUICK GUIDE TO FRUIT PESTS

Pest	Symptoms	Plants affected	Control
Aphids	Masses of small, long-legged, usually green, black or greyish insects clustered on soft, fleshy shoots and leaves. Sometimes white, woolly wax and, usually, sticky honeydew present	Apples, plums and cherries most severely among tree fruits; also currants, raspberries and gooseberries. Woolly wax occurs mainly on apples	Tar oil washes on bark in early to mid winter. Apply insecticides before flowering but check manufacturer's directions for each type of fruit
Beetles	Fruit yield may be affected and individual berries often contain yellow-brown grubs	Raspberry beetle attack on raspberries is the most important type of beetle damage	Spray routinely with fenitrothion immediately after flowering
Birds	Holes pecked in ripening fruits. Buds stripped in late winter, resulting in depleted or almost no crop	Most types of mature fruit can be damaged but bud damage is usually confined to pears and gooseberries	Install scaring devices and change their position frequently. Cover bush fruit with cages. Chemical repellents may work but need regular renewal
Capsid bugs	Fruit disfigured with bumps and other abnormalities. Leaves with irregular ragged holes. Blossom deformed and killed	Fruit symptoms mainly on apples; leaf symptoms on most other tree and bush fruit	Tar oil washes on bark in early to mid winter. Apply a contact or systemic insecticide spray immediately after flowering, or before flowering on raspberries
Caterpillars	Varied. On fruit there may be surface scars and tunnelling, or deeper tunnels, especially in the core. Shoots and leaves are also eaten and, if blossoms are damaged, yield reduced	Most tree fruits but normally apples are affected more seriously than others	Grease bands around the trunk in autumn. Spray with contact insecticides immediately after leaf buds open in spring and/or from early summer onwards

QUICK GUIDE TO FRUIT PESTS

Pest	Symptoms	Plants affected	Control
Red spider mites	Foliage bronzed and speckled. Plants are festooned with cobweb-like webbing and gradually decline in vigour	Most usually on apples, pears, strawberries and plums	Spray with contact insecticide, preferably pyrethrum, immediately after flowering if mite colonies are seen
Sawflies	Ribbon-like scars on fruit surface, often with some tunnelling into the fruit, but less deeply than that caused by caterpillars. Some species are also leaf-eating	Apples are affected by fruit symptoms. Other sawfly species cause leaf damage, especially on gooseberries	Spray with gamma-HCH or malathion (one week after the petals drop in apples).
Wasps	Extensive, often irregular holes eaten in ripening fruit. Wasps often present – handle fruit with care when examining!	Most tree fruit, but plums and apples most importantly	Maintain general control of other insect pests (see above) which usually cause the initial damage the wasps enlarge

Wasps

Red spider mites

QUICK GUIDE TO FRUIT DISEASES

Disease	Symptoms	Plants affected	Control
American gooseberry mildew	Powdery white covering on leaves and shoots, followed later by a brownish, felt-like growth	Gooseberries and blackcurrants	Ensure that bushes are well pruned. Spray with thiophanate-methyl as flowers open and continue at two-week intervals until mid summer
Apple mildew	Powdery white coating to leaves, shoots and blossom. There is often a distinctive tuft of leaves at the end of a bare twig	Apples; occasionally pears	Carefully remove affected shoots. Spray with systemic fungicide as flowers open, and repeat every two weeks until mid to late summer
Canker	Hard, irregular, blister-like lesions on branches or main stem. Plants decline in vigour	Apples and pears	Cut out affected branches and treat cuts with a sealant. Do not plant new stock close to old, cankered trees
Crown gall	Large, more or less rounded swellings on trunks, stems or branches	Many types of fruit tree and bush	Normally no treatment is necessary but if severely disfiguring, cut out and burn
Honey fungus	Trees die in ones and twos; roots and stem base rotten. There may be clusters of honey-coloured toadstools present and black, string-like structures beneath the bark	All fruit trees and bushes	Affected trees must be felled, uprooted and as much as possible of the root system and the surrounding soil dug out. Do not replant the same site with new stock for two years

QUICK GUIDE TO FRUIT DISEASES

Disease	Symptoms	Plants affected	Control
Leaf spots	Brownish spots or larger blotches on the leaves which may ultimately shrivel and drop prematurely	Most fruit trees and bushes but only likely to be serious on currants and gooseberries	Collect and destroy affected leaves in autumn; in the following season, spray with mancozeb after flowering, two weeks later and again after fruit has been picked
Peach leaf curl	Foliage becomes blistered in early summer and later reddens, shrivels and drops	Almonds, peaches, nectarines	Spray with Bordeaux mixture or mancozeb in mid to late winter, repeat as the buds are swelling
Scab	Dark brown or greenish lesions on leaves. Dark, scabby spots on fruit	Apples and pears	With small trees, sweep up and burn affected leaves in autumn. Spray at two-week intervals with benomyl from time of bud burst until the petals drop
Silver leaf	Foliage becomes silvery and shiny. Branches gradually die back and, when cut through, display brown staining within	Plums are by far the most important plants affected	If only slight foliage symptoms occur, the tree may recover naturally. If individual branches are dying, cut these out. If the entire tree shows symptoms, destroy it
Virus	Trees decline gradually over a period of years when there is no obvious reason (such as old age or waterlogged soil) for this. Leaves commonly show yellowish patterns	All fruit trees and bushes	If a virus infection seems the most likely cause of decline and fruit yield is seriously affected, grub up the trees and replace with fresh, certified stock on a new site

QUICK GUIDE TO HOUSE PLANT AND GREENHOUSE PESTS

Pest	Symptoms	Plants affected	Control
Aphids	Clusters of black, green, or grey long-legged, winged or wingless insects on leaves, shoots or flowers	Most indoor plants but tomatoes and cucumbers are probably affected more severely than most	Spray with pirimicarb insecticides as soon as colonies are seen; repeat as necessary
Caterpillars	More or less rounded holes eaten in leaves and fruits. Small caterpillars may be seen	Usually only a problem on tomatoes	Pick off insects by hand; spray with systemic or contact insecticides
Earwigs	Shiny brown insects lurk among blooms of large flowers and bite irregular holes	Chrysanthemums are almost always the major greenhouse plants to be affected	Spray with malathion or gamma-HCH in late evening and maintain good hygiene
Fungus gnats	Masses of tiny, dark-coloured flies in and around the compost. Tiny white grubs with black heads may be found below the surface	Affects almost any pot plant when the compost is over-acid or allowed to become waterlogged	Avoid over-watering
Leaf miners	Blotch-like or irregular, mazelike patterns develop within leaves	Most types of greenhouse plant are liable to be affected at some time	Pick off and burn affected leaves. Spray with gamma-HCH as an added precaution
Mealy bugs	Plants infested with tiny creatures like miniature woodlice, covered in waxy powder	Many indoor plants but especially serious on cacti and succulents	Touch insect colonies with a paint-brush dipped in methylated spirit. Spray with systemic insecticide

QUICK GUIDE TO HOUSE PLANT AND GREENHOUSE PESTS

Pest	Symptoms	Plants affected	Control
Red spider mites	Plants festooned with cobweb-like webbing with masses of minute, reddish mites. Plants become shrivelled	Many different types of plant: common on chrysanthemums, fuchsias, poinsettias and carnations	Apply water mist spray to prevent mites establishing. Attacks may be checked with pyrethrum
Scale insects	Small colonies of insects like fish scales on stems and leaves secreting honeydew and causing sooty moulds	Many indoor plants but also important on grapevines in greenhouses	Spray with systemic insecticide to kill adults and regularly with contact insecticides to eliminate mobile 'crawlers'
Thrips	Leaves, flowers and buds bear pale, fleck-like marks. 'Thunder-flies' may be seen crawling over plants	Orchids, ferns, azaleas and arum lilies among many others	Ensure that plants are not placed under stress which predisposes them to attack. Spray with gamma-HCH when thrip infestations are seen
Whiteflies	Plants infested with masses of minute, moth-like insects. Usually sticky honeydew is present on the foliage	Most types of indoor plant but most serious on tomatoes, cucumbers and egg plants in greenhouses	Spray with a synthetic pyrethroid insecticide as soon as insects are seen, and repeat at regular intervals
Vine weevil	Leaves and young shoots bear holes; plump, white, C-shaped grubs will often be found in the potting compost nearby	Most indoor plants, but especially serious on orchids, begonias, cyclamen, primulas and ferns	Avoid debris in the greenhouse. Check for grubs in the soil when repotting and if any are found, incorporate a little gamma-HCH dust

QUICK GUIDE TO HOUSE PLANT AND GREENHOUSE DISEASES

Disease	Symptoms	Plants affected	Control
Black leg	Stems pinched at base and discoloured dark brown or black	Always commonest on young pelargonium cuttings	Maintain scrupulous hygiene and use sterilized compost. Dip new cuttings in rooting powder containing fungicide
Damping off	Young seedlings keel over and die in patches soon after emergence	All seedlings	Destroy all seedlings from an affected box. Always use clean seed boxes and water and sterile compost
Grey mould	Fluffy grey mould growth associated with a soft brown rot on buds, leaves and shoots	Many. In houses, commonest on pot cyclamen; in greenhouses, most plants are susceptible, particularly late in the season	Maintain thorough hygiene by regular removal of dead leaves and blooms. Spray with benomyl to check attacks
Leaf mould	Yellowish patterns on leaves bearing brown mould growth. Plants may decline after severe attacks	Tomatoes	Ensure that there is good ventilation, especially low down in the greenhouse. Spray fortnightly with benomyl to check severe attacks
Leaf spot	Variously sized and shaped spots on leaves, sometimes accompanied by general leaf deterioration and drop	All houses and greenhouse plants	Determine the cause of spotting. If physical (household sprays etc), avoid these in future. If apparently fungal, spray with benomyl

QUICK GUIDE TO HOUSE PLANT AND GREENHOUSE DISEASES

Disease	Symptoms	Plants affected	Control
Powdery mildew	More or less general powdery white covering to leaves, shoots and other plant parts	Many greenhouse and house plants	Spray at 2-3 week intervals with benomyl
Root rot and crown rot	Foliage turns yellow and may wilt; plants generally decline. Roots and stem base display rotting and, sometimes, mould growth	All house and greenhouse plants	Do not over-water plants. If detected early, repot into fresh compost. Pack compost around the stem base to encourage new rooting
Soft rot	Swollen parts such as corms or cactus stems are reduced to a semi-liquid mass within	All plants with swollen storage organs	If detected early, repot, cut out affected parts and dust with dry Bordeaux mixture
Sooty mould	Black, sticky covering to leaves, fruits, stems and other plant parts	All greenhouse and house plants	Control the insects that secrete honeydew on which moulds grow
Virus	Irregular mottling, crumpling or other distortion of the leaves. Flowering and/or fruiting may be reduced	Most house and greenhouse plants, but always most serious on tomatoes and cucumbers	Protect cucumbers by controlling aphids. Grow resistant tomato varieties and pay rigorous attention to hygiene
Wilt	Leaves droop (usually the lowest first) and become pale yellowish	Many greenhouse and house plants but especially serious on tomatoes and carnations	Prevent by rigorous attention to hygiene; replace affected plants with new stock on a fresh site

A GUIDE TO CHEMICALS

There are two schools of chemical thought on pests and diseases: one is that you should spray immediately at the first sign of attack, the other is that you spray as a preventative measure, before the pest or disease has a chance to raise its ugly head. It is essential to use correct control methods, misusing chemicals can disturb the balance of nature. Take a happy medium and use a combination of both methods – preventative sprays for problems that you know are likely to occur, like blackspot on rose, and quick 'when-you-see-them-spray-them' for unexpected outbreaks – and you won't go far wrong.

PESTICIDES

Chemicals for controlling garden troubles are called pesticides. All are cleared by the Government's Pesticides Safety Precautions Scheme which ensures that no product containing any new chemical is used, no new formulations of an existing product is introduced, and no new use is recommended until results of extensive safety studies have been examined and accepted by the Advisory Committee on Pesticides.

So providing they are used as described on the label, following all instructions and precautions to the letter, pesticides are quite safe to use in the garden.

BUY RIGHT

A bewildering assortment of pesticides is on offer. Before buying look at the label carefully. It will give details of the active ingredients and whether it is an insecticide, fungicide or herbicide. All are available under a variety of trade names.

Insecticides: these are used to control insects and other small pests. There are three basic types.

CONTACT INSECTICIDES are used against sap-sucking insects such as greenfly. They work, as the name suggests, by making contact with the pests, so you need to spray during an attack. Look for malathion or pirimicarb among the list of active ingredients.

STOMACH INSECTICIDES are effective against insects that actually eat the plant, like caterpillars. These, when sprayed on the plant, leave a deposit which the insects then eat, so spray at the first sign of an attack. Look for the ingredient fenitrothion on the label.

SYSTEMIC INSECTICIDES are absorbed into the sap of the plant, killing any sap-sucking insects. Many also kill by contact and give protection for 2-3 weeks once absorbed as they cannot be washed off. Look for the chemical dimethoate among the ingredients.

Insecticides are available in several different formulations. Sprays are economical, efficient and easily applied. Aerosols and dust are a convenient and easy-to-use way of applying them and are available for garden and greenhouse use, and for use on indoor plants. For the greenhouse you can also buy smokes, while some soil insecticides come in granular form.

When it comes to fungal disease, prevention is better than cure. **Fungicides** should be applied in advance of attack to prevent infection. Some fungicides are also systemic, so they are able to enter the sap stream, providing longer protection whatever the weather.

There are three basic types of weed-killer, or **herbicides**: those that kill only green parts of the plant they touch (contact weedkillers); those that are absorbed by the foliage and transported around inside the plant so that they infect the entire sapstream (translocated or systemic) and those that can be watered on to clean soil to prevent weed growth emerging (residual). There are also combination weedkillers that can kill off existing green growth and stop more weeds growing.

Remember, too, that there are selective and total weedkillers. Those used on lawns, for instance, are selective, killing only broadleaved weeds and not the grass. While on the other hand, there are those designed specifically for couch. It is important to note that non-selective weedkillers should only be used on uncultivated land as they will kill everything they come in contact with.

SPRAY SAFE

Before you spray

- Read and follow directions for use given on the product label. Make sure the product is recommended for the plant you wish to spray.
- Stick to the recommended dosage. Higher rates are wasteful and could damage the plant.
- Only if recommended on the label should two chemicals be mixed together.
- If spraying vegetable and fruit crops, check the interval between spraying and harvesting, and adhere to it.

When you spray

- Do not spray in bright sunshine or windy weather.
- During flowering, spray in the evening, when bees have finished working.

- Avoid spraying open delicate blooms.
- Use a fine, forceful spray, and spray until leaves are covered. However, visible wetting of the foliage with aerosol sprays is not recommended.
- Keep sprays off the skin and wash off any splashes immediately.

After you spray

- Wash out all equipment.
- Dispose of surplus spray solution safely, on to the soil, avoiding areas around ponds, watercourses etc.
- Store packs of garden chemicals safely out of reach of children and pets, and in a frost-free place. Do not store chemicals in lemonade or similar bottles. Do not keep unlabelled or illegible packs.

Avoid spraying in windy weather since the chemicals may drift in the wind. The best conditions for spraying are when it is dry, calm and frost free. It is very rare that there is no wind at all and so plastic sheeting may be used to shield nearby plants from the spray.

BIOLOGICAL CONTROL

Research has shown that the overall levels of pest damage in gardens where chemical controls are used and in 'no chemical' gardens is surprisingly similar. This is because pests have their own, natural controlling agents which are always present in the garden and will carry out much of the work for you.

This can be taken a stage further. You can play a part by actually introducing some natural controls to pest-infested plants, and this is what is known as biological control.

To be successful, you must keep a very close watch for the first signs of the pest and obtain the control as soon as it appears. Release the control evenly over the infested plants, then wait. It is important to keep the greenhouse temperature above 68°F/20°C.

For Caterpillars The bacterium *Bacillus thuringiensis* kills caterpillars without harming other insects. It is sold as sachets of dried spores, which are mixed with water and applied as a spray. The bacterium kills caterpillars that eat the sprayed leaves by paralyzing their gut. You may have to repeat the treatment if caterpillars persist.

For Mealy Bugs Mealy bugs are eaten by a ladybird, *Cryptolaemus*, whose larvae, which resemble large mealy bugs, are also voracious feeders. The ladybirds are sold as adults or larvae. They thrive in temperatures of 63-83°F/20-26°C and high humidity.

Release at least one per plant as they search only a small area. Keep the doors and windows closed until they are established in order to stop adults flying away. *Cryptolaemus* should reduce the pest population considerably in a period of two or three months.

For Whitefly A small parasitic wasp (*Encarsia formosa*) can be very effective in controlling whiteflies. It lays its eggs in whitefly scales (larvae) and kills them.

Wasps are supplied in black parasitized scales on a leaf. The wasps hatch out and parasitise more whitefly scales. You must introduce the wasp as soon as you see the first whitefly.

For Red Spider Mite Red spider mite is eaten by a predatory mite (*Phytoseiulus*). The mites arrive on pieces of leaf or card which you tear up and distribute among infested plants. It works best at temperatures of over 80°F/25°C.

A Resident Toad

Before the days of modern biological control, many gardeners kept a toad in the greenhouse to deal with pests. Toads eat insects, grubs, slugs and even earwigs. They need a moist atmosphere and like dense vegetation and secluded corners for hibernation. If you do keep one in your greenhouse, make sure it can get out to find a pond for mating and breeding purposes.

If the controls are very efficient, they will destroy all their prey and die out; you often need to have a low level of pest infestation present all the time to keep the biological controls alive. If the pest species multiplies rapidly, the biological control will do so as well (after a short delay) so it should always keep on top of the problem. It is difficult to keep the populations nicely balanced, so you may need to buy in further batches of controls throughout the growing season.

GARDENING
JARGON

A s with any specialized subject, the craft of gardening is littered with technical terms. What follows is a glossary of just some of the words and expressions that crop up in conversations among gardeners and in gardening books and articles.

Acid soil In practice, this means a soil, or potting compost, containing little or no lime. Acid soils give readings lower than pH7 when tested with an acid/alkaline soil analysis kit (available from garden shops).

Few plants will grow well on very acid soil. Some, such as rhododendrons, must have a soil which is slightly on the acid side. The vast majority of garden plants, including vegetables and fruits, do best on soils which are either slightly acid or slightly alkaline (see **Alkaline Soil**). Soils can be made less acid by treating with hydrated lime (available from garden shops).

Aeration Aeration is the ventilation of soil or potting compost by air seeping down from the surface through tiny gaps between the crumbs of soil.

Fresh air filtering down through the soil is essential for healthy root growth in plants. A soil which is packed down hard and isn't crumbly or well broken up will be poorly aerated; it is also likely to become waterlogged and stagnant after heavy rain or watering.

Digging coarse sand into compacted soil helps to keep it crumbly and open. Regular hoeing, digging and forking will break up the surface of the soil, allowing fresh air in; spiking grass with a fork or spiked roller does the same job on lawns.

Algae Slimy green or brown growths occurring in ponds and on damp stone and wood. A few crystals of potassium permanganate (obtainable from a pharmacist) dissolved in the watering can and poured on to ponds or other affected areas will discourage algae growth.

Alkaline soil More commonly referred to as limy soil. An alkaline soil contains lime, usually in the form of particles of limestone or chalk, and gives a reading higher than pH7 when tested with an acid/alkaline soil analysis kit (see **Acid Soil**).

Certain lime-hating plants, including rhododendrons and camellias, will not grow on alkaline (limy) soils at all. The majority of garden plants are quite happy on soil which is slightly alkaline (and also on slightly acid soil) but some don't grow so well where there is a very high level of lime, such as in areas where there is thin soil overlying chalk.

Always check on the lime-tolerance of plants before buying if your garden soil is extremely limy. Very alkaline soils can be made more acid by the addition of peat and ammonium sulphate fertilizer. Lime-hating plants may be grown in beds or tubs of lime-free potting compost, or a mixture of peat, sand and fertilizer, where the garden soil is too alkaline for them.

Alpines Also commonly referred to as rock plants, these are mainly wild plants from the high mountain ranges of Europe, Asia and America; some are hybrids or varieties raised in cultivation from wild plants. All are neat and low-growing, generally making mats of small leaves, spangled with short-stemmed flowers.

The strongest growing types, such as aubrietas, alyssums, campanulas and geraniums, can be grown in ordinary garden soil at the front of the border. But all alpines prefer a well-drained soil which doesn't become waterlogged during winter, and for the small alpines this is essential.

Soil drainage can be improved by digging in peat, coarse sand and grit before planting, and by raising the level of the bed or rock garden a foot or more. This ensures that excess winter rainwater will drain away fast.

Annuals Plants which are raised from seed, grow rapidly, and flower within a few months, dying after flowering is over; must be raised afresh from seed each year. Useful for colourful spring and summer displays in borders, tubs, windowboxes and hanging baskets.

Hardy annuals may be sown directly into the soil where they are to flower, or in seedtrays to be planted out later. Sow in early autumn for a spring display, from early – mid spring for flowers throughout the summer.

Half-hardy and frost-tender annuals are sown in seedtrays from late winter to mid spring and must be kept in a heated greenhouse or on a windowsill indoors. Plant out after spring frosts are over (usually late spring). Alternatively, sow direct into the garden soil in mid/late spring if the weather is warm.

Annuals need plenty of water and well-prepared soil to flower well. Add peat and compound fertilizer (like Grow-more) to the soil, and water during dry weather. Don't plant or sow annuals too thickly; space them out well.

Aphids Small insects, both winged and wingless, which suck the sap from plants causing distorted growth and poor flowering. More seriously, aphids frequently act as carriers of virus diseases, picking up the virus from infected plants and innoculating previously healthy ones with it. Greenfly and blackfly are typical examples.

Aphids usually cluster around the young growing tips of plants often underneath the leaves. Spray with an insecticide containing malathion, taking care to wet the undersides of the leaves. Watch out for them over the following weeks, repeating the spray if required.

Bark ringing The removal of strips of bark to slow down the growth of a tree; normally used to improve cropping of apples and pears, but can also be used to slow the growth of a tree which is becoming too large for the garden.

A strip of bark ¼-½in/0·5-1cm wide is cut away in a semi-circle around one side of the trunk about 2ft/0·6m up from the base. A similar half-circle of bark is removed on the opposite side of the trunk, 3in/8cm higher.

The cuts in the bark restrict the flow of sap and so reduce the rate of growth. This is done in mid/late spring and must be repeated once the bark has grown together again if continued restriction of growth is desired.

Bedding plants Bedding plants are those used to provide a temporary display of colour in beds and borders. They are grown almost to flowering stage and then planted out in the garden, allowed to flower and then taken up to make room for other plants. This is known as 'bedding out' the plants.

Suitable bedding plants include annuals, biennials, some perennials such as pelargoniums and polyanthus, and bulbs (see entries under **Annuals, Biennials and Perennials**), and can be hardy or half-hardy.

Annuals and biennials used for bedding are thrown away after flowering as they die in any case when flowering is over. Long-lived perennial plants are moved to another part of the garden or potted up. Bulbs are lifted and stored dry once the leaves have died, or may be lifted and planted elsewhere while still green and growing.

Polyanthus, wallflowers, forget-me-nots and spring bulbs are bedded out in autumn for a spring display.

Pelargoniums, marigolds and asters may replace these in late spring to provide summer flowers. Fuschias are excellent for autumn flowering.

Biennials Plants which flower the year after being raised from seed and then die, unlike annuals which flower in the first year. Popular biennials include the foxgloves, wallflowers, Canterbury Bells and forget-me-nots. Seeds are sown in mid – late spring, either in seedtrays or in garden beds. They will not flower until the following year so you may not want them taking up space in the borders during the first summer; in this case keep the young plants in pots or an out-of-the-way corner until autumn, when they can be put in the borders to flower the following spring and summer.

Blanching The process of covering up the stems of celery, leeks and seakale to keep them white and succulent. Celery and leeks are blanched by heaping up earth around them or tying cardboard around them to exclude the light; seakale is usually grown in a shed or greenhouse (or even indoors) to force it into early, soft growth and light is excluded with a large up-turned flower pot over the plant.

Blind Seedling plants are said to be 'blind' if the growing tip dwindles away and growth stops completely. Plants, particularly bulbs, which fail to flower are also sometimes said to be 'blind'.

Seedlings which lose their growing tips and fail to make any new growth should be discarded. Plants which fail to flower properly should be watered regularly around the normal flowering time if the soil is dry and should be fed with a high-potash fertilizer such as Phostrogen. Bulbs may go blind if planted too shallowly; replant deeper and feed as above.

Bolting A salad or root vegetable which starts to produce flowers before it is harvested is said to have bolted. This spoils the hearts of salad vegetables and makes root vegetables tough. It is most commonly caused by a period of hot, dry weather and frequent watering during drought is the best means of prevention. Regular doses of liquid fertilizer (for example, Maxicrop) will also help to prevent bolting.

Bottom heat A slightly rude-sounding phrase which actually means warming pots or soil from below by means of electrical heating cables. Electric propagating units work on this principle, and cables can be bought for burying under soil and pots in the greenhouse.

The extra warmth provided by bottom heating aids the germination of seeds which need high temperatures to sprout. It also speeds up the rooting of cuttings.

However, the soil must only be warm, between 65°F/18°C and 75°F/24°C. Temperatures any higher than this would do more harm than good.

Broadcast sowing Not, unfortunately, a way of growing your own television station, but simply the method of scattering seeds evenly over an area of soil rather than sowing in straight lines (see entry under **Drill**).

Vegetable seeds are normally sown in straight lines, or 'drills', but grass seed is scattered 'broadcast', evenly over the ground, when making a new lawn.

Seeds of annuals and biennials are also sprinkled evenly over the garden border when they're being sown where they are to flower. All seeds sown in trays and pots should also be scattered evenly (and not too thickly).

Cover broadcast sown seeds by gently raking the soil or sprinkling finely-crumbled soil thinly over them.

Budding A method of propagating shrubs and trees, similar to grafting (*see entry under* **Grafting**), used as a fast and reliable way to produce new plants of a good variety of shrub or tree. Not one of the simplest operations for a gardening beginner to try, but widely used by experienced gardeners and nurserymen.

Basically, the leaves and growing point are sliced off a seedling of an easily grown and common shrub or tree, leaving the stem and roots behind. A bud from the tree or shrub to be propagated is grafted on to this stem and the two grow together (just as in a human skin graft). The bud grows away to make a tree or shrub exactly like its parent. The actual techniques vary, but that is the basic theory.

In practice, trees and shrubs which have been propagated by budding sometimes throw up suckers from the roots or the base of the stem in future years. These suckers, which are shoots of the less desirable seedling, must be removed immediately or they will very soon take over.

Many trees and shrubs, in particular roses and fruit trees, are propagated by budding. To be on the safe side, it's best to remove all suckers from the roots or the base of the trunk of any tree or shrub; unless you know that it is meant to produce suckers.

Bud drop Sudden dropping of flower buds is usually caused by frosty weather, cold, blustery winds, or waterlogged soil.

It's a problem most often seen in tomatoes, runner beans, sweet peas and begonias and is most common in spring when night frost and cold winds can kill tender buds, and when garden soil is often wet and cold.

If the weather turns very cold in spring, cover up plants which start to lose buds, to protect the remaining buds from frosts. Make sure greenhouse plants which are in bud are kept warm enough, particularly at night, and don't give them too much water.

Capillary watering Kits for capillary watering of pot plants in the greenhouse and home are available from garden shops. A fibre wick is pushed up through the base of the pot and the pot is then placed on a damp fibre mat in a tray; the compost in the pot draws up moisture from the mat through the wick, as and when it is needed. Capillary watering systems simplify pot plant care, particularly at holiday times, as a number of pots on one mat can be watered in one go simply by soaking the mat when it dries out.

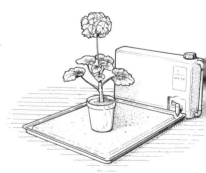

Cloche A glass, plastic or polythene cover placed over plants in the garden to provide protection from frosts and heavy rain; commonly used to protect early-sown vegetable crops (particularly lettuce) from spring frosts and to encourage fast growth, and so produce early crops. Glass cloches give the best protection against cold; plastic and polythene are less effective as they don't retain the sun's warmth so effectively. They are, however, cheaper than glass and, of course, safer, particularly if there are young children or pets about.

Compost Can mean one of two things: a specially prepared compost (soil or peat mixture) for seed sowing and potting plants, or garden compost made from rotted leaves, grass clippings and other vegetable matter.

Garden shops sell a wide range of made-up seed and potting composts, with all the required fertilizers added. Peat-based composts are probably the best for a beginner; they require less frequent watering and give good results.

Making a compost heap is a must for every gardener who has the room to spare. Any vegetable matter, including kitchen scraps, will rot down to produce compost rich in plant foods. Garden compost also improves the texture of the soil (*see* **Humus**). It can be dug into the ground or spread around plants, trees and shrubs as a mulch (*see entry under* **Mulching**).

A compost heap must be open at the bottom, to allow worms to get in and help in breaking down the rotting matter and to allow drainage of water. It need not be closed in around the sides, although this speeds up the rotting process, but it must have a cover on top to keep off the rain.

A compost accelerator (available from garden shops) may be added to hasten the rotting of the heap. Ripe compost should be brown and crumbly, and not too smelly!

Cordon Any tree which is trained to produce a single, upright stem with no large side-branches is known as a cordon.

A cordon is trained into its tall, spindly shape by pinching out and pruning sideshoots.

Sometimes flowering trees are trained this way to make them neat enough for small gardens, but the process is mainly used to produce cordon apple and pear trees.

Cordon-shaped fruit trees can be planted very close together (as close as 2ft/0·6m) so that a number of trees can be squeezed into a small area.

Corms Similar to bulbs but actually swollen underground stems consisting of solid starchy material inside papery tunics; bulbs have fleshy scales or 'rings' (actually the swollen bases of leaves) like an onion. Examples of corms include crocus and colchicums. Treat as bulbs.

Crocks Broken clay pots placed in the bottom of a flower pot to ensure free drainage of excess water. Only really necessary in large pots, tubs, troughs and other large plant containers. In small pots and seedtrays a little grit or gravel will do. When using a peat-based potting compost, crocks and grit are not essential, unless extra good drainage is required for a particular type of plant.

Crown Fleshy, bud-like top of plant roots which protrudes through the soil and from which shoots and leaves grow, as in rhubarb, peonies and delphiniums.

Many herbaceous plants die down to a resting crown on or just below the soil during winter, when they lose their foliage. When planting herbaceous plants in spring and autumn take care not to damage the crowns; watch out for dormant crowns when digging and hoeing.

Plants which form crowns can generally be split up when a number of congested crowns have been formed on one plant (*see* **Division**).

Crown rot is a disease peculiar to rhubarb. It attacks the plant at the crown causing it to turn brown and decay.

Early signs are weak stems and dull-coloured leaves.

The disease is caused by a bacterium and no remedy is known. All affected plants should be burnt.

Cultivar The correct botanical name for a named variety of a plant, e.g. *Rosa* 'Iceberg', which has been raised in cultivation by a gardener or nurseryman rather than having been discovered growing in the wild. Most gardeners simply use the term variety.

Cutting Part of a plant which is cut off and treated in such a way that it grows into a complete new plant with roots, stems and leaves, identical to the parent plant from which the cutting was taken.

Cuttings are most commonly taken as short lengths of stem, complete with two or three leaves, but sometimes individual leaves and buds, and even sections of thick roots, can be used. Stem cuttings are the easiest for beginners to experiment with.

Stem cuttings of herbaceous plants and other non-woody plants, like chrysanthemums, lupins, delphiniums, carnations, pelargoniums and hydrangeas, are taken in late spring or early summer when soft new shoots have been formed.

Stem cuttings of wood plants, i.e. shrubs and trees, are generally taken in late summer or early autumn.

Cuttings are most frequently taken in the form of shoot tips from 2-4in/5-10cm long depending on the size of the plant, cut off just below a leaf joint or pulled off a larger shoot. The lower leaves are pulled off the cutting, leaving about three at the top. Any ragged ends are cut off the base of the cutting and the bottom ½in/1cm is dipped in rooting powder or gel.

Inserted firmly in damp sand with a little peat mixed in, or a ready-made rooting compost, the cuttings should root in time (anything from two weeks to six months, depending on the plant). Cuttings should be kept damp but not wet, in a closed propagating unit or in pots with plastic bags over the tops. Spraying with a fungicide solution helps to prevent rotting of the shoots.

Leaf cuttings are usually taken to propagate house plants like begonias and African violets. A well developed leaf complete with stalk is simply pressed into a bed of very sandy soil or a mixture of sand and peat, so that the lower surface of the leaf lies flat on on the bed.

Damping-off The rotting of young seedling plants, caused by various fungal diseases. The stems of the seedlings rot close to the soil or seed compost, the young plants quickly toppling over and rotting away completely.

Damping-off usually occurs where seedlings are crowded, the seed compost or soil has been overwatered, or the young plants are in a very damp, airless atmosphere such as a constantly closed propagating unit.

It can be avoided by taking care not to overwater, keeping the soil or compost slightly damp but never wet, by sowing seeds thinly to avoid overcrowding, and by keeping the young plants in a light, airy position; not in a constantly closed frame or propagator. If damping-off does start, spray or water lightly with a fungicide solution such as Benlate or Fungus Fighter. Catch it early and that should do the trick.

Deadheading Removal of faded flowers from plants and shrubs. Important to encourage production of further flowers, and to prevent wasted energy being put into seed production instead of plant growth and formation of the next years flower buds.

Deciduous A name given to plants which lose their leaves in winter as opposed to evergreens which retain theirs. It is particularly applied to trees and shrubs.

Such plants are best transplanted during the period that they are leafless, roughly from mid autumn to mid spring.

Die-back The gradual death of plant shoots, starting at the tips and moving down the shoots; a term normally applied to shrubs and trees, but non-woody plants sometimes dieback in a similar way.

Various different diseases cause this type of problem. Cut off all dying shoots,

cutting back to healthy growth and leaving no dying material at all. Burn all diseased shoots after pruning back, to avoid further spread of disease.

Die-back may also be caused by poor growing conditions; i.e. dry soil, waterlogged soil and lack of plant nutrients in the soil. Feeding plants affected by die-back with a high-potash liquid fertilizer such as Phostrogen will aid recovery.

Disbudding The practice of removing most of the flower buds on a plant so that the remaining buds produce very large blooms; often used to produce prize-winning show blooms. Carnations, roses and chrysanthemums are frequently given this treatment by enthusiasts.

For the average gardener this is not necessary, unless he or she wants to try showing a few blooms at the local show or have extra-large flowers for cutting.

Division A large number of garden plants, particularly herbaceous plants, can be increased by division once they have formed good-sized clumps. Many plants benefit from being divided up regularly, growing and flowering better than they would if left to form congested clumps.

Any plant which produces a number of crowns (*see entry under* **Crown**), which forms a spreading mat of rooted shoots, or which spreads by means of suckers with roots, may be increased by division.

The best times to divide plants are autumn and spring when the weather is cool and damp. Small plants can be dug up and pulled apart with the fingers; larger clumps may require splitting up with a garden fork or spade and a sharp knife may be required to cut thick rootstocks.

Make sure that all the divisions have a good share of root, and dust any large cuts or wounds with sulphur powder to guard against disease. Replant the pieces immediately, and water them in well.

Drainage Good soil drainage is essential to healthy plant growth. If rainwater does not drain away quickly through the soil it will become boggy and waterlogged in wet weather, causing plant roots to rot.

Plenty of sand, grit and organic matter like rotted leaves, compost and peat all help to keep the soil 'open' and crumbly so that water can drain through quickly. Ground which has been trampled down hard or which is mainly sticky clay will be poorly drained; digging and adding the above materials will improve drainage. Narrow trenches partly filled with rubble may be necessary in more extreme cases of bad drainage.

Good soil drainage is equally important, and often more important, in pots and other plant containers as in the open garden. Make sure potting and seed composts contain enough sand to aid drainage; ideally, water should drain out of the bottom of the pot very soon after it is watered on to the potting compost.

Drawn plants Plants or seedlings which have grown abnormally tall, weak and spindly as a result of being grown in too dark or shady a position. It occurs where plants, and especially seedlings, are crowded together in greenhouses and frames. Seedtrays should be placed on shelves near the glass or raised on inverted pots on the staging so that they get as much light as possible.

Another way to overcome this problem is to sow seeds thinly in the first place and prick off seedlings early.

It is also a common problem with certain house plants like Busy Lizzies, which are not given enough light.

Drill A shallow groove made in soil for sowing seeds in straight lines; mainly used for sowing vegetable seeds. The drill is made with the edge of a hoe or rake, using a plank or string as a guide.

Small seeds (lettuce, carrots) require only a very shallow drill, no more than ½in/1cm deep and about 1in/3cm wide. Drills for large seeds (peas and beans) should be 1-2in/3-5cm deep.

Smooth soil back over the drills after sowing.

The important point when making drills for sowing is to keep the depth constant. Drills which are deep in places and shallow in others will result in uneven seed germination and crop development; all the seeds should be at about the same depth, evenly spaced and not too thickly.

Small seeds, like carrots and parsnips, are sometimes sown using a method called liquid drilling. The seeds are well mixed with a gel and then squeezed, using something like an empty washing-up liquid bottle, into the prepared drill. This method ensures even spacing of seeds and better germination as they don't dry out.

Earthing-up The process of drawing up earth with a hoe or rake to cover the lower stems of celery, leeks and potatoes.

With celery and leeks, the aim is to blanch the stems (*see entry under* **Blanching**), making them white and tender. Celery plants are earthed-up when mature and full-grown, but leeks are gradually earthed-up as they develop during the summer and early autumn.

Potatoes are earthed-up when the young shoots come through the soil in early spring, soil being piled up around them almost to the tops of the new shoots when they are about 6in/16cm tall. This ensures that the potatoes which develop later are well covered, and also protects the shoots from being damaged by spring frosts.

Ericaceous plants Plants belonging to the heather family, a botanical division known as the *Ericaceae*, which includes not only heathers but rhododendrons (including azaleas), kalmias, arbutus, vacciniums, gaultherias and pernettyas: all shrubby plants.

Most garden centres sell bags of 'Ericaceous Potting Compost', a lime-free, peat-based compost specially made for these lime-hating plants. This type of compost is ideal for all other lime-hating plants, such as autumn-flowering gentians, meconopsis and certain lilies like *Lilium auratum* and *L. speciosum*.

Espalier A method of training fruit trees on wires between strong posts; keeps the trees neat and saves space in a small garden.

The normal system is to train the main stem of the tree straight upwards, vertically, and then to train sideshoots horizontally along the wires. The posts and wires should run from north to south if more than one row is planted, so that the rows do not shade one another unduly.

The same rule applies to soft fruit grown in rows.

F_1 hybrids Plant seed sold as an F_1 hybrid is the result of a carefully controlled cross made in the nursery between two selected parent plants.

The resulting seedlings will produce plants which are uniform in size, flower colour, fruit or vegetable quality in the case of crop plants, vigour of growth and all other characteristics. The parent plants used to produce the seed will have been chosen to give the seedlings an excellent mix of good qualities.

F_1 hybrids will have been tested and tried by the growers and should give reliable results. If the gardener takes seeds from his F_1 plants, however, this will produce very variable seedlings. The only way to produce constantly uniform F_1 plants is to cross the same two parent plants each year, hence the need to buy

fresh F_1 seed every year of annuals and vegetables; the amateur gardener cannot save his or her own seed.

Fan training The normal method of training fruit trees on a wall or fence. The branches are trained up from the base of the young tree in a fan shape, spread out evenly across the wall. Wires or masonry nails and ties are used to support the young branches and keep them in place.

It is essential to start with a young tree which branches close to the ground, so that the branches can be spread out across the whole height of the wall; a long bare trunk at the base means wasted wall space. The main central shoot is pruned out to encourage the growth of the sideshoots across the wall.

As with espalier-trained fruit trees, this method is ideally suited to the smaller garden.

Fertilizers Plant foods; a whole range of nutrients which all plants need for healthy growth just as an animal or human needs a balanced diet. Deficiency of one or more of these nutrients can cause plant disorders.

Fertilizers can be applied in the form of organic manures (horse, cow, pig and chicken manures). These, when well matured and rotted down (about six months should be allowed for this) put a range of nutrients into the soil, and add humus (*see* **Humus**) which improves the quality of the soil generally. The alternative method is to use packaged fertilizers, which may be either organic as in the case of dried blood, bonemeal and fish meal, or chemical fertilizers such as sulphate or potash, ammonium sulphate and superphosphate.

All these types of fertilizers do the same job, but some provide only one kind of plant food or a mixture of foods which isn't very well balanced. For general use on the garden and in potting composts, a balanced compounded fertilizer such as John Innes Base, Growmore, or Blood, Fish and Bone Meal will provide all the required nutrients.

All compounded fertilizers sold in garden shops have the balance of nutrients shown on the package as a set of three numbers; these represent the percentage of each plant food contained in the fertilizer.

Proportions vary from one fertilizer to another. The first number gives the proportion of nitrogen, the second number the proportion of phosphate and the third potash. The compound fertilizer Growmore, for example, has 7:7:7 on the package which shows that it contains equal proportions of all three plant foods.

Nitrogen is the plant food important for producing lots of leafy growth, and vegetable crops need plenty of this. Phosphate aids good root development and is essential for root crops. Potash encourages flowering and fruit production, and also produces tough and frost-resistant shoots on shrubs, trees and evergreen plants. Potash also helps to build up large bulbs.

From the above, it's obvious that all plants need all three nutrients for general health while some (particularly vegetable and fruit crops) may require extra doses of one nutrient. The needs vary, but the above notes should give a basic guide. Applying fertilizers every year will do no harm, provided recommended doses are adhered to.

Liquid fertilizers are useful for giving plants a quick boost, as the dissolved nutrients are quickly taken up by the roots. Liquid feeds containing trace elements are the best, as these contain small amounts of various chemicals which plants require in tiny doses (just as humans need small amounts of vitamins). These trace elements are usually in the soil any-

way, but an extra dose does the plants no harm.

Foliar feeding Plants can absorb water and dissolved nutrients through their leaves, and foliar feeds have been devised to take advantage of this fact. Diluted in water, the foliar fertilizer (available from garden shops) is sprayed or watered on to the plant's foliage. This is a very quick way of giving a boost to an ailing plant, or of boosting growth generally.

Forcing Speeding up the growth or flowering of a plant by bringing it into a warmer temperature, usually in winter and early spring. Early vegetable crops (lettuce, spring onions, etc) can be forced slightly by covering with cloches. Chicory is forced in the dark to blanch the stems making them palatable.

Frost damage Frost may damage many types of plants, including bulbs, shrubs and even trees, by freezing the sap in leaves, stems, buds and flowers. Very severe frosts which freeze deep into the soil may also harm plant roots.

The amount of damage varies considerably, depending on the type of plant. Plants which are killed outright by even slight frosts in autumn, winter and spring are referred to as **tender plants**, and these include the following: most house plants, fuchsias and freesias intended for greenhouse cultivation, summer bedding, such as pelargoniums and dahlias; tender annuals.

All these 'tender' types of plant must be kept in a frost-free greenhouse or frame, or indoors, when the weather is frosty; they will not survive in the open garden over winter.

Plants which are virtually unharmed by even severe frosts are termed **hardy plants**. The majority of spring bulbs, perennial border plants, shrubs and trees are hardy, as are many annuals.

Hardy plants harmed by severe frosts do, however, often recover. Young seedlings are more at risk than mature plants.

Protection from hard frosts can be achieved by keeping pot plants in a heated greenhouse or indoors, or by providing outdoor plants which are suffering damage with some kind of covering.

Glass and polythene provide some protection from cold (in the form of frames or cloches over the plants). But protection from severe cold is better achieved with coverings of such good insulating materials as dry bracken, conifer branches, newspaper, sacking and old blankets. These should be securely fixed or tied around the plants to be protected.

Fungicide Chemical preparations for the treatment of such fungal plant diseases as **grey mould**, **mildews** and **rusts** (*see entries under these diseases*), applied as powders, sprays and fumigating smoke capsules. Sprays are the easiest, and most effective, to use. Most are poisonous, so always wash hands after use.

Fungicides labelled as 'systemic' tend to be more effective (*see entry under* **Systemic sprays**).

Always make sure that you are buying the right fungicide for the disease you have to tackle; check the labels of packs and bottles.

Grafting A method of propagating plants (mainly trees and shrubs) by grafting a shoot from the plant to be propagated on to the stem and roots of a seedling of the same type of plant. The seedling used to provide the stem and roots (known as the 'stock') is normally one that is easy to raise and which is strong growing.

A flowering or fruiting shrub or tree shoot grafted on to such a strong-growing seedling stock grows away strongly, and quickly makes a new tree or shrub identical to the parent from which the shoot was taken.

Grafting is an awkward procedure for the average gardener to tackle, but it is widely used on nurseries to propagate named varieties of flowering shrubs and trees, and fruit trees.

Shrubs and trees which have been grafted usually show a bulge or lump near the base of the trunk where the graft was made; any shoots growing from below this point should be removed.

Grease-banding A method of tying grease-covered bands around the trunks of trees to prevent insects crawling up into the branches to feed on buds, leaves and flowers. Used mainly on apple trees to prevent damage to the blossom and fruit by certain types of moth caterpillar.

It is essential to have the bands in position before the female winter moths begin to emerge from their summer period or pupation and ascend the trees to begin their egg laying.

There's not much point in keeping the bands once the egg laying period is over, so the bands should be fixed by early autumn and removed in early spring.

Bands are available from garden centres and shops.

Grey mould A fungal disease, also known as botrytis. The most obvious symptom is the appearance of very furry grey mould growth on dying stems and leaves. Common on some house plants (cyclamen) and greenhouse plants; also on the foliage of bulbs and on soft fruit. Occurs particularly in damp conditions. Treat with suitable fungicide spray.

Hardening-off The process of preparing plants for the colder conditions they will have to face in the open garden after they have been grown in the warmth of a greenhouse or indoors. This is most important in spring.

If moved outside too quickly, the plants may stop growing for some time because of the shock of the temperature change; they may even be killed by cold, frosty weather. Moving from greenhouse to cold frame and then into the open reduces the risks.

Putting plants outside on mild days and returning them to the warmth when frost is forecast also helps.

But at all times, the appearance of the plants must be your guide. If they continue to grow and remain a healthy colour, then all is well.

Hardy plants Plants which will survive frosts unharmed, or virtually unharmed, and can be left in the open garden during the winter (*see* **Frost damage**).

Herbaceous plants Herbaceous plants are those which lose their leaves in the autumn, producing fresh growth with the arrival of warm spring weather. Most herbaceous plants die down to resting buds (or 'crowns') on or just below the surface of the soil; take care not to damage these when digging and hoeing.

Typical examples include peonies, hardy fuchsias, delphiniums and kniphofias (red hot pokers).

If you've got the room, then a herbaceous border will provide a stunning display of colour throughout the summer. You'll also need a lot of time and patience, as many herbaceous plants require staking.

Weeds will also be a problem in this kind of border, but a good mulch (*see entry under* **Mulching**) will not only help keep these down, but do the plants good as well.

Herbicides Technical term for weed-killers. Basically three types are available; foliar-acting; soil-acting and systemic.

Foliar weedkillers kill leaves and stems when sprayed or watered on to the weeds, but they become inactive once on the soil, so they don't kill deep roots.

Soil-acting weedkillers may kill leaves and stems on contact and also soak into the soil to be taken up by weed roots. Some last a long time in the soil and kill new weed seedlings as they germinate.

Systemic weedkillers are sprayed or watered on to the leaves and are taken down through the sap system of the weed to its stem and roots, giving good kill of deep-rooted and stubborn weeds.

Weedkillers for lawns come in two types: 'spot' treatment, for painting or dabbing on to the leaves of individual weeds and selective weedkillers which kill the weeds without harming the grass. Moss on lawns can be dealt with by using a selective moss killer which doesn't harm the turf.

Take care not to spray or splash garden plants with weedkiller. Don't use soil-acting herbicides too close to garden plants; many of them seep through the soil sideways and may be taken up by the roots of nearby plants.

Some soil-acting weedkillers are recommended for killing weeds (but not the toughest ones) among shrubs and vegetables without doing any harm. Even these should be used with care, however.

Try to keep them away from the roots of garden plants, and use them as little as possible.

Most important of all, it is essential to take great care with weedkillers generally; they may be harmful to both humans and animals. Wash hands after use, and wash off any splashes on the skin straight away.

Humus Decayed vegetable matter in the soil such as decayed leaves and plant stems. Humus is essential to help keeep soil light, crumbly and well-drained, to prevent the soil drying out in hot weather, and to provide valuable plant foods.

It's virtually impossible to put too much humus into your soil; it can only improve it. All humus is gradually destroyed in the soil by the natural processes of decay and the more thorough and more frequent the cultivation of the land, the more rapid will be the loss of humus.

Extra humus can be added by digging in well-rotted garden compost (grass clippings, leaves and any other vegetable matter), well-rotted manure, peat, mushroom compost and the compost from used growing bags.

Insecticides Sprays, powders and granules for dealing with all types of insect pests. Sprays are mainly used to kill insects which feed on the leaves and stems of plants (like greenfly and caterpillars). Powders and granules are generally mixed into the soil to cope with underground slugs, grubs and other soil pests.

Insecticide smoke capsules are also available, for fumigating greenhouses to clean out insect pests; normally used in autumn or spring as a part of general glasshouse hygiene, or to cope with severe pest problems.

Systemic insecticide sprays are useful as they are soaked up by the plants' leaves and kill pests which try to feed on the plants for up to two or three weeks after spraying.

Always check labels carefully to ensure that you are using the correct insecticide for the type of pest you want to deal with. Wash hands after use, and wash off splashes on the skin immediately.

Layering A method of propagating plants by burying a stem or shoot in the soil alongside the parent plant. Once roots have grown on the buried section of stem, it is cut away and grown on as a separate plant.

This method is used mainly for propagating shrubs, but it can also be used on any plant (except annuals) which produces runners or long, floppy stems .

With shrubs it helps to scrape the bark on the underside of the shoot or branch before bending it down and burying it; this will encourage fast rooting. Always ensure that the top few inches of the shoot are left sticking up out of the soil; never bury the entire shoot.

Border carnations, rhododendrons, magnolias and clematis can be propagated in this way.

Lifting Digging up plants to move them. A term often used in reference to bedding plants which are planted out to give a display of spring or summer colour and then lifted to make room for later-flowering plants.

Loam A slightly vague term, normally used to mean a good rich soil with just the right balance of clay particles, sand and humus; a very crumbly, dark soil which is neither too sticky nor too dry. The aim of every gardener should be to create this kind of ideal soil in his or her garden.

Mildews A group of fungal plant diseases which produce powdery or slightly furry, white or grey-white surface mould on leaves and stems. The mould appears on upper leaves and stems as well as lower ones, unlike grey mould (botrytis) which normally starts at the base of the stem.

Mildew thrives in damp conditions, particularly in the stuffy, damp atmosphere of unventilated greenhouses and frames.

Plants liable to be attacked include: roses, chrysanthemums, apple trees, gooseberries, vines, strawberries and some leaf-vegetables. Treat with a fungicide spray recommended for mildew. Always make sure to wash any treated fruit or vegetables thoroughly before eating.

Mulching The practice of spreading a thick layer of humus-forming material (*see* **Humus**) over the soil around plants, shrubs and trees. Suitable materials for mulching include garden compost, well-rotted manure, peat, bark, mushroom compost and the compost from used growing bags.

A mulch can be used to keep down weeds (by smothering seedlings); to prevent the soil drying out too much in summer and to improve the soil (when it is dug into the ground at a later date).

Never mulch over dry ground, as this has the opposite effect of keeping the soil dry. Soak dry ground before mulching and the moisture will then be held in by the mulch. Also ensure that the mulching material is damp.

Naturalizing Growing bulbs and plants in grass, or in a wild garden, so that they appear to be growing in a natural state. It's most important not to space bulbs and plants in a regular fashion in grass, but to place them as clumps, drifts and single plants in a fairly haphazard way. Just, throw handfuls of bulbs on to the grass and plant them where they land.

It's also important to improve the soil under the turf when planting in grass: the plants and bulbs will have to compete with the turf for water and food, and will benefit from any help you can give them.

When lifting a piece of turf for planting, loosen the soil beneath with a trowel or fork and break it up as much as possible. Mix in some damp peat and compound fertilizer (like John Innes base) if possible, or add a handful of potting compost.

Naturalized bulbs should be fed annually for healthy growth and flowering. Scatter compound fertilizer over the turf in autumn or winter, before the bulbs appear and water this in. A scattering of sulphate or potash (watered in) at the same time will improve flowering even more.

Offsets New young plants which sprout around the sides of a large, mature plant and which may be easily removed and grown on as a separate plant; an easy way to propagate clump-forming plants.

This term is also applied to the small bulblets which form around the bases of many types of bulbs and corms. Watch out for them when lifting bulbs.

Plunge bed A frame or bed with a layer of sand, grit, cinders or even peat, into which pots may be plunged to their rims. Plunging protects plants in pots from drying out fast in summer and from excessive cold in winter.

Plunge beds can also be used to grow on forced bulbs for early indoor displays. For this purpose the bed needs to be in a shady spot and the pots, bowls or boxes containing the bulbs (tulips, hyacinths, daffodils, for example) need to be completely covered to a depth of several inches.

Perennials Plants which live and flower for a number of years, unlike annuals and biennials which die after flowering. Some perennials, such as lupins, are termed short-lived. Others, such as peonies, will remain in good health over a fair number of years.

The majority of perennials grown in British gardens are hardy and make excellent garden plants which can be left in the border year after year; some, such as pelargoniums, must be kept in a greenhouse during winter, as they are not hardy.

Typical examples include: peonies, bearded irises, hostas, primroses and polyanthus, hellebores, hemerocallis (day lilies) and asters. All of these are hardy perennials.

Pollinate The fertilization of a flower by the transfer of the dust-like pollen on to the female stigma (usually a sticky protuberance in the centre of the flower); essential for the production of seeds. This can be left to the bees or be done by hand with a small brush.

Potting-on Moving a pot-grown plant into a larger pot once the roots have completely filled the old pot (when the plant is said to be pot-bound). Give the plant a pot just one size larger than its old one; moving it into a much larger pot may cause root problems.

Remove the plant from its old pot by holding it upside-down and tapping the rim of the pot on your hand or a hard surface. Fill in around the roots in the new pot with fresh potting compost; if possible shake a little of the old compost off the roots first.

Pricking out Moving young seedlings from the trays or pots in which the seed was sown and re-planting them, well spaced out, in garden beds or larger pots. It's vital not to leave seedlings crowded together in seedtrays and pots, where they will grow weak and straggly.

Always handle seedlings with great care, holding them by their leaves to avoid crushing the fragile stems. Use a small dibber (a penknife or pencil will do) to get under the roots and lift the seedlings from the seed compost with the minimum of root damage; never tug them out by the leaves.

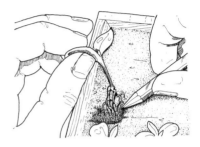

Re-plant in pots or trays of fresh seed compost, or in beds of well-prepared soil (potting compost, intended for mature plants, contains too much fertilizer for tiny young plants). Keep the seedlings watered and fairly warm (on a windowsill indoors, in a greenhouse or in a frame) to ensure that they continue to grow fast.

It's generally best to move seedlings as early as possible; as soon as they've produced their first tiny seed-leaves, or shortly after this. But if only a few seedlings come up in a large tray or pot, and if they have plenty of room to carry on growing, then they can safely be left longer before moving.

Don't re-plant tiny seedlings in large pots; 2½in/6cm or 3in/8cm pots are large enough for the majority of seedlings.

Propagation General term covering all means of increasing plants by seed, dividing clumps, cuttings, grafting and layering.

Pruning Cutting back the shoots of plants, trees and shrubs to produce a neater shape or to improve flowering and fruiting. This can appear to be a very complex and puzzling subject to someone who's a beginner in gardening, but if you follow a few very basic rules then you won't go far wrong.

Generally speaking, all plants, shrubs and trees will grow, flower, produce fruit, etc, quite happily without any pruning at all; just as they would if they were growing in the wild.

When you look at it like that, it's obvious that you can get away with doing far less pruning in the garden than you might have expected. Indeed, most garden plants, shrubs and trees require no regular pruning at all.

Pruning is only strictly necessary when something starts to go wrong. For example, you have to prune if a shrub or tree grows too large or very straggly, or if it starts to flower or fruit poorly due to old age.

Cutting back old wood on shrubs and trees encourages the production of new shoots which will flower and fruit heavily, and that's the basic principle behind most pruning. The same principle applies if a shrub or tree starts to die back; cut out the dead or diseased shoots, and new growth should sprout from the branches that are left.

With some shrubs and trees (particularly fruit trees and soft fruit bushes and canes) pruning is carried out annually to prevent gradual deterioration in flowering and cropping. The same principle applies, but it's prevention instead of cure; regular removal of old wood ensures a constant production of vigorous new flowering and fruiting shoots.

There's one other reason for pruning, and that's to train a shrub or tree into a particular shape. For example, a tree may be trained into a fan shape against a wall or into a tall, thin cordon shape which takes up little space. Fruit trees are also generally trained into an open shape by removing congested and over-lapping branches, to allow fresh air and sunlight in to ripen the fruit.

Pruning times vary from one plant to another, and if in doubt then check for pruning advice in a good general gardening book or a gardening encyclopedia.

The following are very basic guidelines: most pruning is carried out in the cool, damp weather of autumn and spring; avoid pruning in frosty weather and in very hot, dry spells. Prune non-flowering trees and shrubs in autumn or spring. Prune winter and spring-flowering trees and shrubs after flowering is over, but those that bloom during summer should be left until the following spring before pruning.

As a general rule, most pruning of fruit trees and bushes is carried out in autumn or winter, although sometimes summer pruning is also recommended.

Finally, always prune just above a bud or leaf, so that new shoots will sprout from just below the cut; never prune just beneath a bud.

Reversion The sudden change of a plant's leaves or flowers from a highly decorative form to a less attractive type for example, variegated leaves (marked with cream, gold or silver) may revert to plain green; flower colour may alter, or double flowers may revert to singles.

Reversion is often caused by the wrong kind of growing conditions, such as as planting in soil which is too poor and dry or too damp and rich, or planting in shade instead of sun. For example, variegated leaves tend to revert to plain green in dense shade. Moving the plant may, therefore, help. Removing shoots which have reverted will also help, by encouraging new growth of the desired type.

Rotation The practice of changing the crop grown on a particular patch of the vegetable and fruit garden each year.

This process is aimed at making the best use of the plants, foods in the soil (reducing the need for expensive fertilizers) and avoiding the build-up in the soil of pests and diseases which are attracted to a particular type of plant or crop.

Gardening encyclopedias and books on vegetable gardening recommend specific plans for crop rotation, plus correct application of fertilizers. Even if a strict and regular system of rotation isn't used, it's advisable not to plant the same crop on the same ground year after year, for the above reasons.

Root rots A common name for various diseases (mainly fungus diseases) which cause roots to rot away; particularly prevalent in ground which is poorly drained and tends to become waterlogged. All kinds of plants may be affected, including trees and shrubs. Honey fungus, which attacks trees and shrubs, is one example.

Plants, shrubs and trees which die back for no apparent reason, particularly in wet weather, may be suffering from root problems; check to see whether the roots are dying off.

Watering with a fungicide solution may help in the case of a mild attack, but frequently the plants have to be discarded. In the long-term, improving the soil drainage is the best answer.

Rusts The general name for a variety of fungus diseases which cause rusty or orange-coloured spots on leaves and stems. Plants commonly attacked include roses, chrysanthemums, carnations and antirrhinums (snapdragons). Treat by spraying with a fungicide recommended for rust.

Scabs The most important scab diseases are those that produce scabby growths on apples and pears, accompanied by sooty mould on the leaves. Treat by spraying with a suitable fungicide (Dithane 945). If scab is troublesome year after year, spray in spring and again in early summer as a preventative measure.

Potato scab is a totally different disease caused by a fungus carried in the soil. Only the skin is affected, the flesh is not attacked, so the potatoes are usable.

Scorch Damage to leaves in the form of browning and shrivelling. Usually caused by exposure to hot sun, particularly in times of drought. Scorching may be caused by watering plants on sunny summer days; the water droplets focus the sun's rays on to the leaves just as magnifying glasses do, so in summer it's best to water in the morning or evening.

Sooty moulds Black, sooty moulds which grow on the leaves and stems of plants when there has been an infestation of sap-sucking insects such as greenfly or whitefly.

The mould grows on the sticky substances with which the insects cover the plants; it does no real harm but is unsightly and should be washed off to avoid clogging of the leaf pores, through which the plants breathe.

Sour soil A term for a soil which is waterlogged, badly drained and poorly aerated. Like stagnant water, sour soil tends to be full of harmful bacteria and few plants will grow in it. Very sour soil smells of decay and is easily recognized.

Improve the soil by digging in sand

or grit, plus peat, garden compost or other humus-adding and soil lightening materials.

Species A botanical term frequently encountered by the average gardener. Sometimes it is used to denote a plant from the wild, as opposed to a named variety or hybrid raised in cultivation; more correctly, it is one of a number of divisions into which all plants are classified: *Family:* a large group of plants which differ widely but share common characteristics.

Genus: A sub-division of the family, containing plants which are very similar but which still vary slightly (for instance the genus Primula).

Species: an individual plant within a genus (for instance *Primula vulgaris*, the common primrose).

A species may or may not vary slightly in flower colour or habit of growth; if it does vary, the plants are forms, varieties or cultivars of the species. A hybrid is a plant raised by crossing two different species.

Spur A term with two or three meanings in the garden, the commonest being a shoot with fat fruiting buds on a fruit tree.

Apple and pear trees tend to produce too many fruiting spurs if left to grow naturally for too long, leading to crops of small fruits clustered too closely together. To avoid this, fruiting shoots may be thinned out in autumn or winter so that they're not congested and overlapping; and at the same time some of the longest shoots may be shortened to prevent a 'weeping' habit which would shade lower fruits from the sun.

Stopping Removing the upper growing tip of a plant, to force it into making plenty of sideshoots and so take on a good, bushy shape.

This process may be used on any

ornamental plant which starts to grow tall and lanky; it is particularly useful for fast-growing herbaceous plants such as chrysanthemums which otherwise tend to make rather floppy plants requiring staking.

Stratification The process of allowing seeds to be exposed to winter frosts, to hasten germination. Various types of plants (in particular, alpines, shrubs and trees) require a period of freezing before they'll sprout.

Seeds may be stratified after sowing by simply standing the pots outdoors over the winter (don't let them become waterlogged for long periods or the seeds may rot). Large seeds may be buried in pots or boxes of sharp sand, exposed to the frosts, and sown in the spring.

Succulents Plants with thick, fleshy leaves and stems (for instance cacti). These plants come from very dry and desert regions; so consequently they should be kept on the dry side during winter, but should be watered freely in the summer.

Systemic sprays Chemical sprays which soak into plant leaves and are taken into the sap system: the chemical compound is carried to every part of the plant, including the roots.

Systemic insecticide and fungicide

sprays (for dealing with insect pests and fungal diseases) are efficient because they reach all parts of the plants, even those not actually wetted by the spray. Some have a long-lasting effect, remaining in the plant for up to two weeks.

Take care when using these sprays. Always read, and follow the instructions given to the letter, and always wash out the equipment used thoroughly afterwards. Better still, keep a set specifically for this purpose.

Some weedkillers are also systemic in their action, travelling right through the weeds and down into the roots; very effective against deep-rooting weeds.

Tender plants Plants which are not frost-hardy and will not survive the British winter in the open garden. They must be kept in a heated greenhouse, or indoors, during winter.

Typical examples include pelargoniums, dahlias, greenhouse fuschsias, gladioli and freesias.

Tilth The term for a fine, crumbly surface to the soil making it easy to work and perfect for sowing seeds and planting.

Digging in winter, and leaving the clods of soil to be broken down by the frosts, helps to create a fine tilth for spring sowing and planting. Improving the soil in the autumn by digging in humusforming materials, such as peat, garden compost or manure, also helps.

Topdressing The practice of spreading materials such as fertilizers, peat, garden compost, manure, etc, over the soil and leaving them to lie instead of digging them into the ground. This is the best way to provide fresh plant nutrients and improve the soil around established plants, trees and shrubs where you don't want to disturb the roots by digging.

Topdressing of fertilizer is eventually washed down into the soil by rain, and bulky soil-improving material such as garden compost will be dragged down by worms during the course of the year.

Trace elements Minerals which plants need in minute quantities, just as humans require vitamins. Usually available in normal garden soil, but using a liquid fertilizer which contains trace elements (eg Phostrogen) from time to time ensures that there's no shortage.

Variegation More than one colouring in a plant leaf. Most variegated leaves are green with markings of cream, gold or silver, but in some cases the markings may be red, purple or other colours.

Ventilation Adequate ventilation is essential in greenhouses and frames to prevent the build-up of a damp, stuffy atmosphere – the kind of atmosphere in which plant diseases spread like wildfire. This is equally as important in winter as during summer, so provide ventilation on mild winter days.

Virus diseases A number of viruses attack plants, causing symptoms such as white and yellow mottling and streaking on the leaves, curling and distortion of leaves and shoots, and stunted growth.

Any plants showing the above symptoms and showing no signs of recovering should be burned to prevent the spread of the disease. Sap-sucking insects, such as greenfly, spread viruses among plants, so spray at the first signs of these pests.

Wilt The general name for various diseases which cause plants to wilt without apparent reason (ie when they're not short of water). Sometimes spraying with a fungicide may help, but often the plants are unlikely to recover and have to be discarded. Plants commonly affected include asters, sweet peas, carnations, pansies, tomatoes and potatoes.

Wilting may also be caused by the rotting of the plant's roots in soil which is waterlogged, so check the compost.

WHY
USE
LATIN?

Gardeners hate using Latin names. We can't read them, spell them, pronounce them or understand them. Yet we must use them if we are to communicate with other gardeners.

Without the use of Latin plant names, we would be thrown into complete chaos. For example, the pot plant *Clivia miniata* is known as the kaffir lily, but so is the hardy outdoor autumn bulb, *Schizostylis coccinea*. If we merely quoted the common name we would not be sure which plant was being discussed.

We also use Latin to avoid the confusion brought about by the use of colloquialisms and common plant names.

Latin is a truly international language; botanists and gardeners may travel to all corners of the world, and the only way they can converse (and understand) the local horticulturists is by quoting Latin plant names.

The botanical naming of plants is based on the 'binomial' system devised by Carl Linnaeus (1707-78). Every plant receives two names in Latin. The first indicates to what 'genus' or group the plant belongs; similar to our own surnames, although in plants it appears at the beginning of the full name. The second word in a plant's Latin name is the 'specific epithet' and identifies the 'species', a little like our Christian names!

Several related genera are also often grouped together and given a 'family' name which usually ends with the letters - *aceae*. There are, of course, some exceptions.

In addition to the family, genus and species names there are usually additional names given for particular plants. If a species varies and distinct types can be identified, a 'variety', 'sub-species' or 'cultivar' name is added. If this is a natural occurrence it is named in Latin according to the characteristics of the plant. Cultivars (horticultural or cultivated varieties) are distinct forms that originated and are maintained through cultivation (by vegetative means).

The naming of a plant is far from arbitrary as we have already seen, but how do the botanists arrive at these specific epithets? The answers lie with the plants themselves and the names used to describe them fall roughly into four categories – origin, habitat, particular features or to commemorate people or places.

This chapter comprises an alphabetical list of specific epithets and an explanation of their derivation. We have also provided a guideline to their pronunciation although there will invariably be variations in common useage. As a guideline the following rules may help: the consonants b, d, f, h, l, m, n, p, qu, t and z are pronounced just as in English; r is similar but more trilled. In academic Latin, c is hard (as in cat); ch is k or k-h; g is hard (as in gate); j is like y in yell; s is sibilant as in gas; v is as w; and y as a soft u. It is acceptable useage, in the UK, to use the soft c (as in cigar), and the soft g (as in germ), before the vowels i, e and y, though not strictly correct.

WHAT THE WORDS MEAN

acaulis (a-kaw'-lis), stemless
acicularis (a-sik'-u-la'-ris), needle-pointed
aculeatus (a-ku-le-a'-tus), prickly, thorny
adpressus (ad-pres'-sus), pressed against
aestivus (es-ti-'vus), developing in summer
affinis (a-fin'-es), related or similar to
agglomeratus (ag-glo-mer-a'-tus), in a close head
agrarius (ag-ra'-i-us), growing in fields
agrestis (a-gres'-tis), growing in arable fields
alatus (al-a'-tus), winged
albidus (al'-bi-dus), white
albus (al'-bus), dead white
alpestris (al-pes'-tris), of the mountains
alpinus (al-pi'-nus), alpine
alternatus (al-turn-a'-tus), alternate
altissimus (al-tis'-sim-us), very tall
altus (al'-tus), high tall
amabilis (a-ma-bil'-is), pleasing
amarus (a-ma'-rus), bitter
anacanthus (an-a-kan'-thus), thornless
angustifolius (an-gus'-ti-fo-li-us), narrow-
   leaved
annuus (an'-nu-us), annual
apetalus (a-pet'-a-lus), without petals
aphyllus (a-fil'-lus), without leaves
apicatus (a-pi-ka'-tus), decidedly pointed
applanatus (ap-plan-a'-tus), flattened out
appressus (ap-pres'-sus), lying close, adpressed
aquaticus (a-kwat'-ic-kus), living in water
arachnoideus (a-rak-noy'-de-us), cobwebby
arboreus (ar-bor'-e-us), treelike
argentus (ar-gen'-tus), silvery
argutus (ar-gu'-tus), sharply notched
armatus (ar-ma'-tus), armed, with thorns
aromaticus (ar-o-ma'-ti-cus), fragrant
arvensis (ar-ven'-sis), of a cultivated field
asper (as'-per), rough
asperissimus (as-per-is'-i-mus), very rough
aspermus (as-perm'-us), seedless
asperus (as-pers'-us), sprinkled
assimilis (as-sim-i-lis), likened to
atlanticus (at-lan'-tik-us), of the Lesser Atlas
   Mountains
atratus (a-tra'-tus), blackish
augustus (aw-gus'-tus), noble, stately
auratus (aw-ra'-tus), golden

aureus (aw'-re-us), golden yellow
auriculatus (aw-rik-u-la'-tus), ear-shaped
australis (aw-stra'-lis), southern
azureus (az-u'-re-us), sky blue
B
baccatus (bak-a'-tus), baccate, fleshy
barbatus (bar-ba'-tus), bearded
bellus (bel'-lus), beautiful
blandus (blan'-dus), pleasing
borealis (bor-e-a'-lis), northern
bulbosus (bul-bo'-sus), bulbous
bullatus (bul-la'-tus), blistered, puckered
buxifolius (buks-i-fo'li-us), box leaved
C
caeruleus (ke-ru'-le-us), blue
caesius (ke'-si-us), bluish grey
caespitosus (ke-spit'-o-sus), tufted
cambricus (kam'-bri-kus), of Wales
campanulatus (kam-panu-la'-tus), bell-shaped
campestris (kam-pes'-tris), of the plains
candidus (kan'-di-dus), white, shining
canescens (kan-esk'-ens), hoary
cantabilis (kan-tab'-i-lis), worthy of song
canus (ka'-nus), whitish-grey
capillaris (kap-il-la'-ris), hair like
carneus (kar-ne-us), flesh-pink
ceraceus (ker-a'-ke-us), waxy
cernuus (kern-u'-us), drooping
chinensis (chi-nen-sis), Chinese
ciliaris (ki-li-a'-ris), hair fringed
cinereus (kin-er-e-us), ashen, grey
clavatus (kla-va'-tus), club-shaped
coccineus (kok-kin'-e-us), scarlet
comatus (kom-a'-tus), hairy
communis (kom-mu'-nis), common
comosus (kom-o'-sus), growing in tufts
confertus (kon-fer'-tus), crowded
conglomeratus (kon-glom-er-a'-tus), clustered
contortus (kon-tor'-tus), twisted
cordatus (kor-da'-tus), heart-shaped
coriaceus (kor-ri-a'-se-us), leathery, tough
corneus (kor-ne'-us), horny
coronarius (kor-on-a'-ri-us), crowned
crispus (kris'-pus), wavy, curled
cruentus (kru'-en-tus), blood coloured
cuneatus (ku-ne-a'-tus), wedge shaped
cyaneus (ki-an'-e-us), blue
D
debilis (deb'-i-lis), weak
decorus (de-kor'-us), handsome
decurvus (de-kur'-vus), curved downwards
delicatus (del-i-ca'-tus), charming
demersus (de-mer'-sus), living under water
demissus (de-mis'-sus), hanging down
dentatus (den-ta'-tus), toothed
denticulatus (den-tik-u-la'-tus), finely toothed
denudatus (den-nu-da'-tus), stripped, bare

difformis (di-form'-is), unusual form
diffusus (dif-fu'-sus), spreading, diffuse
digitatus (dig-i-ta'-tus), fingered
dispersus (dis-per'-sus), scattered
dulcis (dul'-kis), sweet
dumosus (du-mo'-sus), bushy, compact
durus (du'-rus), hard

E

ebenus (eb'-en-us), ebony black
eburneus (e-bur'-ne-us), ivory white
echinatus (e-kin-a'-tus), prickly
edinensis (e-din-en'-sis), of Edinburgh
edulis (e-du'-lis), edible
effusus (ef-fus'-us), spread out
elatus (e-la'-tus), tall
elegans (el'-e-gans), elegant
ellipticus (el-lip'-ti-kus), elliptical
elongatus (e-lon-ga'-tus), lengthened out
ensifolius (en-si-fo'-li-us), straight, sword-shaped leaves
ensiformis (en-si-form'-is), straight, acute-pointed leaf
equalis (e-kwa'-lis), equal
erectus (e-rek'-tus), upright
ericinus (e-ri-ki'-nus), heath-like
esculentus (es-ku-len'-tus), fit for food
europaeus (u-ro-pe'-us), European
excelsus (ecks-kel'-sus), very tall
excorticatus (ecks-kor-ti-ka'-tus), barkless
exiguus (ecks-ig'-u-us), very small
excapus (ecks-ka'-pus), stemless
extensus (ecks-ten'-sus), wide

F

falcatus (fal-ka'-tus), sickle-shaped
farinosus (fa-ri-no'-sus), mealy
fasciatus (fas-ki-a'-tus), bound together
fastigiatus (fas-tig-i-a'-tus), fastigiate
ferrugineus (fer-ru-gin'-e-us), rust-coloured
fertilis (fer'-til-is), fertile, many seeded
ferus (fe'-rus), wild
festalis (fes-ta'-lis), bright, gay
filiformis (fil-i-form'-is), thread-like
fimbriatus (fim-bri-a'-tus), fringed
flabellatus (fla-bell-a'-tus), fan-like
flaccidus (flak'-kid-us), feeble, weak
flavidus (flav'-i-dus), yellowish
flexuosus (flecks-u'-o-sus), tortuous, zigzag
floribundus (flor-i-bun'-dus), free-flowering
fluitans (flu'-i-tans), floating in water
foetidus (fe'-ti-dus), stinking
formosus (for-mo'-sus), beautiful
fragilis (frag'-i-lis), brittle
fragrans (frag'-rans), sweet-scented
frigidus (frig'-i-dus), cold
frondosus (fron-do'-sus), leafy
fruticosus (fru-ti-co'-sus), shrubby
fulgidus (ful'-gi-dus), shining

fulvus (ful'-vus), tawny
fumosus (fu-mo'-sus), smoky
funebris (fu'-neb-ris), funereal
fuscus (fus'-kus), dark-coloured
fusiformis (fu-si-form'-is), spindle-shaped
futilis (fu'-ti-lis), useless, futile

G

galactinus (gal-ak-ti'-nus), milky
gallicus (gal'-i-kus), French
gelidus (gel'-i-dus), of icy regions
gemmatus (gem-ma'-tus), jewelled
gemmiferus (gem-mif'-er-us), bearing buds
germanicus (ger-man'-i-kus), of Germany
gibbus (gib'-bus), swollen on one side
giganteus (gi-gan'-te-us), very large or tall
glaber (gla'-ber), smooth skinned
glandulosus (glan-du-lo'-sus), with glands
glaucus (glaw'-kus), grey, with waxy bloom
globosus (glo-bo'-sus), round, globular
glutinosus (glu-tin-o'-sus), gluey, sticky
gracilis (grak'-i-lis), slender
graecus (gre'-kus), Grecian
gramineus (gra-min'-e-us), grasslike
grandis (gran'-dis), large
griseus (gris'-e-us), grey
guttatus (gut-ta'-tus), covered with dots

H

haemaleus (hi'-mal-a-us), blood red
hastatus (has-ta'-tus), halberd shaped
hellenicus (hel-len'-i-kus), of Greece
helveticus (hel-vet'-i-kus), of Switzerland
hibernicus (hi-bern'-i-kus), Irish
hibernus (hi-bern'-us), winter-flowering
hiemalis (hi-e-ma'-lis), of the winter
himalaicus (him-a-la'-i-kus), of the Himalayas
hirsutus (hir-su'-tus), hairy
hispanicus (his-pan'-i-kus), Spanish
hispidus (his'-pi-dus), bristly
horizontalis (hori-zon-ta'-lis), flat-growing
horridus (hor'-rid-us), very thorny
hortensis (hor-ten'-sis), belonging to gardens
humifusus (hu-mi-fu'-sus), ground spreading
humilis (hu'-mil-is), low, dwarf or its kind
hupehensis (hu-pe-hen'-sis), of Hupeh, China
hyacinthus (hi-a-kinth'-us), dark purplish-blue
hydrophilus (hi-drof-i'lus), water-loving
hylophilus (hi-lof'-i-lus), wood-loving
hypnoides (hip-noy'-des), moss-like
hypophyllus (hi-po-fil'-lus), whitish beneath

I

ibericus (ib-er'-i-kus), Spanish or Georgian
idaeus (i-de'-us), of Mt. Ida, Crete
ignavus (ig-na'-vus), slothful
igneus (ig'-ne-us), fiery-red
illicinus (il-li-ki'-nus), holly-like
illustris (il-lus'-tris), brilliant
imbricatus (im-bri-ka'-tus), overlapping

immaculatus (im-mak-u-la'-tus), spotless

impeditus (im-pe-di'-tus), tangled

imperialis (imp-er-i-a'-lis), very noble

impressus (imp-res'-sus), sunken

inaequalis (in-e-kwa'-lis), unequal

incanus (in-ka'-nus), grey

incarnatus (in-kar-na'-tus), flesh-coloured

incisus (in-ki'-sus), incised, cut

incomparabilis (in-kom-par-a'-bil-is), unequalled

indicus (in'-di-kus), of India

inermis (in-er'-mis), unarmed, spineless

inflatus (in-fla'-tus), puffed up

innominatus (in-nom-in-a'-tus), unnamed

inodorus (in-o'-dor-us), without scent

insignis (in-sig'-nis), striking

involutus (in-vol-u'-tus), rolled inwards

islandicus (is-land'-i-kus), Icelandic

italicus (i-tal'-i-kus), Italian

J

jackmanii (jaki-man-i), honouring G. Jackman

japonicus (jap-on'-i-kus), Japanese

jubatus (ju-ba'-tus), awned, or maned

juliformis (ju-li-form'-is), downy

junceus (jun'-ke-us), rush-like

juniperinus (jun-i-per-i'-nus), juniper-like

juranus (ju-ra'-nus), of the Jura Mountains, France

K

kewensis (ku-en'-sis), of Kew Gardens, London

Kingdonii (king-don'-i), honouring F. Kingdon-Ward, collector

L

laceratus (lak-er-a'-tus), torn

laciniatus (lak-in-i-a'-tus), jagged

lacteus (lak'-te-us), milk-coloured

laevigatus (lev-i-ga'-tus), smooth

lanatus (lan-a'-tus), woolly

latus (la'-tus), broad

laxus (lacks'-us), loose

lepidus (lep'-i-dus), charming

ligulatus (lig-u-la'-tus), strap-shaped

limosus (lim-o'-sus), slimy, of muddy places

linearis (lin-e-a'-ris), narrow

linneanus (lin-e'-nus), honouring C. Linnaeus

litoralis (lit-or-a'-lis), of the shore

lividus (liv'-i-dus), blue-brown, lead grey

lobatus (lob-a'-tus), lobed

longus (long'-us), long

lucidus (lu'-ki-dus), shining, clear

lunatus (lu-na'-tus), half-moon shaped

lusitanicus (lus-i-tan'-i-kus), Portuguese

luteus (lu'-te-us), yellow

M

macranthus (mac-ran'-thus), large-flowered

macrocarpus (mak-ro-karp'-us), with large fruits

maculatus (mak-u-la'-tus), blotched, spotted

major (ma'-jor), greater

marinus (mari'-nus), growing by the sea

medius (me'-di-us), intermediate, middle

medullaris (med-u-la'-ris), pithy

megeratus (meg-er-a'-tus), very lovely

microphyllus (mi-kro-fil'-lus), small leaved

millefolium (mil-le-fo'-li-um), thousand-leaved

minimus (min'-i-mus), least, small

mollis (mol'-lis), soft

monophyllus (mon-o-fil'-lus), one-leaved

montanus (mon-tan'-us), of the mountains

moschatus (mos-ka'-tus), musky

mucronatus (mu-kron-a'-tus), with short, sharp point

multiflorus (mu-ti-flo'-rus), many-flowered

muralis (mur-a'-lis), growing on walls

muscosus (mus-ko'-sus), mossy, moss-like

N

nanus (na'-nus), dwarf

nebulosus (neb-u-lo'-sus), cloud-like

neglectus (neg-lek'-tus), disregarded

nemoralis (nem-o-ra'-lis), of the woods

niger (nig'-er), black

nikoensis (nik-o-en'-sis), of Niko, Japan

nipponicus (nip-pon'-i-kus), Japanese

nivalis (niv-a'-lis), snow white

nobilis (no-bil'-is), noble, grand

nodosus (no-do'-sus), having nodes, jointed

nudatus (nu-da'-tus), naked, nude

nummularis (num-mu-la'-ris), coin-like

nutans (nu'-tans), nodding

nuttallii (nut-tal'-li), honouring T. Nuttall

O

obliquus (ob-li'-kwus), unequal-sided

oblongus (ob-long'-us), oblong, blunt-ended

occultus (ok-kul'-tus), hidden

odoratus (o-dor-a'-tus), fragrant

officinalis (of-fik-in-a'-lis), used medicinally

olympicus (o-limp'-i-kus), of Olympus, Greece

orbicularis (or-bik-u-la'-ris), disk-shaped

orientalis (o-ri-ent-a'-lis), eastern

ornatus (or-na'-tus), showy

ovalis (o-va'-lis), oval

ovatus (o-va'-tus), egg-shaped

oxyphyllus (ocks-i-fil'-us), sharp-leaved

oxypetalus (ocks-i-pet'-a-lus), sharp petalled

P

pacificus (pa-kif'-i-kus), of Western America

pallidus (pal'-i-dus), pale

palmatus (pal-ma'-tus), five-lobed, palm-like

palustris (pa-lus'-tris), of marshy ground

paniculatus (pan-i-ku-la'-tus), panicle-like

pannosus (pan-no'-sus), woolly, coarse

parciflorus par-ki-flo'-rus), few-flowered

parvus (par'-vus), small

patulus (pa'-tu-lus), spreading, standing open

paucus (paw'-kus), few

pavoninus (pa-vo-ni'-nus), peacock-blue

pectinatus (pek-tin-a'-tus), comb-like

pedatus (ped-a'-tus), like a bird's foot

pendulus (pen'-du-lus), drooping

pennatus (pen-na'-tus), pinnate, feather-like

perfoliatus (per-fo-li-a'-tus), with a stem that
    seems to grow through the leaf

persica (pers'-i-ka), Persian

petraeus (pet-re'-us), grows among rocks

pictus (pik'-tus), painted, strikingly coloured

pileatus (pi-le-a'-tus), with a cap

pilosus (pi-lo'-sus), hairy

pinnatus (pin-na'-tus), feather-like

pisiformis (pi-si-for'-mis), pea-shaped

pissardii (pis-sard'-i), honouring M. Pissard

pleniflorus (plen-i-flo'-rus), double-flowered

plenus (ple'-nus), full, double

plicatus (pli-ka'-tus), pleated

plumarius (plum-a'-ri-us), feathery

plumosus (plu-mo'-sus), feather-like

poeticus (po-e-tik'-us), of the poets

polaris (po-lar'-is), of the North Pole

polyandrus (po-li-an'-drus), many-stamened

polyphyllus (po-li-fil'-lus), many-leaved

ponderosus (pon-de-ro'-sus), large and heavy

ponticus (pon-tik'-us), of the Black Sea area

procerus (prok-e'-rus), very tall

profusus (pro-fu'-sus), very abundant

prolificus (pro-lif'-i-kus), very fruitful

prostratus (pro-stra'-tus), flat on the ground

pudicus (pu-di'-kus), bashful, modest

pulchellus (pul-kel'-lus), pretty

pulcher (pul'-ker), beautiful

pullus (pul'-lus), nearly black

pumilus (pu'-mil-us), low, small

punctatus (punk-ta'-tus), dotted

purpuratus (pur-pur-a'-tus), purplish

pusillus (pu-sil'-lus), weak and slender

pygmaeus (pig-me'-us), dwarf, tiny

pyramidalis (pi-ri-mid-a'-lis), conical

pyriformis (pi-ri-form'-is), pear-shaped

pyxidatus (picks-i-da'-tus), box-like

Q

quadrangularis (kwad-ran-gul-la'-ris), 4-angled

quercifolius (kwer-ki-fo'-li-us), oak leaf-like

quinatus (kwin-a'-tus), with five divisions

R

racemosus (rak-e-mo'-sus), arranged in a
    raceme

radicatus (rad-i-ca'-tus), with distinct root

ramosus (ra-mo'-sus), branching

rarus (ra'-rus), uncommon

rectus (rek'-tus), straight

redivivus (re-di-vi'-vus), renewed

regalis (re-gal'-is), royal

reniformis (reni-for'-mis), kidney-shaped

replicatus (re-plik-a'-tus), doubled

reticulatus (re-tik-u-la'-tus), netted

retusus (re-tu'-sus), retuse, notched

revolutus (re-vol-u'-tus), rolled back

rhombicus (rom'-bi-kus), rhomboid

rigidus (rig'-i-dus), stiff

rivalis (ri-va'-lis), growing by streams

robustus (ro-bus'-tus), strong, stout-growing

romanus (ro-ma'-nus), of Rome

roseus (ro'-se-us), rose-coloured

rotundus (ro-tun'-dus), round in outline

rubellus (ru-bel'-lus), reddish

ruber (ru'-ber), red

rudentus (ru-den'-tus), rope-like

rudis (ru'-dis), wild

rufus (ru'-fus), reddish-brown

rugosus (ru-go'-sus), wrinkled

rupestris (ru-pes'-tris), growing on rocks

ruralis (ru-ral'-is), of country places

russatus (rus-sa'-tus), reddened

rutilus (ru-til'-us), rich, deep red

S

saccatus (sak-ka'-tus), bag-shaped

sagittatus (sag-it-ta'-tus), arrow-shaped

salicifolius (sal-i-ki-fo'-li-us), willow-leafed

sanguineus (san-gwin'-e-us), blood-red

sativus (sat-i'-vus), sown or planted

saxatilis (sacks-a-til'-is), growing on rocks

scaber (ska'-ber), rough

scalaris (ska-la'-ris), ladder-like

sceleratus (skel-er-a'-tus), wicked, noxious

scoparius (sko-pa'ri-us), broom-like

scoticus (sko-ti'-cus), Scottish

scriptus (skrip'-tus), marked with lines

semperflorens (sem-per-flo'-rens), everflowering

senilis (sen-i'-lis), grey-haired

sensibilis (sen-sib'-i-lis), sensative

serratus (ser-ra'-tus), edged with teeth

sessilis (ses'-sil-is), without a stalk

setosus (set-o'-sus), bristly

signatus (sig-na'-tus), well-marked

silvaticus (sil-vat'-i-cus), of woods

silvicola (sil-vik'-o-la), wood-dwelling

sinensis (si-nen'-sis), of China

singularis (sin-gu-la'-ris), unusual

sinuatus (sin-u-a'-tus), with a waved edge

solidus (sol-i'-dus), not hollow, solid

sparsus (spars'-sus), scattered

spathulatus (spath-u-la'-tus), spatula-like

speciosus (spek-i-o'-sus), showy

spicatus (spik-a'-tus), spike-like

spinosus (spi-no'-sus), spiny, thorny

spiralis (spi-ra'-lis), twisted

squalidus (skwall'-i-dus), dingy, untidy

squamatus (skwa-ma'-tus), scaly

stellatus (stel-la'-tus), star-like

sterilis (ste'-ri-lis), barren, bearing useless fruit

stramineus (stra-min'-e-us), straw-coloured

striatus (stri-a'-tus), finely-streaked

strictus (strik'-tus), erect, very straight

stylosus (sti-lo'-sus), with prominent style

suavis (su-a'-vis), agreeable, sweet

suberosus (sub-er-o'-sus), corky

succulentus (suk-ku-len'-tus), juicy, soft

suffruticosus (suf-fru-ti-co'-sus), shrubby

sulphureus (sul-fu'-re-us), pale yellow

superbus (su-perb'-us), magnificent

susianus (su-si-a'-nus), of Susa, Persia

suspensus (sus-pen'-sus), pendent

syriacus (si-ri'-a-kus), Syrian

syrmaticus (sir-mat'-i-kus), sleep inducing

T

tabularis (tab-u-la'-ris), flat, board-like

tardus (tard'-us), late, slow

tauricus (taw'-ri-kus), of the Crimea

taxifolius (tacks-i-fo'-li-us), yew-like

tectus (tek'-tus), roofed, covered

tenerus (ten-e'-rus), delicate, soft

tenuis (ten'-u-is), thin, slender

ternatus (tern-a'-tus), whorls of three

terrestris (ter-res'-tris), grows on ground

tessellatus (tes-sel-la'-tus), chequered

testaceus (tes-ta'-ke-us), brownish yellow

texanus (tecks-a'-nus), of Texas, USA

textilis (tecks'-til-is), used in weaving

thibeticus (thi-bet-i'-kus), of Thibet

thymifolius (time-i-fo'-li-us), thyme-like

tiliaceus (ti-i-a'-ke-us), like a lime

tinctus (tink'-tus), coloured

tomentosus (to-men-to'-sus), thickly hairy

tonsus (ton'-sus), shaven, smooth

torridus (tor'-ri-dus), parched, tropical

tortuosus (tor-tu-o'-sus), tortuous, twisted

torvus (tor'-vus), fierce, sharp

toxicarius (tocks-i-ka'-ri-us), poisonous

triandrus (tri-and'-rus), with 3 stamens

trichlorophilus (tri-ko'-fil-us), strongly hairy

tricolor (tri-ko'-lor), three-coloured

trilobus (tri-lo'-bus), three-lobed

trimestris (trem-es'-tris), exists for 3 months

truquetrus (tri-kwe'-trus), 3-edged or cornered

tristris (tris'-tris), sad, dull coloured

tropicus (trop'-i-kus), of the tropics

truncatus (trun-ka'-tus), broken-off abruptly

tuberculatus (tu-ber-ku-la'-tus), warted

turgidus (tur-gi'-dus), distended, swollen

turpis (tur'-pis), ugly, unsightly

U

uber (u'-ber), fruitful, luxuriant

uliginosus (u-lig-in-o'-sus), of swamps

umbellatus (um-bel-la'-tus), in umbels

umbrosus (um-bro'-sus), shade-loving

uncinatus (un-kin-a'-tus), hooked

undulatus (un-dul-la'-tus), hooked

urbicus (ur'-bik-us), of towns

urceolatus (ur-ke-o-la'-tus), urn-shaped

utilis (u'-til-is), useful

uticulatus (u-trik-u-la'-tus), bladdery

uviformis (u-vi-form'-is), clustered with swarming bees

V

vaccinus (vak-ki'-nus), relating to cows

vaginatus (va-gin-a'-tus), having a sheath

validus (va'-li-dus), strong, well developed

variabilis (var-i-a'-bil-is), variable

variegatus (var-i-ga'-tus), variegatedly coloured

vasculosus (vas-ku-lo-sus), pan- or pot-shaped

vegetus (ve'-get-us), vigorous growing

velutinus (vel-u-ti'-nus), velvety

venenatus (ven-en-a'-tus), poisonous

vermicularis (ver-mic-u-la'-ris), worm-like

vernus (ver'-nus), of the spring

verticillatus (ver-tik-il-la'-tus), whorled

verus (ve'-rus), true

vestalis (vest-a'-lis), white

vialis (vi-a'-lis), by or of the wayside

vicinus (vi-kin'-us), neighbouring

villosus (vil-lo'-sus), shaggy with hairs

viminalis (vim-in-a'-lis), with slender shoots

virens (vi'-rens), green

virgatus (vir-ga'-tus), twiggy

virginalis (vir-gin-a'-lis), virginal, pure white

viridis (vi'-ri-dus), green

virosus (vir-o'-sus), poisonous

viscatus (vis-ka'-tus), clammy

viscidus (vis'-ki-us), viscous, sticky

vitifolius (vi-ti-fo'-li-us), vine-leaved

vitreus (vit'-re-us), glassy

volubilis (vol-u'-bil-is), twining

vulgaris (vul-ga'-ris), common

vulpinus (vul-pi'-nus), foxy

W

warleyensis (war-le-en'-sis), from Warley Place

wolgaricus (wol-ga'-ri-kus), from the Volga

X

xalapensis (sal-a-pen'-sis) of Xalapa, Mexico

xerophilus (ser-o-fil'-us), loving dry places

xiphophyllus (sif-o-fil'-lus), sword-leaved

Y

yedoensis (ye-do-en'-sis), of Yedo, Japan

yunnanensis (yun-nan-en'-sis), of Yunnan, Japan

Z

zaleucus (za-lu'-kus), very white

zanzibaricus (zan-zi-bar'-i-cus), of Zanzibar, East Africa

zebrinus (zeb-ri'-nus), striped colours

zephyinus (zef-i'-in-us), of the wild west

zeylanicus (zee-la'-ni-kus), of Ceylon

zonatus (zon-a'-tus), with a zone of colour

Top 450
Hardy
Plants

The best garden centres and nurseries have an amazing range of plants available these days, but there are always going to be some plants that are more popular than others. The following list, compiled by the Hardy Plant Society, details the 450 plants that nurseries have found to be their overall best sellers. These plants should be widely available from most good, general nurseries and garden centres.

However, not everyone has a good garden centre nearby, and for those who are not so lucky, mail order is the answer. Many nurseries unfortunately no longer offer a mail order service, but the list that follows the top 450 plants gives details of those that do. We also give details of their specialities, if any. Although catalogues are often free, most nurseries would no doubt appreciate a large, stamped addressed envelope with catalogue requests.

While every care has been taken to ensure accuracy, changes are obviously occurring all the time, and it is possible that some nurseries may well alter their methods of trading during the lifetime of this publication.

The Hardy Plant Society

The Hardy Plant Society was formed to foster interest in hardy herbaceous plants on the widest possible scope. It aims to give its members information about the wealth of both well-known and little-known plants, how to grow them to the best advantage and where they may be obtained.

Members are eligible to join their nearest regional or local group. These organize many events in their area, including plant sales and garden visits; most issue their own newsletters. Members may also join any of the specialized groups within the Society, such as the Geranium Group, Euphorbia Group or the Variegated Plant Group.

The Society produces a bulletin, 'The Hardy Plant', which is currently issued twice a year. This contains major articles on a wide range of plants and gardens. There is also a regular newsletter which keeps members informed of current events, and a central publications and slide library.

For details of how to join the society write to Pam Adams, Little Orchard, Great Comberton, Pershore, Worcestershire, WR10 3DP.

For Australian gardeners, contact one of the following addresses to gain specialist advice: Society for Growing Australian Plants NSW Ltd, PO Box 410, Padstow, NSW 2211; The Royal Horticultural Society of NSW, Mrs J W Slattery, 12 Eddystone Road, Bexley, Sidney, NSW 2207; The Royal Horticultural Society of Queensland, Mrs D L Young, PO Box 1921, Brisbane.

TOP 450 HARDY PLANTS

Genus	Species	Variety/Cultivar	Type
Abelia	× *grandiflora*		S
	× *grandiflora*	'Francis Mason'	S
Abies	*koreana*		CO
Acanthus	*spinosus*		HP
Acer	*griseum*		TR
	negundo	'Flamingo'	TR
	palmatum	'Osakazuki'	TR
Achillea	× *huteri*		HP
Actinidia	*kolomikta*		CL
Agapanthus		'Headbourne hybrids'	HP
Ajuga	*reptans*	'Atropurpurea'	HP
Alchemilla	*mollis*		HP
Allium	*cernuum*		B
Aloysia	*triphylla*		S
Anemone	× *hybrida*	'Honorine Jobert'	HP
	multifida		HP
	sylvestris		HP
Anthemis	*punctata cupaniana*		HP
	tinctoria	'E C Buxton'	HP
Aquilegia	*vulgaris*	'Nora Barlow'	HP
Arabis	*ferdinandi-coburgii*	'Variegata'	R
Araucaria	*araucana*		TR
Arbutus	*unedo*		TR
Argyranthemum		'Jamaica Primrose'	HHP
Arisarum	*proboscideum*		B
Artemisia	*abrotanum*		S
		'Powis Castle'	S
	schmidtiana	'Nana'	S
Arum	*italicum italicum*		HP
Aruncus	*dioicus*	'Kneiffii'	HP
Asphodeline	*lutea*		HP
Aster	*novae-angliae*	'Andenken an Alma Pötschke'	HP
Astilbe	*chinensis*	*pumila*	HP
	multifida		HP
		'Sprite'	HP
Astrantia	*major*	'Sunningdale Variegated'	HP
	major		HP
	maxima		HP
Ballota	*pseudodictamnus*		HHP
Berberis	*darwinii*		S
	× *stenophylla*		S
	thunbergii	*atropurpurea*	S
	thunbergii	'Atropurpurea Nana'	S
	thunbergii	'Aurea'	S
	thunbergii	'Rose Glow'	S
Betula	*pendula*		TR
Brunnera	*macrophylla*		HP
Buddlea	*alternifolia*		S

HP–Hardy perennial   HHP–Half-hardy perennial   B–Bulb   CL–Climber   CO–Garden conifer
R–Rock plant   S–Shrub   TR–Tree

TOP 450 HARDY PLANTS

Genus	Species	Variety/Cultivar	Type
Buddlea	*davidii*	'Black Knight'	S
	davidii	'Harlequin'	S
	davidii	'Royal Red'	S
		'Lochinch'	S
		'Pink Delight'	S
Buxus	*sempervirens*		S
	sempervirens	'Elegantissima'	S
Caltha	*palustris*	'Plena'	HP
Camellia	× *williamsii*	'Donation'	S
Campanula	*alliariifolia*		HP
	cochleariifolia		HP
	cochleariifolia	'Elizabeth Oliver'	HP
	takesimana		HP
Carex	*oshimensis*	'Evergold'	HP
Ceanothus	× *delileanus*	'Gloire de Versailles'	S
	thyrsiflorus	*repens*	S
Cedrus	*deodara*		TR
	libani	*atlantica* 'Glauca Group'	TR
Cephalaria	*gigantea*		HP
Ceratostigma	*plumbaginoïdes*		S
	willmottianum		S
Cercidiphyllum	*japonicum*		TR
Cercis	*siliquastrum*		TR
Chamaecyparis	*lawsoniana*	'Ellwoodii'	CO
	lawsoniana	'Ellwood's Gold'	CO
	lawsoniana	'Minima Aurea'	CO
	lawsoniana	'Minima Glauca'	CO
	lawsoniana	'Pembury Blue'	CO
	obtusa	'Nana Gracilis'	CO
	pisifera	'Boulevard'	CO
Cheiranthus	*cheiri*	'Harpur Crewe'	S
Chiastophyllum	*oppositifolium*		R
Chimonanthus	*praecox*		S
Choisya	*ternata*		S
	ternata	'Sundance'	S
Chrysanthemopsis	*hosmariense*		HP
Cistus	× *hybridus*		S
	× *purpureus*		S
Clematis	*alpina*	'Frances Rivis'	CL
		'Bill Mackenzie'	CL
	cirrhosa	*balearica*	CL
		'Comtesse de Bouchaud'	CL
		'Ernest Markham'	CL
		'Hagley Hybrid'	CL
		'Jackmanii Superba'	CL
		'Lasurstern'	CL
	macropetala		CL
	macropetala	'Markham's Pink'	CL
	montana		CL
	montana	'Elizabeth'	CL
	montana	*rubens*	CL

TOP 450 HARDY PLANTS

Genus	Species	Variety/Cultivar	Type
Clematis	*montana*	'Tetrarose'	CL
		'Nelly Moser'	CL
	tangutica		CL
		'The President'	CL
		'Ville de Lyon'	CL
		'Vyvyan Pennell'	CL
Clianthus	*puniceus*		S
Convallaria	*majalis*		HP
Convolvulus	*cneorum*		S
	sabatius		HP
Coreopsis	*verticillata*	'Moonbeam'	HP
Cornus	*alba*	'Elegantissima'	S
	alba	'Sibirica'	S
	alba	'Spaethii'	S
	canadensis		S
	mas		S
	stolonifera	'Flaviramea'	S
Corylus	*avellana*	'Contorta'	TR
	maxima	'Purpurea'	TR
Cosmos	*atrosanguineus*		HHP
Cotinus	*coggygria*	'Royal Purple'	S
Cotoneaster	*congestus*		S
	horizontalis		S
	horizontalis	'Variegatus'	S
Crinodendron	*hookerianum*		S
Crocosmia	× *crocosmiiflora*	'Emily McKenzie'	B
		'Lucifer'	B
Cryptomeria	*japonica*	'Vilmoriniana'	CO
Cupressocyparis	× *leylandii*	'Castlewellan'	CO
Cyclamen	*cilicium*		B
	coum		B
	hederifolium		B
	hederifolium	album	B
Cytisus	*battandieri*		S
	× *kewensis*		S
Daphne	*mezereum*		S
	odora	'Aureomarginata'	S
	retusa		S
	tangutica		S
Desfontainia	*spinosa*		S
Dianthus		'Little Jock'	HP
		'Mrs Sinkins'	HP
		'Pike's Pink'	HP
Diascia	*rigescens*		HP
		'Ruby Field'	HP
	vigilis		HP
Dicentra	*formosa*		HP
	formosa	alba	HP

HP–Hardy perennial   HHP–Half-hardy perennial   B–Bulb   CL–Climber   CO–Garden conifer
R–Rock plant   S–Shrub   TR–Tree

▶

TOP 450 HARDY PLANTS

Genus	Species	Variety/Cultivar	Type
Dicentra	*formosa*	'Stuart Boothman'	HP
	spectabilis		HP
	spectabilis	*alba*	HP
Dierama	*pulcherrimum*		HP
Digitalis	*grandiflora*		HB
	× *mertonensis*		HB
Dodecatheon	*meadia*		HP
Dryas	*octopetala*		R
Elaeagnus	× *ebbingei*		S
	pungens	'Maculata'	S
Enkianthus	*campanulatus*		S
Epilobium	*canum angustifolium*	'Dublin'	HP
Epimedium	× *youngianum*	'Niveum'	HP
Erica	*carnea*	'Foxhollow'	S
	carnea	'Myretoun Ruby'	S
	carnea	'Springwood White'	S
	carnea	'Vivellii'	S
Erodium	*chrysanthum*		R
	× *variabile*	'Album'	R
	× *variabile*	'Roseum'	R
Eryngium	*bourgatii*		HP
	variifolium		HP
Erysimum		'Bowles' Mauve'	S
Escallonia		'Apple Blossom'	S
Eucalyptus	*gunnii*		TR
	pauciflora	*niphophila*	TR
Euonymus	*alatus*		S
	europaeus	'Red Cascade'	S
	fortunei	'Emerald Gaiety'	S
	fortunei	'Emerald and Gold'	S
Euphorbia	*amygdaloïdes*	*robbiae*	HP
	amygdaloïdes	'Rubra'	HP
	characias wulfenii		HP
	griffithii	'Dixter'	HP
	griffithii	'Fireglow'	HP
	× *martinii*		HP
	mellifera		HP
	myrsinites		HP
	polychroma		HP
Euryops	*acraeus*		HHP
Exochorda	× *macrantha*	'The Bride'	S
Fatsia	*japonica*		S
Festuca	*glauca*		HP
Fritillaria	*meleagris*		B
Fuchsia		'Genii'	S
		'Lady Thumb'	S
	magellanica	'Versicolor'	S
		'Mrs Popple'	S
		'Tom Thumb'	S
Garrya	*elliptica*		S
Gaultheria	*procumbens*		S

TOP 450 HARDY PLANTS

Genus	Species	Variety/Cultivar	Type
Gaura	lindheimeri		S
Genista	lydia		S
Gentiana	acaulis		R
Geranium	× cantabrigiense	'Biokovo'	HP
	cinereum	'Ballerina'	HP
	cinereum	subcaulescens	HP
	clarkei	'Kashmir White'	HP
	dalmaticum		HP
	dalmaticum	'Album'	HP
	endressii	'Wargrave Pink'	HP
	himalayense	'Plenum'	HP
		'Johnson's Blue'	HP
	macrorrhizum	'Album'	HP
	macrorrhizum	'Ingwersen's Variety'	HP
	nodosum		HP
	orientalitibeticum		HP
	× oxonianum	'Claridge Druce'	HP
	phaeum		HP
	phaeum	'Album'	HP
	psilostemon		HP
	renardii		HP
	sanguineum		HP
	sanguineum	'Album'	HP
	sanguineum	striatum	HP
	sessiliflorum	novae-zelandiae nigricans	HP
	wallichianum	'Buxton's Variety'	HP
Ginkgo	biloba		TR
Griselinia	littoralis		S
Gunnera	manicata		HP
Hebe	pinguifolia	'Pagei'	S
	rakaiensis		S
		'Youngii'	S
Hedera	algeriensis	'Gloire de Marengo'	CL
	colchica	'Sulphur Heart'	CL
	helix helix	'Oro di Bogliasco'	CL
Helianthemum		'Jubilee'	HP
		'Wisley Pink'	HP
		'Wisley Primrose'	HP
Helleborus	argutifolius		HP
	foetidus		HP
	niger		HP
	orientalis		HP
Heuchera	cylindrica	'Greenfinch'	HP
	micrantha	'Palace Purple'	HP
		'Snow Storm'	HP
Hosta	fortunei	aureomarginata	HP
	fortunei	albopicta	HP
	sieboldiana	elegans	HP

HP–Hardy perennial HHP–Half-hardy perennial B–Bulb CL–Climber CO–Garden conifer
R–Rock plant S–Shrub TR–Tree

▶

◀

TOP 450 HARDY PLANTS

Genus	Species	Variety/Cultivar	Type
Hosta	*sieboldiana*	'Francis Williams'	HP
	× *tardiana*	'Halcyon'	HP
	undulata	*albomarginata*	HP
	undulata	*undulata*	HP
Houttuynia	*cordata*	'Chameleon'	HP
Humulus	*lupulus*	'Aureus'	CL
Hydrangea	*anomala petiolaris*		S
	aspera	*villosa*	S
		'Preziosa'	S
	quercifolia		S
Hypericum		'Hidcote'	S
	× *moserianum*	'Tricolor'	S
Ilex	× *altaclerensis*	'Golden King'	S
	crenata	'Golden Gem'	S
Incarvillea	*delavayi*		B
Indigofera	*heterantha*		S
Iris	*foetidissima*		HP
	pallida	'Variegata'	HP
	pseudacorus	'Variegata'	HP
Itea	*ilicifolia*		S
Jasminum	*nudiflorum*		CL
	officinale		CL
	× *stephanense*		CL
Juglans	*regia*		TR
Juniperus	*communis*	'Compressa'	CO
	scopulorum	'Skyrocket'	CO
	squamata	'Blue Carpet'	CO
	squamata	'Blue Star'	CO
Kerria	*japonica*	'Picta'	S
Knautia	*macedonica*		HP
Lamium	*maculatum*	'Beacon Silver'	HP
	maculatum	'White Nancy'	HP
Laurus	*nobilis*		S
Lavandula	*angustifolia*	'Hidcote'	S
	angustifolia	'Munstead'	S
	angustifolia	'Nana Alba'	S
	angustifolia	'Rosea'	S
	stoechas		S
	stoechas	*leucantha*	S
	stoechas pendunculata		S
Lavatera		'Barnsley'	S
		'Burgundy Wine'	S
	maritima		S
		'Rosea'	S
Leucothoe	*fontanesiana*	'Rainbow'	S
Leycesteria	*formosa*		S
Liatris	*spicata*		HP
Ligustrum	*ovalifolium*	'Aureum'	S
Liquidambar	*styraciflua*		TR
Liriodendron	*tulipifera*		TR
Lithodora	*diffusa*	'Heavenly Blue'	R

TOP 450 HARDY PLANTS

Genus	Species	Variety/Cultivar	Type
Lobelia	×*gerardii*	'Vedrariensis'	HHP
	pedunculata		HHP
		'Queen Victoria'	HHP
Lonicera	×*brownii*	'Dropmore Scarlet'	CL
	japonica	'Aureoreticulata'	CL
	japonica	'Halliana'	CL
	nitida	'Baggesen's Gold'	CL
	periclymenum	'Belgica'	CL
	periclymenum	'Serotina'	CL
	×*tellmanniana*		CL
Lotus	*hirsutus*		HP
Lysimachia	*clethroïdes*		HP
	ephemerum		HP
	nummularia	'Aurea'	HP
Magnolia	×*loebneri*	'Leonard Messel'	S
	×*soulangeana*		S
	stellata		S
Mahonia	×*media*	'Charity'	S
Malus	*domestica*	'Bramley's Seedlings'	TR
	domestica	'James Grieve'	TR
		'Golden Hornet'	TR
		'John Downie'	TR
Malva	*moschata*	*alba*	HHP
Meconopsis	*betonicifolia*		HP
Melissa	*officinalis*	'Aurea'	HP
Mentha	×*gentilis*	'Variegata'	HP
	requienii		HP
Metasequoia	*glyptostroboïdes*		TR
Milium	*effusum*	*aureum*	HP
Mitraria	*coccinea*		S
Molinia	*caerulea*	*caerulea* 'Variegata' (grass)	HP
Myrtus	*communis*		S
	communis tarentina		S
Nepeta	*racemosa*		HP
Oenothera	*missouriensis*		HP
Olearia	*macrodonta*		S
Ophiopogon	*planiscapus*	*nigrescens*	HP
Origanum	*vulgare*	'Aureum'	HP
Osmanthus	×*burkwoodii*		S
	delavayi		S
Osteospermum		'Buttermilk'	HP
		'Silver Sparkler'	HP
		'Whirligig'	HP
Oxalis	*adenophylla*		B
Pachysandra	*terminalis*		S
Parahebe	*perfoliata*		S
Parthenocissus	*henryana*		CL
Passiflora	*caerulea*		CL

HP–Hardy perennial   HHP–Half-hardy perennial   B–Bulb   CL–Climber   CO–Garden conifer
R–Rock plant   S–Shrub   TR–Tree

Top 450 Hardy Plants

Genus	Species	Variety/Cultivar	Type
Penstemon		'Andenken an Friedrich Hahn'	HHP
		'Evelyn'	HHP
	pinifolius		HHP
	pinifolius	'Mersea Yellow'	HHP
		'Schoenholzeri'	HHP
		'Sour Grapes'	HHP
Persicaria	*bistorta*	'Superba'	HP
	vacciniifolia		HP
Phaiophleps	*nigricans*	'Aunt May'	B
Philadelphus		'Belle Etoile'	S
	coronarius	'Aureus'	S
	coronarius	'Variegatus'	S
Phlomis	*fruticosa*		S
Phlox	*subulata*	'G F Wilson'	R
Photinia	×*fraseri*	'Red Robin'	S
Phuopsis	*stylosa*		S
Phygelius	*aequalis*	'Yellow Trumpet'	HP
Picea	*glauca*	*albertiana* 'Conica'	CO
	pungens	'Hoopsii'	CO
Pieris		'Forest Flame'	S
	japonica	'Variegata'	S
Pleioblastus	*auricomus* (grass)		HP
Polemonium	*caeruleum*		HP
	caeruleum	*album*	HP
Polygonatum	×*hybridum*		HP
Potentilla	*fruticosa*	'Daydawn'	S
	fruticosa	'Elizabeth'	S
	fruticosa	'Tangerine'	S
	megalantha		S
	nepalensis	'Miss Willmott'	S
Primula	*bulleyana*		HP
		'Dawn Ansell'	HP
	denticulata		HP
	florindae		HP
	japonica	'Postford White'	HP
		'Lady Greer'	HP
		'Miss Indigo'	HP
	veris		HP
	vialii		HP
Prunus	*domestica*	'Victoria'	TR/S
	laurocerasus	'Otto Luyken'	TR/S
Pulmonaria	*officinalis*	'Sissinghurst White'	HP
Pulsatilla	*vulgaris*		R
Pyrus	*communis*	'Conference'	TR
	salicifolia	'Pendula'	TR
Rhododendron	hybrid	'Blue Diamond'	S
	hybrid	'Curlew'	S
	hybrid	'Elizabeth'	S
	hybrid	'Percy Wiseman'	S
	hybrid	'Pink Drift'	S
	hybrid	'Praecox'	S

TOP 450 HARDY PLANTS

Genus	Species	Variety/Cultivar	Type
Rhododendron	hybrid	'Princess Anne'	S
	impeditum		S
	williamsianum		S
Rosmarinus	*officinalis*		S
Rubus		'Benenden'	S
Ruta	*graveolens*	'Jackman's Blue'	S
Salix	*hastata*	'Wehrhahnii'	S
	integra	'Hakuro-nishiki'	S
	lanata		S
Salvia	*officinalis*	'Icterina'	S
	officinalis	'Purpurascens'	S
	officinalis	'Tricolor'	S
	rutilans		S
	uliginosa		S
Sambucus	*nigra*	'Guincho Purple'	S
	nigra	'Marginata'	S
	racemosa	'Plumosa Aurea'	S
Santolina	*chamaecyparissus*		S
	rosmarinifolia rosmarinifolia		S
		'Primrose Gem'	S
Schizostylis	*coccinea*		B
	coccinea	*alba*	B
	coccinea	'Sunrise'	B
Scrophularia	*auriculata*	'Variegata'	HP
Sedum	*spathulifolium*	'Cape Blanco'	R
	spathulifolium	'Purpureum'	R
	spurium	'Variegatum'	R
Sisyrinchium	*angustifolium*		HP
	idahoense	*album*	HP
Skimmia	*japonica*	*reevesiana*	S
	japonica	'Rubella'	S
Solanum	*crispum*	'Glasnevin'	CL
	jasminoïdes	'Album'	CL
Sorbus	*cashmiriana*		TR
	reducta		TR
Spiraea		'Arguta'	S
	japonica	'Anthony Waterer'	S
	japonica	'Goldflame'	S
	japonica	'Little Princess'	S
Stipa	*gigantea*		HP
Syringa	*meyeri*	'Palibin'	S
Taxodium	*distichum*		CO
Taxus	*baccata*	'Standishii'	CO
Tellima	*grandiflora*	*rubra*	HP
Teucrium	*fruticans*		HP
	× *lucidrys*		HP
Thuja	*occidentalis*	'Rheingold'	CO
	orientalis	'Aurea Nana'	CO

HP–Hardy perennial   HHP–Half-hardy perennial   B–Bulb   CL–Climber   CO–Garden conifer
R–Rock plant   S–Shrub   TR–Tree

Top 450 Hardy Plants

Genus	Species	Variety/Cultivar	Type
Thymus	× *citriodorus*	'Variegatus'	R
	'Doone Valley'		R
	serpyllum	*coccineus*	R
Tiarella	*cordifolia*		HP
Trachelospermum	*jasminoïdes*	'Variegatum'	CL
Tropaeolum	*speciosum*		CL
Ulmus	× *hollandica*	'Jacqueline Hillier'	TR
Veronica	*prostrata*	'Trehane'	R
Viburnum	× *bodnantense*	'Dawn'	S
	× *burkwoodii*		S
	× *carlcephalum*		S
	plicatum	'Mariesii'	S
	sargentii	'Onondaga'	S
	tinus		S
	tinus	'Eve Price'	S
Vinca	*major*	'Variegata'	S/HP
Viola	*cornuta*	*alba*	HP/R
		'Irish Molly'	HP/R
		'Molly Sanderson'	HP/R
	sororia	'Freckles'	HP/R
Vitis	*coignetiae*		CL
Waldsteinia	*ternata*		HP/R
Weigela	*florida*	'Foliis Purpureis'	S
		'Florida Variegata'	S
Yucca	*filamentosa*		S

HP–Hardy perennial   CL–Climber   CO–Garden conifer   R–Rock plant   S–Shrub
R–Tree

Top 100
Roses

Mention the names of 'Zephirine Drouhin', 'Peace' or 'Golden Showers' to a gardener and they will instantly be recognized as rose varieties. But how many others crop up time and time again?

In this directory we have catalogued in order of widest distribution, the 100 roses most easily available in this country. Each rose has been listed with the codes of British Rose Growers' Association members offering the variety for sale at the time of issue. Their full addresses are given at the end of this section.

A classification is also given (shown in brackets) under which the rose is likely to appear in other publications; and a basic colour code is given after this bracket code.

The key to the codes is as follows:

Classification code breakdown:

- **(c)** – climber or rambler
- **(f)** – floribunda
- **(gc)** – ground cover
- **(h)** – hybrid tea
- **(m)** – miniature
- **(p)** – patio
- **(pl)** – dwarf polyantha
- **(s)** – shrub or species

Colour code breakdown:

- **1** – white
- **2** – cream to light yellow
- **3** – medium yellow
- **4** – deep golden yellow
- **5** – yellow blends
- **6** – soft apricot
- **7** – deep apricot to bronze
- **8** – orange vermillion to scarlet
- **9** – light pink
- **10** – medium pink
- **11** – pink blends
- **12** – salmon and coral
- **13** – deep pink to light red
- **14** – medium red
- **15** – dark red
- **16** – lilac to magenta
- **17** – brown shades

Various heights and types are reflected by the use of . . .
Standard, Weeping Standard, Half Standard, Quarter Standard, Patio Standard, Miniature Standard

Explanation Three letters appear as a code to each grower, followed by a number. The number reflects the type of grower i.e.

- 1 – Retailer
- 2 – Retailer/Wholesaler
- 3 – Mainly Wholesaler
- 4 – Strictly Wholesaler

This is an example of the first line to a typical entry.

Albertine (c) 10   Abb2, Act2, And2, Apu2,

Information for this directory was extracted from the British Rose Growers' Association handbook *Find That Rose!*. For further details of this annual publication, which includes information on over 2,600 varieties please send a stamped self addressed envelope to: The Editor of Find That Rose, Dept. GF, 303 Mile End Road, Colchester, Essex CO4 5EA.

1 0 0   R O S E S

Zephirine Drouhin (c) 10   Abb2, Act2, And2, Apu2, Aus2, Bls1, Bnt3, Bra2, Brw1, Can1, Ces4, Cgr1, Cly1, Coc2, Col3, Crl4, Cro2, Dlv4, Doy3, Ess3, Fry2, Gdy2, Gly1, Har2, Hay2, Hdy2, Hgh1, Hll2 Hpn1, Jon2, Jus1, Lay3, Leg2, Mat2, Nts1, Okr2, Pal2, Pen4, Phi2, Poc1, Rea2, Red3, Rog2, Rss2, Rum2, San2, Sbr2, Sck2, Sha2, Stl2, Str2, Sty2, Tim3, Van3, War2, Web3, Wha4, Whe3, Wht3, Wis3, Wye4.

Albertine (c) 12   Abb2, Act2, And2, Apu2, Aus2, Bat2, Bls1, Bnt3, Bra2, Brw1, Can1, Ces4, Cgr1, Cly1, Coc2, Col3, Crl4, Cro2, Dlv4, Doy3, Ess3, Fry2, Gdy2, Gly1, Har2, Hay2, Hdy2, Hgh1, Hll2, Hpn1, Jon2, Jus1, Lay3, Leg2, Mat2, Nts1, Okr2, Pal2, Phi2, Poc1, Rea2, Red3, Rog2, Rss2, Rum2, San2, Sbr2, Sha2, Stl2, Str2, Sty2, Tim3, Van3, War2, Web3, Wha4, Whe3, Wht3, Wis3, Wye4.
Weeping Standard   Bls1, Bnt3, Ces4, Cly1, Gdy2, Hoc4, Nts1, Rog2, Sbr2, Str2, War2, Web3.

Golden Showers (c) 3   Abb2, Act2, Apu2, Aus2, Bat2, Bls1, Bnt3, Bra2, Brw1, Can1, Ces4, Cly1, Coc2, Col3, Crl4, Cro2, Dlv4, Doy3, Ess3, Fry2, Gdy2, Gly1, Har2, Hay2, Hdy2, Hgh1, Hll2, Hpn1, Jon2, Jus1, Lay3, Leg2, Mat2, Nts1, Okr2, Pal2, Phi2, Poc1, Rea2, Red3, Rog2, Rss2, Rum2, San2, Sbr2, Sck2, Sha2, Stl2, Str2, Sty2, Tim3, Van3, War2, Web3, Wha4, Whe3, Wht3, Wis3, Wye4.

Ballerina (s) 9   Abb2, Act2, Apu2, Aus2, Bat2, Bls1, Bnt3, Bra2, Brw1, Can1, Ces4, Cgr1, Cly1, Coc2, Col3, Crl4, Cro2, Doy3, Fry2, Gdy2, Gly1, Har2, Hay2, Hdy2, Hgh1, Hll2, Hpn1, Jon2, Jus1, Lay3, Leg2, Mat2, Nts1, Okr2, Pal2, Pen4, Phi2, Poc1, Rea2, Red3, Rog2, Rss2, Rum2, San2, Sbr2, Sck2, Sha2, Str2, Tim3, Van3, War2, Web3, Wha4, Whe3, Wht3, Wis3, Wye4.
Standard   Bls1, Can1, Ces4, Col3, Fry2, Gdy2, Har2, Hdy2, Hll2, Hoc4, Hpn1, Jon2, Leg2, Mat2, Nts1, Okr2, Pal2, Poc1, Rog2, Rum2, Sbr2, Str2, Tim3, Van3, War2, Web3, Whe3.
Half Standard   Bls1, Ces4, Fry2, Gdy2, Har2, Hoc4, Jon2, Rea2, Red3, Tim3, Wha4.
Quarter Standard   Doy3.

Just Joey (h) 7   Abb2, And2, Apu2, Aus2, Bat2, Bls1, Bnt3, Bra2, Brw1, Can1, Ces4, Cly1, Coc2, Col3, Crl4, Cro2, Dlv4, Doy3, Ess3, Fry2, Gdy2, Gly1, Har2, Hay2, Hdy2, Hgh1, Hll2, Hpn1, Jon2, Jus1, Lay3, Leg2, Mat2, Nts1, Okr2,

Pal2, Phi2, Poc1, Rea2, Red3, Rog2, Rss2, Rum2, San2, Sbr2, Sck2, Sha2, Stl2, Str2, Tim3, Van3, War2, Web3, Wha4, Whe3, Wis3, Wye4.
Standard   Abb2, Aus2, Bnt3, Brw1, Can1, Ces4, Coc2, Col3, Doy3, Fry2, Gdy2, Gly1, Har2, Hdy2, Hgh1, Hll2, Hoc4, Hpn1, Jon2, Lay3, Leg2, Mat2, Okr2, Pal2, Rea2, Rum2, Sbr2, Str2, Tim3, Van3, War2, Web3, Wha4, Whe3, Wis3.
Half Standard   Can1, Ces4, Gdy2, Gly1, Hll2, Rum2, Str2, War2.

Handel (c) 2/14   Abb2, Act2, Apu2, Aus2, Bat2, Bls1, Bnt3, Bra2, Brw1, Can1, Ces4, Cly1, Coc2, Col3, Crl4, Cro2, Dlv4, Ess3, Fry2, Gdy2, Gly1, Har2, Hay2, Hdy2, Hgh1, Hll2, Hpn1, Jon2, Jus1, Lay3, Leg2, Mat2, Nts1, Okr2, Pal2, Phi2, Poc1, Rea2, Red3, Rog2, Rss2, Rum2, San2, Sbr2, Sck2, Sha2, Stl2, Str2, Tim3, Van3, War2, Web3, Wha4, Whe3, Wis3, Wye4.

Iceberg (f) 1   Abb2, Act2, Apu2, Aus2, Bat2, Bls1, Bnt3, Bra2, Can1, Ces4, Cly1, Coc2, Col3, Crl4, Cro2, Dlv4, Doy3, Ess3, Fry2, Gdy2, Gly1, Har2, Hay2, Hdy2, Hgh1, Hll2, Hpn1, Jon2, Jus1, Lay3, Leg2, Mat2, Nts1, Okr2, Pal2, Phi2, Poc1, Rea2, Red3, Rog2, Rss2, Rum2, San2, Sbr2, Sck2, Sha2, Stl2, Str2, Sty2, Tim3, Van3, War2, Web3, Wha4, Whe3, Wye4.
Climbing   Abb2, Act2, Aus2, Bls1, Bnt3, Bra2, Ces4, Cgr1, Col3, Dlv4, Ess3, Gdy2, Har2, Hay2, Hll2, Hpn1, Jon2, Jus1, Lay3, Leg2, Mat2, Nts1, Pal2, Phi2, Poc1, Red3, Rog2, Rss2, Rum2, San2, Str2, Tim3, Van3, War2, Web3, Wha4, Wht3, Wye4.
Standard   Abb2, Aus2, Ces4, Coc2, Col3, Cro2, Fry2, Gdy2, Har2, Hdy2, Hgh1, Hll2, Hoc4, Hpn1, Jon2, Jus1, Leg2, Mat2, Nts1, Okr2, Pen4, Poc1, Rog2, Rum2, San2, Str2, Tim3, Van3, War2, Web3.
Half Standard   Bls1, Ces4, Gdy2, Hll2, Red3, Rum2, San2, Str2.

New Dawn (Also known as The New Dawn) **(c) 9**   Abb2, Act2, Apu2, Aus2, Bat2, Bls1, Bnt3, Brw1, Can1, Cgr1, Cly1, Coc2, Col3, Crl4, Cro2, Dlv4, Doy3, Ess3, Fry2, Gdy2, Gly1, Har2, Hay2, Hdy2, Hgh1, H112, Hpn1, Jon2, Jus1, Lay3, Leg2, Mat2, Nts1, Okr2, Pal2, Phi2, Poc1, Rea2, Red3, Rog2, Rss2, Rum2, San2, Sbr2, Sha2, Stl2, Str2, Sty2, Tim3, Van3, War2, Web3, Wha4, Wht3, Wis3, Wye4.

Weeping Standard   Can1, Ces4, Cly1, Coc2, Hoc4, Str2, War2.
Silver Jubilee (h) 11   Abb2, And2, Apu2, Aus2,

Bat2, Bls1, Bnt3, Bra2, Brw1, Can1, Ces4, Cly1, Coc2, Col3, Crl4, Cro2, Dlv4, Doy3, Ess3, Fry2, Gdy2, Gly1, Har2, Hay2, Hdy2, Hgh1, Hll2, Hpn1, Jon2, Jus1, Lay3, Leg2, Mat2, Nts1, Okr2, Pal2, Phi2, Poc1, Rea2, Red3, Rog2, Rss2, Rum2, San2, Sbr2, Sha2, Stl2, Str2, Tim3, Van3, War2, Web3, Wha4, Whe3, Wis3, Wye4.
Standard Abb2, And2, Aus2, Bls1, Bnt3, Brw1, Can1, Ces4, Cly1, Coc2, Col3, Cro2, Fry2, Gdy2, Gly1, Har2, Hdy2, Hgh2, Hgh1, Hll2, Hoc4, Hpn1, Jon2, Lay3, Leg2, Mat2, Nts1, Okr2, Pal2, Poc1, Rea2, Red3, Rog2, Rum2, San2, Sbr2, Stl2, Str2, Tim3, Van3, War2, Web3, Wha4, Whe3, Wis3.
Half Standard Bnt3, Can1, Ces4, Coc2, Fry2, Gdy2, Gly1, Har2, Hll2, Pal2, Red3, San2, Str2, War2, Web3, Wis3.

Canary Bird (Also known as Rosa Xanthina) **(s) 4** Abb2, Act2, And2, Apu2, Aus2, Bat2, Bls1, Bnt3, Bra2, Brw1, Can1, Cgr1, Chi4, Cly1, Coc2, Col3, Cro2, Dlv4, Ess3, Fry2, Gdy2, Gly1, Har2, Hay2, Hgh1, Hll2, Hpn1, Jon2, Jus1, Lay3, Leg2, Mat2, Nts1, Pen4, Phi2, Poc1, Rea2, Red3, Rss2, Rum2, San2, Sbr2, Sck2, Sha2, Str2, Sty2, Tim3, Van3, War2, Web3, Wha4, Whe3, Wht3, Wis3, Wye4.
Standard Abb2, Aus2, Bls1, Bnt3, Can1, Cly1, Col3, Gdy2, Hll2, Hoc4, Hpn1, Jon2, Jus1, Leg2, Mat2, Nts1, Pen4, Poc1, Rea2, Rum2, Sbr2, Str2, Tim3, Van3, War2, Web3, Whe3, Wht3.
Half Standard Hdy2, Rum2.

Fragrant Cloud (h) 13 Abb2, And2, Apu2, Bat2, Bls1, Bnt3, Bra2, Brw1, Can1, Ces4, Coc2, Col3, Crl4, Cro2, Dlv4, Doy3, Ess3, Fry2, Gdy2, Gly1, Har2, Hay2, Hdy2, Hgh1, Hll2, Hpn1, Jon2, Jus1, Lay3, Leg2, Mat2, Nts1, Okr2, Pal2, Phi2, Poc1, Rea2, Red3, Rog2, Rss2, Rum2, San2, Sbr2, Sck2, Sha2, Stl2, Str2, Tim3, Van3, War2, Web3, Wha4, Whe3, Wis3, Wye4.
Climbing Col3, Gdy2, Hdy2, Red3, Sbr2.
Standard Abb2, Aus2, Bls1, Bnt3, Can1, Ces4, Crl4, Cro2, Fry2, Gdy2.
Half Standard Bnt3, Can1, Ces4, Gdy2, Hll2, Rum2, San2, Str2, War2, Wis3.

Peace (h) 5 Abb2, And2, Apu2, Aus2, Bat2, Bls1, Bnt3, Bra2, Brw1, Can1, Ces4, Coc2, Col3, Crl4, Cro2, Dlv4, Ess3, Fry2, Gdy2, Gly1, Har2, Hay2, Hdy2, Hgh1, Hll2, Hpn1, Jon2, Jus1, Lay3, Leg2, Mat2, Nts1, Okr2, Pal2, Phi2, Poc1, Rea2, Red3, Rog2, Rss2, Rum2, San2, Sbr2, Sck2, Sha2, Stl2, Str2, Tim3, Van3, War2, Web3, Wha4, Whe3, Wis3, Wye4.

Climbing Col3, Ess3, Sbr2.
Standard Abb2, Bnt3, Ces4, Col3, Crl4, Cro2, Fry2, Gdy2, Gly1, Har2, Hdy2, Hll2, Hoc4, Hpn1, Jon2, Lay3, Mat2, Nts1, Okr2, Pal2, Red3, San2, Sbr2, Str2, Van3, War2, Web3, Wha4, Wis3.
Half Standard Bnt3, Ces4, Gdy2, Gly1, Hll2, Rum2, San2, Str2, War2.

The Queen Elizabeth (Also known as Queen Elizabeth) **(f) 10** Abb2, Apu2, Aus2, Bat2, Bls1, Bnt3, Bra2, Brw1, Can1, Ces4, Cly1, Coc2, Col3, Crl4, Cro2, Dlv4, Ess3, Fry2, Gdy2, Gly1, Har2, Hay2, Hdy2, Hgh1, Hll2, Hpn1, Jon2, Jus1, Lay3, Leg2, Mat2, Nts1, Okr2, Pal2, Phi2, Poc1, Rea2, Red3, Rog2, Rss2, Rum2, San2, Sbr2, Sck2, Sha2, Stl2, Str2, Tim3, Van3, War2, Web3, Wha4, Whe3, Wis3, Wye4.
Climbing Bls1, Col3, Gdy2, Hay2, Phi2, Rum2, Sbr2, Van3, Web3.
Standard Gdy2, Hoc4, Jon2, Web3, Wha4, Wis3.
Half Standard Gdy2.

Compassion (c) 11 Abb2, Act2, Apu2, Aus2, Bat2, Bls1, Bnt3, Brw1, Can1, Ces4, Cly1, Coc2, Col3, Crl4, Cro2, Dlv4, Doy3, Ess3, Fry2, Gdy2, Gly1, Har2, Hay2, Hgh1, Hll2, Hpn1, Jon2, Jus1, Lay3, Leg2, Mat2, Nts1, Okr2, Pal2, Phi2, Poc1, Rea2, Red3, Rog2, Rss2, Rum2, San2, Sbr2, Sck2, Sha2, Stl2, Str2, Tim3, Van3, War2, Web3, Wha4, Whe3, Wis3.

Danse du Feu (Also known as Spectacular) **(c) 8** Abb2, Act2, Apu2, Aus2, Bat2, Bls1, Bnt3, Bra2, Ces4, Coc2, Col3, Crl4, Cro2, Dlv4, Doy3, Ess3, Fry2, Gdy2, Gly1, Hay2, Hdy2, Hgh1, Hll2, Hpn1, Jon2, Jus1, Lay3, Leg2, Mat2, Nts1, Okr2, Pal2, Phi2, Poc1, Rea2, Red3, Rog2, Rss2, Rum2, San2, Sbr2, Sck2, Sha2, Stl2, Str2, Tim3, Van3, War2, Web3, Wha4, Whe3, Wht3, Wis3, Wye4.

Margaret Merril (f) 1 Abb2, Act2, And2, Apu2, Aus2, Bat2, Bls1, Bnt3, Bra2, Brw1, Can1, Ces4, Cly1, Coc2, Col3, Crl4, Dlv4, Doy3, Ess3, Fry2, Gdy2, Gly1, Har2, Hay2, Hdy2, Hgh1, Hll2, Hpn1, Jon2, Jus1, Lay3, Leg2, Mat2, Nts1, Okr2, Pal2, Phi2, Poc1, Rea2, Red3, Rog2, Rss2, Rum2, San2, Sbr2, Stl2, Str2, Tim3, War2, Whe3, Wis3, Wye4.
Standard Abb2, Bnt3, Can1, Ces4, Doy3, Fry2, Gdy2, Har2, Hgh1, Hll2, Hoc4, Hpn1, Jon2, Leg2, Mat2, Okr2, Red3, Sbr2, War2, Wis3.
Half Standard Bnt3, Can1, Ces4, Gdy2, Gly1, Har2, Hll2, Pal2, Poc1, Rea2, Red3, Wis3.

Pink Perpetue (c) 10   Abb2, Act2, Apu2, Aus2, Bat2, Bls1, Bnt3, Bra2, Brw1, Can1, Ces4, Cly1, Col3, Crl4, Cro2, Dlv4, Ess3, Fry2, Gdy2, Gly1, Hay2, Hdy2, Hgh1, Hll2, Hpn1, Jon2, Jus1, Lay3, Leg2, Mat2, Nts1, Okr2, Pal2, Rea2, Red3, Rog2, Rss2, Rum2, San2, Sbr2, Sck2, Sha2, Stl2, Str2, Sty2, Tim3, Van3, War2, Web3, Wha4, Whe3, Wis3, Wye4.

Whisky Mac (h) 6   Abb2, Apu2, Aus2, Bat2, Bls1, Bnt3, Bra2, Brw1, Can1, Ces4, Coc2, Col3, Crl4, Cro2, Dlv4, Ess3, Fry2, Gdy2, Gly1, Hay2, Hdy2, Hgh1, Hll2, Hpn1, Jon2, Jus1, Lay3, Leg2, Mat2, Nts1, Okr2, Pal2, Phi2, Poc1, Rea2, Red3, Rog2, Rss2, Rum2, San2, Sbr2, Sck2, Sha2, Stl2, Str2, Tim3, Van3, War2, Web3, Wha4, Whe3, Wis3, Wye4.
Standard Bls1, Ces4, Col3, Crl4, Cro2, Fry2, Gdy2, Hdy2, Hgh1, Hll2, Hoc4, Hpn1, Jon2, Lay3, Leg2, Okr2, Poc1, Rog2, Rum2, San2, Sbr2, Tim3, Van3, War2, Web3, Whe3, Wis3.
Half Standard Ces4, Gdy2, Hll2, Rum2, San2, War2, Wis3.

Sweet Dream (Fryminicot) **(p) 6**   Abb2, And2, Apu2, Bat2, Bls1, Bnt3, Bra2, Brw1, Can1, Ces4, Cly1, Coc2, Col3, Crl4, Cro2, Dlv4, Doy3, Fry2, Gdy2, Gly1, Har2, Hdy2, Hgh1, Hll2, Hpn1, Jon2, Jus1, Lay3, Leg2, Mat2, Nts1, Okr2, Pal2, Phi2, Poc1, Rea2, Red3, Rog2, Rss2, Rum2, San2, Sbr2, Sck2, Sha2, Str2, Tim3, Van3, War2, Web3, Wha4, Wis3, Wye4.
Standard Hdy2, Mat2, Web3.
Half Standard Ces4, Cly1, Coc2, Col3, Har2, Hoc4, Hpn1, Jon2, Rum2, Van3, War2, Web3.
Patio Standard And2, Can1, Ces4, Hll2, Wha4.
Miniature Standard Ces4, Gly1, Pal2, Rum2, Wis3.

The Fairy (s/pl/gc) 9   Abb2, Act2, Apu2, Aus2, Bls1, Bnt3, Bra2, Brw1, Can1, Ces4, Cgr1, Chi4, Cly1, Coc2, Col3, Cro2, Dlv4, Doy3, Fry2, Gdy2, Gly1, Har2, Hay2, Hdy2, Hgh1, Hll2, Hpn1, Jon2, Jus1, Lay3, Leg2, Mat2, Nts1, Pal2, Poc1, Rea2, Red3, Rog2, Rum2, San2, Sbr2, Sck2, Str2, Sty2, Tim3, Van3, War2, Web3, Wha4, Whe3, Wht3, Wye4.
Standard Aus2, Bls1, Can1, Ces4, Coc2, Fry2, Hdy2, Hll2, Hoc4, Jon2, Leg2, Mat2, Nts1, Sbr2, Tim3, Van3, Wht3.
Half Standard Aus2, Ces4, Har2, Hoc4, Hpn1, Jon2, Str2, Tim3.
Quarter Standard   Doy3.
Miniature Standard Pal2, Rea2.
Polar Star (Tanlarpost) **(h) 1**   Abb2, Apu2, Aus2, Bat2, Bls1, Bnt3, Bra2, Can1, Ces4, Cly1,

Coc2, Col3, Crl4, Dlv4, Doy3, Fry2, Gdy2, Gly1, Har2, Hay2, Hdy2, Hgh1, Hll2, Hpn1, Jon2, Jus1, Lay3, Leg2, Mat2, Nts1, Okr2, Pal2, Phi2, Poc1, Rea2, Red3, Rog2, Rss2, Rum2, San2, Sbr2, Sha2, Stl2, Str2, Tim3, Van3, War2, Web3, Whe3, Wis3, Wye4.
Standard Abb2, Can1, Ces4, Gdy2, Gly1, Hdy2, Hgh1, Hoc4, Hpn1, Nts1, Okr2, Pal2, Poc1, Rea2, Rog2, Rum2, Van3, War2, Web3, Wis3.
Half Standard Can1, Ces4, Gdy2, Gly1, War2, Wis3.

Alec's Red (h) 14   Abb2, Apu2, Aus2, Bat2, Bls1, Bnt3, Bra2, Coc2, Col3, Crl4, Cro2, Dlv4, Doy3, Ess3, Fry2, Gdy2, Har2, Hay2, Hdy2, Hgh1, Hll2, Hpn1, Jon2, Lay3, Leg2, Mat2, Nts1, Okr2, Pal2, Phi2, Poc1, Rea2, Red3, Rog2, Rss2, Rum2, San2, Sbr2, Sck2, Sha2, Stl2, Str2, Tim3, Van3, War2, Web3, Wha4, Whe3, Wis3, Wye4.
Climbing Hdy2, Lay3, Wis3.
Standard Abb2, Bls1, Ces4, Coc2, Col3, Crl4, Doy3, Gdy2, Hdy2, Hgh1, Hll2, Hoc4, Jon2, Leg2, Mat2, Nts1, Pal2, Rea2, San2, Sbr2, Str2, Tim3, Van3, Web3, Wha4, Wis3.
Half Standard Ces4, Coc2, Doy3, Gdy2, Hll2, Okr2, Pal2, San2, Str2.

Blessings (h) 12   Abb2, Apu2, Aus2, Bat2, Bls1, Bnt3, Bra2, Brw1, Can1, Ces4, Coc2, Col3, Crl4, Dlv4, Ess3, Fry2, Gdy2, Gly1, Hay2, Hgh1, Hll2, Hpn1, Jon2, Jus1, Lay3, Leg2, Mat2, Nts1, Okr2, Pal2, Phi2, Poc1, Rea2, Red3, Rog2, Rss2, San2, Sbr2, Sck2, Sha2, Stl2, Str2, Tim3, Van3, War2, Web3, Wha4, Whe3,Wis3, Wye4.
Climbing Col3, Hpn1.
Standard Abb2, Aus2, Bls1, Bnt3, Ces4, Crl4, Fry2, Gdy2, Gly1, Hll2, Hoc4, Hpn1, Jon2, Lay3, Mat2, Okr2, Poc1, Rea2, Red3, Rog2, Sbr2, Str2, Tim3, Van3, War2, Whe3, Wis3.
Half Standard Bnt3, Gdy2, Gly1, Hll2, Str2.

Mountbatten (Harmantelle) **(f) 3**   Abb2, Apu2, Aus2, Bat2, Bls1, Bnt3, Bra2, Can1, Ces4, Cly1, Coc2, Col3, Crl4, Dlv4, Ess3, Fry2, Gdy2, Gly1, Har2, Hay2, Hgh1, Hll2, Hpn1, Jon2, Jus1, Lay3, Leg2, Mat2, Nts1, Okr2, Pal2, Phi2, Poc1, Rea2, Red3, Rog2, Rss2, Rum2, Sbr2, Sha2, Stl2, Str2, Tim3, Van3, War2, Web3, Wha4, Whe3, Wis3, Wye4.
Standard Ces4, Doy3, Gdy2, Har2, Hll2, Hoc4, Hpn1, Red3, Rum2, Tim3, Web3.
Half Standard Ces4, Gdy2, Hoc4, Red3, Web3.

Nevada (s) 1 Abb2, Act2, And2, Apu2, Aus2, Bls1, Bnt3, Bra2, Brw1, Can1, Cgr1, Chi4, Cly1, Coc2, Col3, Cro2, Fry2, Gdy2, Gly1, Har2, Hgh1, Hll2, Jon2, Jus1, Lay3, Leg2, Mat2, Nts1, Okr2, Pen4, Phi2, Rea2, Red3, Rog2, Rss2, Rum2, San2, Sbr2, Sck2, Stl2, Str2, Sty2, Tim3, Van3, War2, Web3, Wha4, Wht3, Wis3, Wye4.

Royal William (Korzaun) **(h) 15** Abb2, And2, Apu2, Aus2, Bls1, Bnt3, Brw1, Can1, Ces4, Cly1, Coc2, Col3, Crl4, Cro2, Dlv4, Doy3, Ess3, Fry2, Gdy2, Gly1, Har2, Hay2, Hgh1, Hpn1, Jon2, Jus1, Lay3, Leg2, Mat2, Nts1, Okr2, Pal2, Phi2, Poc1, Rea2, Red3, Rog2, Rss2, Rum2, Sbr2, Sha2, Str2, Tim3, Van3, War2, Web3, Wha4, Whe3, Wis3, Wye4.
Standard Abb2, And2, Aus2, Bnt3, Brw1, Can1, Ces4, Gdy2, Gly1, Har2, Hgh1, Hoc4, Hpn1, Jon2, Mat2, Nts1, Okr2, Rum2, Sbr2, Str2, Tim3, Van3, War2, Web3, Wis3.
Half Standard Bnt3, Can1, Ces4, Gdy2, Gly1, War2.

Schoolgirl (c) 6 Abb2, Apu2, Aus2, Bat2, Bls1, Bnt3, Bra2, Brw1, Can1, Ces4, Col3, Crl4, Cro2, Dlv4, Ess3, Fry2, Gdy2, Gly1, Hay2, Hll2, Hpn1, Jon2, Lay3, Leg2, Mat2, Nts1, Okr2, Pal2, Phi2, Poc1, Rea2, Red3, Rog2, Rss2, Rum2, San2, Sbr2, Sck2, Sha2, Stl2, Str2, Tim3, Van3, War2, Web3, Wha4, Whe3, Wht3, Wis3, Wye4.

Doris Tysterman (h) 8 Abb2, And2, Aus2, Bat2, Bls1, Bnt3, Bra2, Brw1, Ces4, Coc2, Col3, Crl4, Cro2, Dlv4, Doy3, Ess3, Fry2, Gdy2, Gly1, Hay2, Hgh1, Hll2, Hpn1, Jon2, Jus1, Lay3, Leg2, Okr2, Pal2, Phi2, Poc1, Rea2, Red3, Rog2, Rss2, Rum2, San2, Sbr2, Sck2, Sha2, Stl2, Str2, Tim3, Van3, War2, Web3, Whe3, Wis3.
Standard Ces4, Gdy2, Hgh1, Hll2, Hoc4, Hpn1, Jon2, Lay3, Leg2, Okr2, Pal2, Pen4, Rea2, Rum2, Sbr2, Tim3, Van3, Web3, Wha4, Wis3.
Half Standard Gdy2, Hll2.

Piccadilly (h) 3/14 Abb2, Apu2, Aus2, Bat2, Bls1, Bnt3, Bra2, Brw1, Ces4, Coc2, Col3, Crl4, Cro2, Dlv4, Ess3, Fry2, Gdy2, Gly1, Hay2, Hgh1, Hll2, Hpn1, Jon2, Lay3, Leg2, Mat2, Nts1, Okr2, Pal2, Phi2, Poc1, Rea2, Red3, Rog2, Rss2, Rum2, San2, Sbr2, Sck2, Sha2, Stl2, Str2, Tim3, Van3, War2, Web3, Wha4, Whe3, Wis3.
Climbing Hpn1.
Standard Abb2, Bnt3, Ces4, Crl4, Cro2, Hgh1, Hll2, Hoc4, Hpn1, Lay3, Leg2, Mat2, Nts1, Okr2,

Rog2, Rum2, San2, War2, Web3, Wha4, Wis3.
Half Standard Bnt3, Ces4, Hll2, San2, War2, Wis3.

Amber Queen (Harroony) **(f) 4** Abb2, Apu2, Aus2, Bls1, Bnt3, Brw1, Can1, Ces4, Cly1, Coc2, Col3, Crl4, Doy3, Ess3, Fry2, Gdy2, Gly1, Har2, Hay2, Hdy2, Hgh1, Hpn1, Jon2, Jus1, Lay3, Leg2, Mat2, Okr2, Pal2, Phi2, Poc1, Rea2, Rog2, Rss2, Rum2, San2, Sbr2, Sha2, Stl2, Str2, Tim3, Van3, War2, Web3, Wha4, Whe3, Wis3, Wye4.
Standard Ces4, Cly1, Coc2, Gdy2, Har2, Hdy2, Hoc4, Jon2, Leg2, Mat2, Poc1, Rog2, Str2, War2, Wis3.
Half Standard Ces4, Fry2, Gdy2, Gly1, Har2, Hoc4, Hpn1, Jon2, Pal2, Poc1, Rea2, War2.

Gentle Touch (Diclulu) **(p) 9** Abb2, And2, Apu2, Bat2, Bls1, Bnt3, Brw1, Can1, Ces4, Coc2, Col3, Crl4, Dic2, Fry2, Gdy2, Gly1, Har2, Hay2, Hdy2, Hgh1, Hpn1, Jon2, Jus1, Lay3, Leg2, Mat2, Nts1, Okr2, Poc1, Rea2, Red3, Rog2, Rss2, Rum2, San2, Sbr2, Sck2, Sha2, Stl2, Str2, Tim3, Van3, War2, Web3, Wha4, Whe3, Wis3, Wye4.
Half Standard Ces4, Col3, Har2, Hoc4, Hpn1, Jon2, Mat2, Van3, Web3.
Quarter Standard Doy3, Rea2, Str2.
Patio Standard And2, Can1, Wha4.
Miniature Standard Gly1.

Pascali (h) 1 And2, Apu2, Aus2, Bls1, Bnt3, Bra2, Brw1, Can1, Ces4, Coc2, Col3, Crl4, Cro2, Dlv4, Ess3, Fry2, Gdy2, Gly1, Har2, Hll2, Hpn1, Jon2, Jus1, Lay3, Leg2, Mat2, Nts1, Okr2, Pal2, Phi2, Poc1, Rea2, Red3, Rog2, Rss2, Rum2, San2, Sha2, Stl2, Str2, Tim3, Van3, War2, Web3, Wha4, Whe3, Wis3, Wye4.
Climbing Gdy2.
Standard And2, Aus2, Bls1, Ces4, Hll2, Hoc4, Jon2, Leg2, Mat2, Okr2, Pen4, Rea2, Rum2, San2, Str2, Tim3, Van3, Web3, Whe3, Wis3.
Half Standard Ces4, Hll2, San2, Str2.

Evelyn Fison (f) 14 Abb2, And2, Apus2, Aus2, Bnt3, Bra2, Brw1, Ces4, Coc2, Col3, Crl4, Cro2, Dlv4, Ess3, Fry2, Gdy2, Gly1, Hay2, Hdy2, Hgh1, Hll2, Hpn1, Jon2, Jus1, Lay3, Leg2, Nts1, Okr2, Pal2, Phi2, Poc1, Red3, Rog2, Rss2, Rum2, Sbr2, Sck2, Stl2, Str2, Tim3, Van3, War2, Web3, Wha4, Whe3, Wis3, Wye4.
Standard Aus2, Ces4, Coc2, Cro2, Hoc4, Okr2, Pen4, Rog2, Sbr2, Web3, Wha4, Wis3.
Half Standard Bls1, Web3, Wis3.

Grandpa Dickson (h) 2   Abb2, Apu2, Aus2, Bat2, Bls1, Bnt3, Bra2, Brw1, Ces4, Coc2, Col3, Crl4, Cro2, Dlv4, Ess3, Fry2, Gdy2, Gly1, Hay2, Hgh1, Hll2, Hpn1, Jon2, Lay3, Leg2, Mat2, Nts1, Okr2, Pal2, Phi2, Poc1, Rea2, Red3, Rog2, Rss2, Rum2, Sbr2, Sck2, Sha2, Stl2, Tim3, Van3, War2, Web3, Wha4, Whe3, Wis3.
Standard Ces4, Crl4, Hll2, Jòn2, Okr2, Pen4, Rea2, Red3, Rum2, Sbr2, Tim3, Van3, Wha4, Whe3, Wis3, Wye4.
Half Standard Ces4, Hll2, Wis3.

Nozomi (gc/s) 9   Abb2, Act2, Apu2, Aus2, Bat2, Bls1, Bnt3, Bra2, Can1, Ces4, Chi4, Coc2, Col3, Cro2, Fry2, Gdy2, Har2, Hgh1, Hll2, Hpn1, Jon2, Jus1, Lay3, Leg2, Mat2, Nts1, Okr2, Pal2, Pen4, Poc1, Rea2, Red3, Rog2, Rss2, Rum2, San2, Sbr2, Sha2, Stl2, Str2, Tim3, Van3, War2, Web3, Wha4, Wis3, Wye4.
Standard Abb2, Bls1, Can1, Ces4, Fry2, Gdy2, Har2, Hll2, Hoc4, Jon2, Leg2, Mat2, Nts1, Okr2, Pal2, Poc1, Rea2, Rog2, San2, Sbr2, Str2, Tim3, Van3, War2, Web3.
Half Standard Ces4, Coc2, Gdy2, Hoc4, Jon2, Tim3, Web3, Wha4.
Miniature Standard Ces4, Hoc4, Hpn1, Jon2, Rum2, War2.

Prima Ballerina (h) 10   Abb2, Act2, Aus2, Bat2, Bls1, Bnt3, Bra2, Ces4, Coc2, Col3, Crl4, Cro2, Dlv4, Doy3, Ess3, Fry2, Gdy2, Hay2, Hgh1, Hll2, Hpn1, Jon2, Lay3, Leg2, Mat2, Nts1, Okr2, Pal2, Phi2, Poc1, Rea2, Red3, Rog2, Rss2, Rum2, San2, Sbr2, Sck2, Stl2, Str2, Tim3, Van3, Web3, Wha4, Whe3, Wis3, Wye4.
Standard Ces4, Hgh1, Hoc4, Jon2, Nts1, Pal2, Pen4, Sbr2, Str2, Web3, Wha4, Wis3.
Half Standard Pal2.

Sweet Magic (Dicmagic) (p) 7   And2, Apu2, Bat2, Bls1, Bnt3, Brw1, Can1, Ces4, Cly1, Coc2, Col3, Crl4, Dic2, Dlv4, Doy3, Fry2, Gdy2, Gly1, Har2, Hdy2, Hgh1, Hpn1, Jon2, Jus1, Lay3, Leg2, Mat2, Nts1, Phi2, Poc1, Rea2, Red3, Rss2, Rum2, San2, Sbr2, Sck2, Sha2, Stl2, Str2, Tim3, Van3, War2, Web3, Wha4, Whe3, Wis3.
Standard Mat2, Web3.
Half Standard Ces4, Cly1, Har2, Hoc4, Jon2, Rum2, Van3.
Quarter Standard Rea2, Red3.
Miniature Standard Ces4, Gly1, Pal2, Rum2, Wis3.
Wendy Cussons (h) 13   Abb2, Apu2, Aus2, Bat2, Bls1, Bnt3, Bra2, Brw1, Ces4, Coc2, Crl4, Cro2, Dlv4, Doy3, Ess3, Fry2, Gdy2, Hay2, Hgh1, Hll2, Hpn1, Jon2, Lay3, Leg2, Nts1,

Okr2, Pal2, Phi2, Poc1, Rea2, Red3, Rog2, Rss2, Rum2, San2, Sbr2, Sck2, Stl2, Str2, Tim3, Van3, War2, Web3, Wha4, Whe3, Wis3, Wye4.
Climbing Hay2.
Standard Crl4, Gdy2, Hgh1, Hoc4, Hpn1, Rum2, San2, War2, Web3, Wis3.
Half Standard Gdy2, Rum2, San2.

Ernest H Morse (h) 14   Abb2, And2, Apu2, Aus2, Bls1, Bnt3, Bra2, Brw1, Ces4, Coc2, Col3, Crl4, Cro2, Dlv4, Ess3, Fry2, Gdy2, Har2, Hay2, Hgh1, Hll2, Jon2, Lay3, Nts1, Okr2, Pal2, Phi2, Poc1, Rea2, Red3, Rog2, Rss2, Rum2, Sbr2, Sck2, Sha2, Stl2, Str2, Tim3, Van3, War2, Web3, Wha4, Whe3, Wis3, Wye4.
Climbing Gdy2.
Standard Ces4, Gdy2, Hoc4, Rog2, Web3, Wis3.
Half Standard Gdy2, Wis3.

Korresia (Friesia) (f) 4   Abb2, Aus2, Bat2, Bnt3, Bra2, Can1, Ces4, Cly1, Coc2, Col3, Crl4, Dlv4, Fry2, Gdy2, Gly1, Har2, Hay2, Hdy2, Hgh1, Hll2, Hpn1, Jon2, Jus1, Lay3, Leg2, Mat2, Nts1, Pal2, Phi2, Poc1, Rea2, Rog2, Rss2, Rum2, San2, Sbr2, Sha2, Stl2, Str2, Tim3, Van3, War2, Web3, Wha4, Whe3, Wis3.
Standard Aus2, Bnt3, Can1, Ces4, Col3, Fry2, Gdy2, Hll2, Hoc4, Hpn1, Jon2, Leg2, Mats, Nts1, Rog2, Sbr2, Van3, War2, Web3.
Half Standard Bnt3, Can1, Ces4, Fry2, Gdy2, Har2, Hll2, Pal2, Poc1, Rea2, Web3.

Rosa Rubrifolia (Also known as Rosa Glauca) **(s) 10**   Abb2, Act2, Apu2, Aus2, Bls1, Bnt3, Can1, Ces4, Cgr1, Chi4, Cly1, Coc2, Col3, Cro2, Dlv4, Fry2, Gdy2, Gly1, Har2, Hay2, Hgh1, Hll2, Hpn1, Jon2, Jus1, Lay3, Leg2, Mat2, Nts1, Phi2, Poc1, Rea2, Red3, Rog2, Rum2, San2, Sbr2, Sha2, Stl2, Str2, Sty2, Web3, Wha4, Whe3, Wht3, Wis2.
Weeping Standard Abb2.

Super Star (h) 8   Abb2, Aus2, Bls1, Bnt3, Bra2, Brw1, Ces4, Coc2, Col3, Crl4, Cro2, Dlv4, Ess3, Fry2, Gdy2, Hay2, Hdy2, Hll2, Hpn1, Jon2, Jus1, Lay3, Mat2, Nts1, Okr2, Pal2, Phi2, Poc1, Rea2, Red3, Rog2, Rss2, Rum2, San2, Sbr2, Sha2, Stl2, Str2, Tim3, Van3, War2, Web3, Wha4, Whe3, Wis3, Wye4.
Climbing Aus2, Col3, Dlv4, Gdy2, Hay2, Hdy2, Hll2, Lay3, Leg2, Nts1, Phi2, Rum2, Sbr2, Tim3.
Standard Ces4, Gdy2, Hll2, Hoc4, Jon2, Lay3, Nts1, Pen4, San2, Str2, War2, Web3, Wha4, Wis3.

Half Standard Ces4, Gdy2, Hll2, San2, Str2, War2, Wis3.

Maigold (c) 4 Abb2, Act2, Aus2, Bat2, Bls1, Bnt3, Bra2, Can1, Coc2, Col3, Cro2, Dlv4, Ess3, Gdy2, Gly1, Har2, Hay2, Hll2, Hpn1, Jon2, Jus1, Lay3, Leg2, Mat2, Nts1, Pal2, Phi2, Poc1, Rea2, Red3, Rog2, Rss2, Rum2, San2, Sbr2, Sck2, Stl2, Str2, Sty2, Tim3, War2, Wha4, Whe3, Wht3, Wis3.

Alexander (h) 8 Abb2, Apu2, Aus2, Bat2, Bls1, Bnt3, Bra2, Can1, Coc2, Col3, Crl4, Cro2, Dlv4, Ess3, Fry2, Gdy2, Gly1, Har2, Hay2, Hdy2, Hgh1, Hll2, Hpn1, Jon2, Lay3, Leg2, Mat2, Nts1, Okr2, Pal2, Phi2, Rea2, Red3, Rog2, San2, Sbr2, Sha2, Stl2, Str2, Tim3, War2, Whe3, Wis3, Wye4.
Standard Abb2, Aus2, Ces4, Cro2, Gdy2, Har2, Hoc4, Okr2, Wis3.
Half Standard Gdy2.

Chinatown (f/s) 3 Abb2, Apu2, Aus2, Bls1, Bnt3, Bra2, Ces4, Coc2, Col3, Crl4, Cro2, Dlv4, Gdy2, Hay2, Hgh1, Hll2, Hpn1, Jon2, Jus1, Lay3, Leg2, Nts1, Okr2, Pal2, Pen4, Phi2, Red3, Rog2, Rss2, Rum2, Sbr2, Sck2, Sha2, Stl2, Str2, Sty2, Tim3, Van3, War2, Web3, Wha4, Whe3, Wis3, Wye4.
Standard Ces4, Web3.
Half Standard Rum2.

Harvest Fayre (Dicnorth) **(f) 6** Abb2, Apu2, Bat2, Bls1, Bnt3, Bra2, Brw1, Can1, Ces4, Cly1, Coc2, Col3, Crl4, Dic2, Doy3, Ess3, Gdy2, Gly1, Har2, Hay2, Hdy2, Hgh1, Hpn1, Jus1, Lay3, Leg2, Mat2, Nts1, Okr2, Phi2, Poc1, Rea2, Red3, Rog2, Rss2, Rum2, Sbr2, Stl2, Str2, Tim3, Van3, War2, Web3, Wha4.
Standard Bnt3, Can1, Ces4, Gdy2, Hoc4, Hpn1, Mat2, Sbr2, Wha4.
Half Standard Can1, Ces4, Cly1, Gdy2, Van3.

Penelope (s) 9 Act2, And2, Apu2, Aus2, Bls1, Bnt3, Brw1, Can1, Cgr1, Chi4, Coc2, Col3, Cro2, Doy3, Fry2, Gdy2, Har2, Hay2, Hgh1, Hll2, Hpn1, Jon2, Jus1, Lay3, Leg2, Mat2, Nts1, Okr2, Poc1, Rea2, Red3, Rog2, Rum2, San2, Sbr2, Str2, Sty2, Tim3, Van3, War2, Wha4, Whe3, Wht3, Wye4.
Weeping Standard Hll2.

Rosa Mundi (Also known as Rosa Gallica Versicolor) **(s) 1/13** Act2, Apu2, Aus2, Bls1, Bnt3, Bra2, Brw1, Can1, Ces4, Cgr1, Coc2, Col3, Dlv4, Doy3, Fry2, Gdy2, Har2, Hay2,

Hgh1, Hll2, Hpn1, Jon2, Jus1, Lay3, Leg2, Mat2, Nts1, Phi2, Poc1, Rea2, Red3, Rog2, Rum2, San2, Sbr2, Sck2, Str2, Sty2, Tim3, War2, Wha4, Wht3, Wis3, Wye4.
Standard Aus2, Ces4.

Baby Masquerade (m) 5/13 Aus2, Bls1, Bnt3, Bra2, Brw1, Ces4, Coc2, Dlv4, Ess3, Fry2, Gdy2, Gly1, Har2, Hay2, Hgh1, Hll2, Hpn1, Jon2, Jus1, Lay3, Leg2, Mat2, Nts1, Okr2, Pal2, Phi2, Poc1, Rea2, Red3, Rog2, San2, Sbr2, Sck2, Sha2, Stl2, Tim3, Van3, War2, Web3, Wha4, Whe3, Wis3, Wye4.
Half Standard Hll2.
Miniature Standard Ces4, Har2, Hll2, Hoc4, Jon2, Web3, Wha4.

Buff Beauty (s) 2 Act2, Apu2, Aus2, Bls1, Bnt3, Bra2, Brw1, Can1, Cgr1, Chi4, Col3, Doy3, Fry2, Gdy2, Har2, Hay2, Hll2, Hpn1, Jon2, Jus1, Lay3, Leg2, Mat2, Nts1, Okr2, Phi2, Poc1, Rea2, Red3, Rog2, Rum2, San2, Sbr2, Str2, Sty2, Tim3, Van3, Web3, Wha4, Whe3, Wht3, Wis3, Wye4.
Standard Hll2, Red3, Wht3.

Fruhlingsgold (s) 2 Abb2, Act2, Apu2, Aus2, Bls1, Bnt3, Bra2, Brw1, Ces4, Cgr1, Chi4, Coc2, Col3, Cro2, Fry2, Gdy2, Gly1, Hay2, Hll2, Jus1, Lay3, Leg2, Mat2, Nts1, Pen4, Phi2, Red3, Rog2, Rum2, San2, Sbr2, Sck2, Stl2, Str2, Sty2, Tim3, Van3, War2, Web3, Whe3, Wht3, Wis3, Wye4.

Roseraie de L'Hay (s) 15+16 Act2, Apu2, Aus2, Bls1, Bnt3, Brw1, Can1, Cgr1, Chi4, Coc2, Col3, Dlv4, Doy3, Fry2, Gdy2, Har2, Hgh1, Hll2, Hpn1, Jon2, Jus1, Lay3, Leg2, Mat2, Nts1, Pal2, Poc1, Rea2, Red3, Rog2, Rum2, San2, Sck2, Str2, Sty2, Tim3, War2, Web3, Wha4, Whe3, Wht3, Wis3, Wye4.

Ruby Wedding (h) 15 Aus2, Bat2, Bls1, Bnt3, Bra2, Brw1, Can1, Ces4, Coc2, Crl4, Cro2, Dlv4, Ess3, Fry2, Gdy2, Gly1, Har2, Hay2, Hdy2, Hgh1, Hpn1, Jon2, Jus1, Lay3, Mat2, Pal2, Phi2, Poc1, Rea2, Red3, Rog2, Rss2, Rum2, San2, Sbr2, Sha2, Str2, Tim3, Van3, War2, Web3, Wha4, Whe3.
Standard Bnt3, Ces4, Coc2, Fry2, Gdy2, Har2, Hdy2, Hoc4, Jon2, Poc1, Red3, Rum2, Sbr2, Str2, Tim3, War2.
Half Standard Bnt3, Ces4, Gdy2, Hpn1, Pal2, Rum2.

Arthur Bell (f) 3 Abb2, Apu2, Aus2, Bat2, Bls1, Bnt3, Bra2, Brw1, Ces4, Col3, Crl4, Cro2, Ess3, Gdy2, Hay2, Hgh1, Hll2, Hpn1, Lay3, Leg2,

Mat2, Nts1, Okr2, Pal2, Phi2, Poc1, Rea2, Red3, Rog2, Rss2, Rum2, San2, Sbr2, Sha2, Stl2, Str2, Tim3, War2, Wha4, Whe3, Wis3, Wye4.
Climbing Abb2, Apu2, Bra2, Doy3, Hdy2, Jus1, Lay3, Rog2, Rum2, Sbr2, Van3, Web3.
Standard Abb2, Ces4, Pen4, Poc1, Sbr2, Tim3, Web3, Wha4, Wis3.
Half Standard Ces4, Rum2, Wha4, Wis3.

Blue Moon (h) 16 Abb2, Apu2, Aus2, Bls1, Bnt3, Bra2, Brw1, Ces4, Col3, Crl4, Ess3, Fry2, Gdy2, Gly1, Hay2, Hgh1, Hll2, Hpn1, Jon2, Jus1, Nts1, Okr2, Pal2, Phi2, Poc1, Red3, Rog2, Rss2, Rum2, San2, Sck2, Sha2, Stl2, Tim3, Van3, War2, Web3, Wha4, Whe3, Wis3, Wye4.
Climbing Brw1, Col3, Ess3, Gdy2, Phi2, Van3, Web3, Wis3.
Standard Abb2, Ces4, War2, Web3.
Half Standard Ces4.

Glad Tidings (Tantide) **(f) 15** Abb2, Apu2, Bat2, Bnt3, Bra2, Brw1, Can1, Ces4, Cly1, Coc2, Col3, Crl4, Doy3, Gdy2, Har2, Hay2, Hdy2, Hgh1, Hpn1, Jon2, Lay3, Leg2, Mat2, Nts1, Okr2, Pal2, Phi2, Poc1, Rea2, Red3, Rog2, Rss2, Rum2, Sbr2, Stl2, Str2, Tim3, War2, Web3, Wha4, Whe3, Wis3.
Standard Bnt3, Can1, Ces4, Col3, Hdy2, Hoc4, Hpn1, Jon2, Leg2, Red3, Str2, Tim3, War2, Wha4.
Half Standard Bnt3.

Graham Thomas (Ausmas) **(s) 4** Act2, Apu2, Aus2, Bat2, Bls1, Bnt3, Bra2, Can1, Ces4, Cly1, Coc2, Col3, Dlv4, Doy3, Fry2, Gdy2, Gly1, Har2, Hay2, Hpn1, Jon2, Jus1, Lay3, Leg2, Mat2, Nts1, Pal2, Phi2, Poc1, Rea2, Red3, Rog2, Rum2, San2, Str2, Tim3, Van3, War2, Web3, Wha4, Whe3, Wht3.
Standard Aus2, Ces4.

Lovers Meeting (h) 8 And2, Apu2, Bat2, Bnt3, Brw1, Can1, Ces4, Coc2, Col3, Crl4, Cro2, Dlv4, Ess3, Fry2, Gdy2, Hay2, Hll2, Hpn1, Jon2, Jus1, Lay3, Leg2, Mat2, Okr2, Pal2, Phi2, Poc1, Rea2, Red3, Rog2, Rss2, San2, Sbr2, Sha2, Str2, Tim3, Van3, War2, Web3, Wha4, Whe3, Wis3.
Standard And2, Bnt3, Brw1, Ces4, Col3, Fry2, Gdy2, Hll2, Hoc4, Hpn1, Jon2, Okr2, Rea2, Red3, San2, Str2, Web3.
Half Standard Ces4, Gdy2, Hll2.
Melody Maker (Dicqueen) **(f) 8** Abb2, Apu2, Bat2, Bls1, Bnt3, Brw1, Can1, Ces4, Cly1, Coc2, Col3, Crl4, Dic2, Ess3, Fry2, Gdy2, Har2, Hay2,

Hdy2, Hgh1, Hpn1, Jon2, Lay3, Leg2, Mat2, Nts1, Okr2, Pal2, Phi2, Poc1, Rea2, Red3, Rss2, Rum2, Sbr2, Str2, Tim3, Van3, War2, Wha4, Whe3.
Standard Abb2, Bnt3, Ces4, Har2, Hdy2, Tim3, Van3, War2, Web3.
Half Standard Bnt3, Ces4, Hoc4, Sbr2, War2, Web3.

Glenfiddich (f) 4 Abb2, And2, Apu2, Aus2, Bat2, Bnt3, Ces4, Coc2, Col3, Crl4, Cro2, Dlv4, Fry2, Gdy2, Gly1, Hay2, Hdy2, Hgh1, Hll2, Jon2, Jus1, Lay3, Nts1, Okr2, Pal2, Phi2, Poc1, Rea2, Red3, Rog2, Rum2, Sbr2, Sha2, Stl2, Str2, Tim3, Van3, War2, Whe3, Wis3.
Standard Ces4, Coc2, Fry2, Hgh1, Hoc4, Jon2, Okr2, Rog2.
Half Standard Ces4, Coc2, Hll2.

Paul's Scarlet Climber (c) 14 Apu2, Aus2, Bls1, Bnt3, Brw1, Can1, Ces4, Col3, Crl4, Dlv4, Ess3, Gdy2, Gly1 Har2, Hay2, Hll2, Hpn1, Jon2, Lay3, Leg2, Mat2, Nts1, Pal2, Phi2, Poc1, Rea2, Rum2, San2, Sbr2, Stl2, Str2, Sty2, Tim3, Van3, War2, Web3, Wha4, Whe3, Wht3, Wis3.

Savoy Hotel (Harvintage) **(h) 9** Abb2, Apu2, Aus2, Bls1, Bnt3, Brw1, Can1, Ces4, Cly1, Coc2, Col3, Doy3, Fry2, Gdy2, Gly1, Har2, Hay2, Hdy2, Hgh1, Hpn1, Jon2, Jus1, Lay3, Leg2, Mat2, Okr2, Rea2, Red3, Rog2, Rss2, San2, Sbr2, Stl2, Str2, Tim3, War2, Web3, Wha4, Whe3, Wis3.
Standard Abb2, Brw1, Can1, Ces4, Col3, Fry2, Gly1, Har2, Hoc4, Poc1, Str2, War2, Web3, Wha4, Wis3.
Half Standard Can1, Ces4, Fry2, Gly1, Har2, War2.

Beautiful Britain (Dicfire) **(f) 8** Abb2, Apu2, Aus2, Bls1, Bnt3, Can1, Ces4, Cly1, Coc2, Dic2, Dlv4, Doy3, Fry2, Gdy2, Gly1, Har2, Hay2, Hgh1, Hll2, Hpn1, Jon2, Jus1, Lay3, Leg2, Okr2, Phi2, Poc1, Rea2, Red3, Rog2, Rss2, Rum2, Sbr2, Stl2, Str2, Tim3, War2, Wha4, Whe3.
Standard Ces4, Hgh1, Hoc4, Jon2, Rog2.
Half Standard Ces4, Rea2.

Filipe 'Kiftsgate' (Also known as Rosa Filipes Kiftsgate) **(c) 1** Act2, Apu2, Aus2, Bls1, Bnt3, Bra2, Can1, Ces4, Cgr1, Cly1, Col3, Doy3, Fry2, Gdy2, Har2, Hay2, Hdy2, Hgh1, Hll2, Hpn1, Jon2, Jus1, Lay3, Leg2, Mat2, Nts1, Poc1, Rea2, Red3, Rog2, Rum2, San2, Str2, Sty2, Tim3, Wha4, Whe3, Wht3, Wye4.

Chicago Peace (h) 5 Abb2, Aus2, Bls1, Bnt3, Bra2, Ces4, Cly1, Coc2, Crl4, Cro2, Dlv4, Ess3, Fry2, Gdy2, Gly1, Hpn1, Jon2, Lay3, Leg2, Okr2, Pal2, Phi2, Red3, Rog2, Rss2, Rum2, Sbr2, Sck2, Sha2, Stl2, Str2, Tim3, Van3, War2, Web3, Wha4, Whe3, Wis3.
Standard Abb2, Crl4, Lay3, Rum2, War2, Web3, Wis3.
Half Standard Rum2.

Frau Dagmar Hartopp (Also known as Fru Dagmar Hastrup) **(s) 9** Act2, Apu2, Aus2, Bls1, Bnt3, Can1, Cgr1, Chi4, Coc2, Col3, Dlv4, Fry2, Gdy2, Har2, Hll2, Jon2, Jus1, Lay3, Leg2, Mat2, Nts1, Pen4, Rea2, Red3, Rog2, Rum2, San2, Sck2, Str2, Sty2, Tim3, Van3, War2, Web3, Wha4, Whe3, Wht3, Wis3.

Heritage (Ausblush) **(s) 10** Act2, Apu2, Aus2, Bat2, Bls1, Bnt3, Can1, Ces4, Cly1, Coc2, Crl4, Dlv4, Doy3, Fry2, Gly1, Hay2, Hdy2, Hgh1, Hpn1, Jon2, Jus1, Lay3, Leg2, Mat2, Nts1, Pal2, Poc1, Rea2, Red3, Rog2, Rum2, San2, Stl2, Tim3, Van3, Wha4, Whe3.
Standard Aus2, Ces4.

Kings Ransom (h) 3 Apu2, Aus2, Bls1, Bnt3, Bra2, Brw1, Ces4, Col3, Crl4, Cro2, Dlv4, Ess3, Fry2, Gdy2, Hay2, Hgh1, Hll2, Jon2, Lay3, Leg2, Nts1, Okr2, Phi2, Poc1, Rea2, Red3, Rum2, Sbr2, Sck2, Sha2, Stl2, Str2, Tim3, Van3, War2, Web3, Wis3, Wye4.
Standard Aus2, Bls1, Ces4, Hgh1, Hll2, Hoc4, Nts1, Rum2, Sbr2, Van3, Web3, Wis3.
Half Standard Ces4, Hll2.

Madame Alfred Carriere (c) 1 Act2, Apu2, Aus2, Bls1, Bnt3, Can1, Cgr1, Cly1, Coc2, Col3, Doy3, Gdy2, Har2, Hdy2, Hgh1, Hll2, Hpn1, Jon2, Jus1, Lay3, Leg2, Mat2, Nts1, Pal2, Phi2, Poc1, Rea2, Red3, Rog2, Rss2, Rum2, San2, Sck2, Str2, Sty2, Tim3, War2, Wht3.

Trumpeter (Mactru) **(f) 13** Abb2, Apu2, Aus2, Bat2, Bnt3, Can1, Ces4, Cly1, Coc2, Cro2, Fry2, Gdy2, Gly1, Har2, Hay2, Hdy2, Hgh1, Hll2, Hpn1, Jon2, Jus1, Lay3, Leg2, Mat2, Nts1, Okr2, Pal2, Rea2, Red3, Rss2, San2, Sbr2, Sha2, Stl2, Tim3, War2, Web3, Wha4.
Standard Abb2, Can1, Ces4, Coc2, Fry2, Hll2, Hoc4, Hpn1, Jon2, Mat2, Nts1, Pen4, Sbr2, Wha4.
Half Standard Can1, Ces4, Fry2, Har2, Hll2, Hpn1, Pal2, Red3, Web3, Wha4.

American Pillar (c) 12 Act2, And2, Apu2, Aus2, Bat2, Bls1, Bnt3, Bra2, Can1, Col3, Doy3, Ess3, Gdy2, Gly1, Hay2, Hll2, Hpn1, Jus1, Lay3, Leg2, Mat2, Nts1, Okr2, Phi2, Poc1, Rog2, Rum2, San2, Sbr2, Sha2, Stl2, Str2, Sty2, War2, Web3, Wha4, Wht3.

Breath of Life (Harquanne) **(c) 6** Apu2, Aus2, Bat2, Bnt3, Can1, Ces4, Cly1, Coc2, Col3, Dlv4, Ess3, Fry2, Gdy2, Gly1, Har2, Hay2, Hgh1, Hll2, Hpn1, Jon2, Jus1, Lay3, Leg2, Nts1, Poc1, Rea2, Rss2, Rum2, San2, Sbr2, Sha2, Stl2, Str2, Tim3, War2, Web3, Wye4.

Elizabeth of Glamis (f) 11 Abb2, And2, Aus2, Bls1, Bnt3, Bra2, Ces4, Coc2, Crl4, Cro2, Dlv4, Fry2, Gdy2, Hdy2, Hgh1, Leg2, Mat2, Nts1, Okr2, Pal2, Phi2, Red3, Rog2, Rss2, Rum2, Sbr2, Sck2, Sha2, Stl2, Str2, Tim3, Van3, War2, Web3, Whe3, Wis3, Wye4.
Standard Cro2, Hdy2, Okr2, Pen4, Rog2, Sbr2, Web3, Wis3.
Half Standard Bls1.

Fragrant Delight (f) 12 And2, Apu2, Bat2, Bnt3, Bra2, Brw1, Can1, Ces4, Coc2, Col3, Cro2, Ess3, Fry2, Gdy2, Har2, Hpn1, Jon2, Jus1, Lay3, Leg2, Okr2, Pal2, Phi2, Rea2, Red3, Rss2, Sbr2, Sha2, Str2, Tim3, Van3, War2, Web3, Wha4, Whe3, Wis3, Wye4.
Standard Bnt3, Ces4, Col3, Gdy2, Leg2, Sbr2, Tim3, Van3, Web3, Wha4, Wis3.
Half Standard Bnt3, Gdy2, Wha4, Wis3.

Lilli Marlene (f) 15 Abb2, And2, Aus2, Bls1, Bra2, Brw1, Ces4, Coc2, Col3, Crl4, Cro2, Dlv4, Ess3, Gdy2, Hll2, Lay3, Leg2, Mat2, Nts1, Okr2, Pal2, Phi2, Red3, Rog2, Rss2, Rum2, Sbr2, Sck2, Sha2, Stl2, Str2, Tim3, Van3, Web3, Wha4, Wis3, Wye4.
Standard H112, Leg2, Web3, Wis3.
Half Standard H112, Wis3.

Mary Rose (Ausmary) **(s) 10** Act2, Apu2, Aus2, Bat2, Bls1, Bnt3, Bra2, Can1, Ces4, Coc2, Doy3, Gdy2, Gly1, Har2, Hay2, Hgh1, Hpn1, Jus1, Lay3, Leg2, Mat2, Nts1, Phi2, Poc1, Rea2, Red3, Rog2, Rum2, San2, Sbr2, Str2, Tim3, Van3, War2, Web3, Wha4, Whe3.
Standard Aus2, Ces4, Hoc4.

Mischief (h) 12 Abb2, Aus2, Bls1, Bnt3, Bra2, Brw1, Ces4, Coc2, Col3, Crl4, Cro2, Dlv4, Gdy2, Hdy2, Hgh1, Hpn1, Jus1, Lay3, Okr2, Pal2, Phi2, Poc1, Red3, Rog2, Rss2, Rum2, San2, Sck2, Stl2, Str2, Tim3, Van3, War2, Wha4, Wis3.

Standard Crl4, Hpn1, Lay3, Pen4, San2, Wis3.
Half Standard San2.

Rose Gaujard (h) 13/1 Abb2, Aus2, Bls1, Bnt3, Brw1, Ces4, Col3, Crl4, Cro2, Dlv4, Ess3, Gdy2, Gly1, Hay2, Hdy2, Hll2, Leg2, Nts1, Okr2, Pal2, Phi2, Poc1, Red3, Rss2, Rum2, Sbr2, Sck2, Sha2, Stl2, Str2, Tim3, Van3, War2, Web3, Wha4,Wis3,Wye4.
Standard Red3, Web3.

Cornelia (s) 11 Act2, Apu2, Aus2, Bls1, Bnt3, Can1, Cgr1, Cly1, Col3, Cro2, Fry2, Har2, Hay2, Hll2, Jon2, Jus1, Lay3, Leg2, Mat2, Nts1, Okr2, Poc1, Rog2, Rum2, San2, Sbr2, Str2, Sty2, Tim3, War2, Web3, Wha4, Whe3, Wht3, Wis3, Wye4.
Standard Hll2.

Dearest (f) 12 Abb2, Aus2, Bls1, Bnt3, Bra2, Ces4, Col3, Crl4, Cro2, Dlv4, Doy3, Ess3, Gdy2, Hay2, Hll2, Hpn1, Jon2, Nts1, Okr2, Phi2, Poc1, Rea2, Red3, Rog2, Rss2, Rum2, Sbr2, Sck2, Stl2.
Standard Hoc4, Pen4, Sbr2, War2, Wis3.

Excelsa (c) 14 Abb2, Act2, Aus2, Bls1, Bnt3, Bra2, Ces4, Cly1, Col3, Cro2, Doy3, Ess3, Gdy2, Gly1, Hay2, Hll2, Jon2, Jus1, Leg2, Okr2, Phi2, Poc1, Rea2, Rog2, Rss2, Rum2, San2, Sbr2, Sck2, Stl2, Str2, Sty2, Tim3, Van3, Web3, Wha4.
Weeping Standard Abb2, And2, Bls1, Bnt3, Can1, Ces4, Cly1, Coc2, Col3, Cro2, Fry2, Gdy2, Gly1, Hll2, Hoc4, Jon2, Leg2, Nts1, Okr2, Poc1, Rog2, Rum2, San2, Sbr2, Str2, Van3, Web3.

Top Marks (Fryminstar) (p/m) 8 Abb2, Apu2, Bat2, Bnt3, Brw1, Can1, Coc2, Col3, Crl4, Doy3, Fry2, Gdy2, Har2, Hdy2, Hpn1, Jon2, Lay3, Leg2, Mat2, Nts1, Okr2, Pal2, Poc1, Rea2, Red3, Rog2, Rss2, Rum2, Sha2, Stl2, Str2, Tim3, Van3, War2, Wha4, Whe3.
Patio Standard Ces4, Har2.
Miniature Standard Ces4, Har2.

Fruhlingsmorgen (s) 10/2 Abb2, Act2, Apu2, Aus2, Bls1, Bnt3, Brw1, Ces4, Chi4, Coc2, Col3, Cro2, Dlv4, Gdy2, Hll2, Jus1, Lay3, Leg2, Mat2, Nts1, Pen4, Red3, Rog2, Sck2, Stl2, Str2, Sty2, Tim3, Van3, War2, Web3, Whe3, Wht3, Wis3, Wye4.

Orange Sensation (f) 8 And2, Aus2, Bls1, Bnt3, Bra2, Ces4, Col3, Cro2, Dlv4, Fry2, Gdy2,

Hay2, Hdy2, Hgh1, Jon2, Lay3, Leg2, Nts1, Okr2, Phi2, Red3, Rog2, Rss2, Rum2, Sbr2, Sck2, Stl2, Tim3, Van3, War2, Web3, Wha4, Whe3, Wis3, Wye4.
Standard Cro2, Hdy2, Hll2.

Paul Shirville (Harqueterwife) **(h) 11** Abb2, And2, Apu2, Aus2, Bat2, Bnt3, Can1, Ces4, Coc2, Crl4, Dlv4, Fry2, Gdy2, Har2, Hay2, Hgh1, Hpn1, Jus1, Lay3, Leg2, Mat2, Okr2, Pal2, Phi2, Poc1, Rea2, Red3, Rog2, Rss2, San2, Sbr2, Str2, Tim3, War2, Wha4.
Standard Ces4, Fry2, Gdy2, Har2, Hgh1, Hoc4, Hpn1, Leg2, Rea2, Red3, Sbr2.
Half Standard Ces4, Gdy2, Har2, Red3.

Gertrude Jekyll (Ausbond) **(s) 13** Act2, Apu2, Aus2, Bls1, Bnt3, Can1, Cly1, Coc2, Crl4, Dlv4, Doy3, Fry2, Har2, Hdy2, Hpn1, Jon2, Jus1, Lay3, Mat2, Nts1, Pal2, Phi2, Poc1, Rea2, Red3, San2, Sbr2, Stl2, Str2, Tim3, War2, Wha4, Whe3, Wht3.
Standard Ces4.

National Trust (h) 14 Aus2, Bls1, Bnt3, Ces4, Col3, Crl4, Dlv4, Fry2, Gdy2, Gly1, Hay2, Hgh1, Hll2, Jon2, Leg2, Mat2, Nts1, Okr2, Phi2, Rea2, Red3, Rog2, Rss2, Sbr2, Sck2, Stl2, Str2, Tim3, War2, Web3, Wha4, Whe3, Wis3.
Standard Ces4, Col3, Crl4, Hoc4, Okr2, Red3, Sbr2, Tim3, Wha4, Wis3, Wye4.

Remember Me (Cocdestin) **(h) 8** Apu2, Bat2, Bnt3, Bra2, Can1, Ces4, Cly1, Coc2, Cro2, Dlv4, Fry2, Gdy2, Gly1, Har2, Hay2, Hgh1, Hpn1, Jon2, Lay3, Leg2, Mat2, Okr2, Pal2, Phi2, Poc1, Rea2, Red3, Rog2, Rss2, Sha2, Str2, Tim3, War2.
Standard Bnt3, Can1, Ces4, Coc2, Fry2, Gdy2, Gly1, Hgh1, Hoc4, Hpn1, Jon2, Mat2, Pal2.
Half Standard Can1, Ces4, Coc2, Gdy2, Gly1,

Tip Top (f) 10 Aus2, Bls1, Bnt3, Ces4, Coc2, Col3, Crl4, Cro2, Dlv4, Fry2, Gdy2, Gly1, Hay2, Hgh1, H112, Hpn1, Lay3, Nts1, Okr2, Poc1, Red3, Rog2, Rum2, Sck2, Stl2 Str2, Tim3, Van3, War2, Web3, Wha4, Whe3, Wis3.
Climbing Sck2.
Half Standard Rum2, Web3, Wis3.
Miniature Standard Rum2.

Allgold (f) 3 Apu2, Aus2, Bat2, Bls1, Bra2, Coc2, Col3, Cro2, Dlv4, Ess3, Gdy2, Hll2, Jon2, Lay3, Leg2, Okr2, Phi2, Poc1, Red3, Rss2, Rum2, San2, Sbr2, Sck2, Sha2, Stl2, Str2, Tim3, Van3, War2, Whe3, Wis3, Wye4.

Climbing Hdy2, Lay3, Wis3.
Standard Abb2, Bls1, Ces4, Coc2, Col3, Crl4, Doy3, Gdy2, Hdy2, Hgh1, Hll2, Hoc4, Jon2, Leg2, Mat2, Nts1, Pal2, Rea2, San2, Sbr2, Stl2, Tim3, Van3, Web3, Wha4, Wis3.
Half Standard Ces4, Coc2, Doy3, Gdy2, Hll2, Okr2, Pal2, San2, Str2.

Blanc Double de Coubert (s) 1 Act2, Apu2, Aus2, Bls1, Bnt3, Can1, Cgr1, Chi4, Coc2, Col3, Doy3, Fry2, Har2, Hll2, Hpn1, Jon2, Jus1, Lay3, Leg2, Mat2, Nts1, Poc1, Red3, Rog2, Rum2, San2, Str2, Sty2, Tim3, War3, Whe3, Wht3, Wis3.

Deep Secret (h) 15 Abb2, Bnt3, Bra2, Brw1, Can1, Ces4, Col3, Cly1, Crl4, Dlv4, Ess3, Fry2, Gdy2, Hgh1, Hpn1, Jon2, Jus1, Leg2, Pal2, Rea2, Red3, Rog2, Rss2, Rum2, San2, Sck2, Sha2, Tim3, Van3, War2, Web3, Wha4, Whe3.
Standard Brw1, Can1, Ces4, Col3, Gdy2, Hoc4, Hpn1, Jon2, Leg2, Pal2, Rea2, Tim3, Van3, Web3, Wha4, Whe3.
Half Standard Can1, Ces4, Gdy2, Rum2, Wha4.

Dorothy Perkins (c) 10 Abb2, Act2, Apu2, Aus2, Bls1, Bnt3, Bra2, Ces4, Cly1, Col3, Cro2, Ess3, Gdy2, Hll2, Hpn1, Jon2, Jus1, Mat2, Okr2, Pal2, Phi2, Rea2, Rog2, Rss2, Rum2, San2, Sbr2, Sck2, Stl2, Str2, Tim3, War2, Wht3.
Weeping Standard Abb2, Act2, And2, Bnt3, Can1, Ces4, Cly1, Coc2, Col3, Fry2, Gdy2, Hll2, Hoc4, Hpn1, Mat2, Pal2, Rog2, Rum2, San2, Sbr2, Str2, Web3, Wht3.

Peek A Boo (Dicgrow) **(p) 6** Abb2, Apu2, Aus2, Bnt3, Can1, Ces4, Cly1, Coc2, Col3, Crl4, Dic2, Doy3, Fry2, Gdy2, Gly1, Har2, Hgh1, Hpn1, Jus1, Lay3, Leg2, Mat2, Nts1, Phi2, Poc1, Rea2, Stl2, Str2, Tim3, Van3, War2, Web3, Wha4.
Half Standard Ces4, Cly1, Hoc4, Hpn1, Web3.
Quarter Standard Rea2, Str2.
Miniature Standard Ces4, Web3.

Alberic Barbier (c) 2 Act2, Apu2, Aus2, Bls1, Bnt3, Brw1, Can1, Cgr1, Col3, Gdy2, Har2, Hay2, Hgh1, Hll2, Jon2, Jus1, Lay3, Leg2, Mat2, Nts1, Poc1, Rea2, Red3, Rog2, Rum2, San2, Sbr2, Str2, Sty2, Tim3, War2, Wht3.
Weeping Standard Bls1, Ces4, Gdy2, Har2, Hll2, Leg2, Mat2, Rum2, Sbr2, Str2, Wht3.

Double Delight (h) 13/2 Apu2, Bnt3, Can1, Ces4, Cly1, Col3, Dlv4, Gdy2, Har2, Hay2,

Hgh1, Hpn1, Jon2, Jus1, Lay3, Leg2, Phi2, Poc1, Rog2, Rss2, Rum2, Sbr2, Sck2, Sha2, Stl2, Str2, Tim3, Van3, Wha4, Whe3, Wis3, Wye4.
Standard Ces4, Wis3.
Half Standard Ces4.

Gloire de Dijon (c) 2 Act2, Apu2, Aus2, Bls1, Bnt3, Brw1, Can1, Coc2, Col3, Gdy2, Har2, Hgh1, Hll2, Hpn1, Jon2, Jus1, Leg2, Mat2, Nts1, Phi2, Poc1, Rog2, Rum2, San2, Sbr2, Stl2, Sty2, Tim3, Van3, War2, Wht3, Wye4.

Max Graf (s/gc) 11 Act2, Apu2, Aus2, Bls1, Brw1, Can1, Ces4, Chi4, Col3, Cro2, Gdy2, Hgh1, Hll2, Jon2, Lay3, Leg2, Mat2, Nts1, Pen4, Red3, Rog2, Rum2, San2, Sbr2, Stl2, Sty2, Tim3, Web3, Wha4, Whe3, Wht3, Wye4.

Orange Sunblaze (Meijaktar) **(m) 8** Abb2, Act2, Apu2, Bls1, Bnt3, Can1, Ces4, Cly1, Gdy2, Gly1, Har2, Hay2, Hpn1, Jon2, Lay3, Leg2, Nts1, Pen4, Poc1, Rea2, Red3, Rss2, San2, Sbr2, Sck2, Tim3, Van3, War2, Web3, Wha4, Wis3, Wye4.
Half Standard Web3.
Quarter Standard Rea2. **Patio Standard** Wha4.
Miniature Standard Can1, Ces4, Har2, Hoc4, Pen4, War2, Wis3.

Southampton (f) 6 Abb2, Apu2, Aus2, Bls1, Bnt3, Can1, Ces4, Col3, Cro2, Dlv4, Ess3, Gdy2, Har2, Hay2, Hll2, Hpn1, Lay3, Leg2, Mat2, Nts1, Phi2, Poc1, Rog2, Rss2, San2, Sck2, Stl2, Str2, Tim3, War2, Whe3, Wis3.
Standard & Half Standard Ces4.

Abb2 **Abbey Rose Gardens**
Burnham, Bucks SL1 8NJ
Tel (0628) 603000

Act2 **Acton Beauchamp Roses**
Nr Worcester WR6 5AE
Tel (0531) 640433

And2 **Anderson's Rose Nurseries**
Friarsfield Road, Cults, Aberdeen AB1 9QT.
Tel (0224) 868881

Apu2 **Apuldram Roses**
Apuldram Lane, Dell Quay,
Chichester, West Sussex PO20 7EF
Tel (0243) 785769

Aus2 **David Austin Roses**
Bowling Green Lane, Albrighton,
Nr Wolverhampton WV7 3HB
Tel (0902) 373931

Bat2 **Battersby Roses**
Pear Tree Cottage, Old Battersby,
Great Ayton, Cleveland TS9 6LU
Tel (0642) 723402

Bls1 **Peter Beales Roses**
London Road, Attleborough,
Norfolk NR17 1AY
Tel: (0953) 4548707

Bnt3 **Walter Bentley & Sons Ltd**
The Nurseries, Loughborough Road,
Wanlip, Leicester LE7 8PN
Tel (0533) 673702

Bra2 **Brannel Farm Roses**
Brannel Farm, St. Stephens, Coombe,
St. Austell, Cornwall PL25 7LG
Tel (0726) 882468

Brw1 **Burrows Roses**
Meadowcroft, Spondon Road,
Dale Abbey, Nr Ilkeston, Derby DE7 4PQ
Tel (0332) 668289

Can1 **Cants of Colchester Ltd.**
Rose Specialists, Nayland Road (A134),
Mile End, Colchester CO4 5EB
Tel (0206) 844008

Ces4 **Paul Chessum Wholesale Rose Grower**
21 High Street, Great Barford,
Nr. Bedford MK44 3JH
Tel (0234) 870182

Cgr1 **Cottage Garden Roses**
Woodlands House, Stretton,
Nr. Stafford ST19 9LG
Tel (0785) 840217

Chi4 **Chichester Roses Ltd.**
Chalder Farm, Sidlesham, Chichester,
West Sussex PO20 7RN
Tel (0243) 641219

Cly1 **Cley Nurseries Ltd.**
Holt Road, Cley-Next-The-Sea,
Holt, Norfolk NR25 7TX
Tel (0263) 740892

Coc2 **James Cocker & Sons**
Whitemyres, Lang Stracht, Aberdeen
AB9 2XH
Tel (0224) 313261

Col3 **W. H. Collins & Sons (Roses) Ltd.**
The Manor House, Knossington,
Oakham, Leics LE15 8LX
Tel (066 477) 323

Crl4 **John Charles Nurseries Ltd.**
64 Derby Road, Risley, Derby DE7 3SU
Tel (0602) 396024

Cro2 **D & W Croll Ltd.**
Dalhousie Nurseries, Broughty Ferry,
Dundee DD5 2PP
Tel (0382) 78921

Dic2 **Dickson Nurseries Ltd.**
Milecross Road, Newtownards,
Co. Down, N. Ireland BT23 4SS
Tel (0247) 812206

Dlv4 **Peter Delves** Rose Grower
Woolhouse Nursery, Redford, Midhurst,
Sussex GU29 0QH
Tel (0428) 76257

Doy4 **Doubleday & Co.**
Walnut Hill, Surlingham, Norwich,
Norfolk NR14 7DQ
Tel (05088) 8097

Ess3 **Leo Esser & Son**
Grange Farm Nursery, Barton Road
(B1441), Wisbech, Cambs PE13 4TH
Tel (0945) 582262

Fry2 **Fryer's Nurseries Ltd.**
Manchester Road, Knutsford,
Cheshire WA16 0SX
Tel (0565) 755455

Gdy2 **Gandy's Roses**
North Kilworth, Nr. Lutterworth,
Leics LE17 6HZ
Tel (0858) 880398

Gly1 **Godly's Roses**
Dunstable Road (A5183), Redbourn,
St. Albans, Herts AL3 7PS
Tel (0582) 792255

Har2 **R. Harkness & Co. Ltd.**
The Rose Gardens, Cambridge Road,
Hitchin, Herts SG4 0JT
Tel (0462) 420402

Hay2 **F. Haynes & Partners**
56 Gordon Street, Kettering,
Northants NN16 PRX
Tel (0536) 519836

Hdy2 **Handley Rose Nurseries**
Lightwood Road, Marsh Lane,
Nr Sheffield S31 9RG
Tel (0246) 432921

Hgh1 **Highfield Nurseries**
Whitminster, Gloucester GL2 7PL
Tel (0452) 740266

Hll2 **Hills Nurseries**
Netherton Road, Appleton,
Nr Abingdon, Oxon OX13 5QN
Tel (0865) 862081

Hpn1 **Hill Park Nurseries**
Kingston By Pass (A309), Surbiton,
Surrey KT6 5HN
Tel (081) 398 0022

Hoc4 **Hockenhull Roses**
28 Hallfields Road, Tarvin, Chester
CH3 8LL
Tel (0829) 40045

Jon2 **C & K Jones** (Rose Specialists)
Golden Fields Nursery, Barrow Lane,
Tarvin, Chester CH3 8JF
Tel (0829) 40663

Jus1 **Just Roses**
Beales Lane, Northian, Nr Rye,
Sussex TN31 6QY
Tel (0797) 252355

Lay3 **Layham Nurseries & Garden Centre**
Summerfield, Staple, Canterbury,
Kent CT3 1LD
Tel (0304) 611380
Retail from own Garden Centre only

Leg2 **LeGrice Roses**
Norwich Road, North Walsham,
Norfolk NR28 0DR
Tel (0692) 402591

Mat2 **Mattock Roses**
Nuneham Courtenay, Oxford OX9 9PY
Tel (086 738) 265

Nts1 **Notcutts Nurseries Ltd.**
Woodbridge, Suffolk IP12 4AF
Tel (0394) 383344

Okr **O.K. Roses**
Ferriby High Road, North Ferriby,
North Humberside HU14 3LA
Tel (0482) 634237

Pal2 **A. J. Palmer & Son**
Denham Court Nursery, Denham Village,
Denham, Nr. Uxbridge, Bucks UB9 6BQ
Tel (0895) 832035

Pen4 **Pennine Nurseries**
J & W Blackburn Ltd. Pennine Nurseries,
Shelley, Huddersfield HD8 8LG
Tel (0484) 605511

Phi2 **J. B. Philp & Son Ltd.**
Elm Park Garden Centre, Pamber End,
Basingstoke, Hants RG26 5QW
Tel (0256) 850587

Poc1 **Pocock's Nurseries**
Dandys Ford Lane, Sherfield English,
Romsey, Hants S051 6FT
Tel (0794) 23514

Rea2 **Rearsby Roses Ltd.**
Melton Road, Rearsby, Leics LE7 8YP
Tel (0533) 601211

Red3 **Redhill Roses**
Thurlby Farm, Thurlby Lane,
Stanton-on-the-Wolds, Notts NG12 5PL
Tel (06077) 4359

Rog2 **R. V. Roger Ltd.**
The Nurseries, Pickering, North
Yorkshire Y018 7HG
Tel (0751) 72226

Rss2 **Rosslow Roses**
North Street Farm, North Street,
Hellingly, Hailsham, East Sussex
BN27 4DZ
Tel (0323) 440888

Rum2 **Rumwood Nurseries**
Langley, Maidstone, Kent ME17 3ND
Tel (0622) 861477

San2 **John Sanday (Roses) Ltd.**
Over Lane, Almondsbury,
Bristol BS12 4DA
Tel (0454) 612195

Sbr2 **St. Bridget Nurseries Ltd.**
Old Roydon Lane, Exeter,
Devon EX2 7JY
Tel (0392) 873672

Sck2 **Slacks Roses**
White Post, Farnsfield, Nottingham
NG22 8HX
Tel (0623) 882773
Retail from nursery only

Sha2 **Shaw Rose Trees**
2 Hollowgate Hill, Willoughton,
Gainsborough, Lincs DN21 5SF
Tel (0427) 668230

Stl2 **J. A. Steele & Sons Ltd.**
The Market Place, Regent Street,
Newtownards, Co. Down, N. Ireland
Tel (0247) 818378

Str2 **Henry Street**
Swallowfield Road Nurseries,
Arborfield, Reading, Berks
Tel (0734) 761223

Sty2 **Stydd Nursery**
Stonygate Lane, Ribchester,
Nr Preston, Lancs PR3 3YN
Tel (0254) 878797

Tim3 **Timmermans Roses**
Lowdham Lane, Woodborough,
Nottingham NG14 6DN
Tel (0602) 663193

Van3 **L. W. Van Geest (Farms) Ltd.**
Wool Hall Farm, Wykeham, Spalding,
Lincs PE12 6HW
Tel (0775) 725041

War2 **Warley Rose Gardens Ltd.**
The Garden Centre, Warley Street, Great
Warley, Brentwood, Essex CM13 3JH
Tel (0277) 221966

Web3 **F. & G. F. Webb** (Orchard Nurseries),
90 Peters Point, Sutton Bridge,
Spalding, Lincs PE12 9UX
Tel (0406) 350098
Orders in minimum 10 per variety

Wha4 **Whartons Nurseries (Harleston) Ltd.**
Station Road, Harleston, Norfolk
IP20 9EY
Tel (0379) 852157

Whe3 **Wheatcroft Ltd.**
Edwalton, Nottingham NG12 4DE
Tel (0602) 216061

Wht3 **Trevor White Old-Fashioned Roses**
'Chelt Hurst', 10 Sewell Road,
Norwich, Norfolk NR3 4BP
Tel (0603) 418240

Wis3 **Wisbech Plant Co. Ltd.**
Walton Road, Wisbech, Cambs
PE13 3EF
Tel (0945) 582588
Orders in minimum of 10 per variety

Wye4 **Wyevale Nurseries Ltd.**
Kings Acre, Hereford HR4 7AY
Tel (0432) 352255